THE
TELEVISION
SERIES

Paul Abbott

MANCHESTER
1824

Manchester University Press

THE TELEVISION SERIES

series editors

JONATHAN BIGNELL
STEVEN PEACOCK

former editor

SARAH CARDWELL

BETH JOHNSON

Paul Abbott

Manchester University Press

MANCHESTER AND NEW YORK

distributed in the United States exclusively by Palgrave Macmillan

Published by Manchester University Press
Oxford Road, Manchester M13 9NR, UK
and Room 400, 175 Fifth Avenue, New York, NY 10010, USA
www.manchesteruniversitypress.co.uk

Distributed in the United States exclusively by
Palgrave Macmillan, 175 Fifth Avenue, New York, NY 10010, USA

Distributed in Canada exclusively by
UBC Press, University of British Columbia, 2029 West Mall,
Vancouver, BC, Canada V6T 1Z2

British Library Cataloguing-in-Publication Data
A catalogue record for this book is available from the British Library

Library of Congress Cataloging-in-Publication Data applied for

ISBN 978 0 7190 8629 8 *hardback*

First published 2013

Typeset in Scala with Meta display by
Koinonia, Manchester
Printed in Great Britain by
TJ International Ltd, Padstow

Contents

List of illustrations

Foreword

I never wanted to be a writer. From seven, I wanted to be a surgeon. It's taken me this long to realise that the jobs really aren't that far apart. Most of the best of what you do is as a result of editing.

As the seventh of eight kids, I wasn't popular because I had a big mouth. I think I learnt how to write as a means of talking without being contradicted, venting my spleen without getting another smart-arsed busted lip.

When Beth first approached me about writing this book, and then composing a foreword, in all honesty, I got cold belly-butterflies. I loathe being examined or having to explain myself. And yet, here I am.

And I've only just realised why I'm compelled to.

And I've only just realised why. I'm compelled to.

Wherever I came from, across the last 35 years of dedicated writing-as-a-weapon, I'm one of the very few writers you will ever meet who enjoys passing the shortcuts on. Sad, but true.

Paul Abbott
August 2012

General editors' preface

Television is part of our everyday experience, and is one of the most significant aspects of our cultural lives today. Yet its practitioners and its artistic and cultural achievements remain relatively unacknowledged. The books in this series aim to remedy this by addressing the work of major television writers and creators. Each volume provides an authoritative and accessible guide to a particular practitioner's body of work, and assesses his or her contribution to television over the years. Many of the volumes draw on original sources, such as specially conducted interviews and archive material, and all of them list relevant bibliographic sources and further reading and viewing. The author of each book makes a case for the importance of the work considered therein, and the series includes books on neglected or overlooked practitioners alongside well-known ones.

In comparison with some related disciplines, Television Studies scholarship is still relatively young, and the series aims to contribute to establishing the subject as a vigorous and evolving field. This series provides resources for critical thinking about television. While maintaining a clear focus on the writers, on the creators and on the programmes themselves, the books in this series also take account of key critical concepts and theories in Television Studies. Each book is written from a particular critical or theoretical perspective, with reference to pertinent issues, and the approaches included in the series are varied and sometimes dissenting. Each author explicitly outlines the reasons for his or her particular focus, methodology or perspective. Readers are invited to think critically about the subject matter and approach covered in each book.

Although the series is addressed primarily to students and scholars of television, the books will also appeal to the many people who are interested in how television programmes have been commissioned, made and enjoyed. Since television has been so much a part of personal and public life in the twentieth and twenty-first centuries, we hope that the series will engage with, and sometimes challenge, a broad and diverse readership.

Jonathan Bignell
Steven Peacock

Acknowledgements

First, I would like to express my sincere thanks to Paul Abbott, who kindly provided me with copies of his work, prized scripts and wonderful interview material. It was Paul's work that motivated me to write this book, and his work that has inspired and excited me from my childhood to the present day. I feel truly honoured.

I would also like to express my gratitude to the Humanities Research Institute and my wonderful colleagues at Keele University for allowing me the time and space to complete my research. Matthew Frost at Manchester University Press, series editors Steven Peacock and Jonathan Bignell, I want to thank you for your support and patience throughout the writing and editing process. Deborah Goodman and Jan Bradley – many thanks go to you for your wealth of knowledge and continuous aid. Nicky Johnston, thank you so much for allowing me to include your beautiful *Shameless* image in this monograph. Thanks also go to Dave Woodward and Justine Rhodes at ITV as well as Steve McInerny at FremantleMedia Enterprises.

On a personal note, this book is lovingly dedicated to two Pauls.

First, to Paul Abbott: a giant amongst men and the most brilliant television writer and creator of our age. You are a true inspiration. Thank you for your work, your time, your kindness, your friendship, your voice. I hope this book 'shouts' for you.

Secondly, to Paul Smith: my husband, best friend and love. On our wedding day, you read this passage to me and today, I want to dedicate it to you.

You trip along through life minding your own business until one day – bang – someone steps in front of you, stops you in your tracks, leans in to kiss you and rips your heart right out of your chest. And it's all right, you know. It doesn't hurt. Not at first. Not so long as they look after it and maybe give you theirs in return. And you might be lucky that the last person to rip your heart out is the one who'll look after it, the one who'll wrap it in tissue paper, and tinsel and stars. Being married means you join a club. You see a load of other people with rings on their fingers and you go 'oh yeah, I did that. I stood up in front of the world and told someone that I love them and I wanted to be with them for the rest of my life'. And it really doesn't matter how you do it, when and where you do it. Just as long as there's truth and honesty. If there's no truth and honesty, there'll never be love. No beauty. (*Shameless* Series 7, Episode 8 (Kelly Marie Maguire – closing))

Introduction

What inspires me to write, more than anything if I'm really honest, is spotting things in real life that you never see on TV. Conversations, looks, tiny looks, social behaviour. You don't literally watch someone you've had round for dinner or at a party, you don't literally lift what you have just seen; you learn how to use that frequency.[1]

Paul Abbott

Paul Abbott is one of the most profound, passionate and political television screenwriters and showrunners of the twenty-first century, having created, crafted and contributed to projects and programmes as varied as *Coronation Street* (1960–), *Children's Ward* (1989–2000), *Cracker* (1993–96), *Reckless* (1997), Royal Television Society-nominated *Touching Evil* (1997–99), *Linda Green* (2001–2), BAFTA- and RTS-winning *Clocking Off* (2000–3), Broadcasting Press Guild Award-winning *State of Play* (2003) and BAFTA- and RTS-winning comedy-drama, *Shameless* (2004–). At the 2004 British Academy Television Awards, Abbott was presented with an honorary Award for Outstanding Writing in Television, and, that same summer was positioned by *Radio Times* magazine at number 5 in a poll of industry professionals to find 'the Most Powerful People in Television Drama'. This is the first book-length academic study of the television programmes created, written by and/or executive-produced by Abbott. It is also the first academic study to attempt to consider his complete oeuvre. Within a broadly chronological structure this volume elucidates, decodes and discusses key examples of Abbott's output, exhibiting a vital evaluation of Abbott's work over the past three decades and assessing his contribution to British television. Engaging with thematic and ideological notions of the personal, the autobiographical, the honest, the shameless, the pleasurable and the painful recourse of the specificity of 'ordinary life', the book seeks to combine close textual analysis of Abbott's work with archival research and specially commissioned interviews with Abbott and other important industry practitioners.

Primarily, the volume presents an aesthetic analysis of televisual case studies. Following Sarah Cardwell (2006: 73), who suggests that the term aesthetic ought to imply a study that is both 'analytical', 'close', 'theoretical' and 'critical', the analysis of Abbott's programmes pays close attention to matters of theme, form and style. The case studies presented in this book explore the 'grammar' of the televisual, including colour, sound, diegetic and extra-diegetic music, point of view, shot size, shot length, dialogue, the creation of space and place, on-location shooting, temporality, televisual narrative, performance, mise-en-scène and shot punctuation. These technical elements of television style are considered alongside Abbott's role as creator/writer/director/producer/ executive of the various television texts. The disclosures of the close textual analysis are to be associated with a range of thematic, stylistic and representational motifs across the range of Abbott's work, thereby inaugurating discussions based upon the authorial voice, definitions of 'quality' television – such as the debates offered up by Kim Akass and Janet McCabe (2007) plus Mark Jancovich and James Lyons (2003) – and the negotiation of generic boundaries (Cardwell, 2007).

Chapter 1 offers up a biographical sketch of Paul Abbott. Demonstrating both Abbott's career development and the breadth of his early talents, this chapter briefly considers Abbott's early life and three projects that saw Abbott work for the first time as a television writer, television-series drama creator and finally, a television producer – *Coronation Street*, *Children's Ward* and *Cracker*.

Chapter 2 explores *Reckless*: a drama written by Abbott broadcast on ITV in the UK in 1997 and on PBS in the USA in 1998. Through the close analysis of segments from six individual episodes (1.1–1.6), this chapter considers how Abbott draws on generic paradigms of love, illicit passion, human motivation, friendship and miscommunication in order to present a vision that makes visible the chaos of human connections. Considering perspectives of desire, this chapter focuses on the disclosures of the camera via analyses of bodily performance and close-up shots of the three main characters: Dr Owen Springer (Robson Green), Anna Fairley (Francesca Annis) and Dr Richard Crane (Michael Kitchen). Dominated by principal themes of power and perspective, segments are analysed in order to render visible that which dialogue fails to communicate and, through doing so, this chapter begins to situate Abbott as a patently recognisable author of his work.

Chapter 3 explores and illuminates the televisual aesthetics of *Clocking Off*, paying attention to the exploration of space, place and location in order to highlight personal perspectives and the extraordinary nature of ordinary lives seen and lived in and around the northern English Mackintosh Textiles factory. In the opening of the series, establishing cityscape shots of Manchester are coupled with tight framing. As such, framing across the first series is analysed – framing utilised to invoke distinct character perspectives and unveil personal secrets of the factory and familial communities presented. The slow pacing in Episode 1:1 reinforces the confusion of the central characters (life appears to be going along at a normal pace; however, reactions to events are extreme). Entitled 'Stuart', this episode sees the return of Stuart (John Simm), a husband and father who, having disappeared for 13 months (presumed dead), returns to the family home citing memory loss. Oscillating between medium and close-up shots, the camera records the pain, pleasure and confusion of both Stuart and the family and community he left behind. Constant movement between inside (the factory, the family home/s) and outside (the open road, the docks) reflects, I argue, the collapse of the distinct and yet parallel places and spaces in which Stuart had previously lived his two separate lives.

The central aim of Chapter 4 is to explore how Abbott has created a text that critiques and partially refuses (via comedic undermining) traditional gender expectations in relation to the thirty-something single British woman in the comedy serial *Linda Green*. Positioning Linda Green as a strong, ironic, humorous and determined character, the chapter begins by considering the performance of Liza Tarbuck as Linda Green. Closely analysing facial expressions, mannerisms and speech, the chapter explores how Tarbuck transforms the character from potentially tragic to promiscuously comic. Unusual shot transitions and surreal inserts serve here to highlight Linda's fantasies and undermine the indexical nature of the real – again making visible to the viewer that which the main character, Linda, refuses or is unable to articulate. In addition, the interaction between Linda and her friends, co-workers and lovers reveals identity to be negotiated, comparative and dynamic rather than fixed. While Linda Green (with her 'ordinary' physique) at once stands for every woman and, simultaneously, is situated as an extrovert or extraordinary woman, scenes that focus upon Linda's comparison of herself with others are analysed in order to illuminate the transformative and infectious nature of identity politics. Specific segment analyses of episodes entitled 'Pete', 'Sexual Harassment', 'Fitness Freak' and 'Motherhood' thus form the basis of this chapter.

Chapter 5 explores the spectacular drama series *State of Play*. An important aspect of this chapter is the exploration of the darker side of public life, particularly in relation to the interconnections between the political, the private and the public – often made visible via the press.

In order to explore this, the chapter considers the symbiotic relationship between the mass media and the political machine. The series repeatedly highlights and sketches the complex and contrived relationship between the real and the perception of the real as well as making visible the constraints and problems associated with press revelations of political/personal connections. Conspiracy and conscience are probed, pierced and intersected in this drama via explicit and often devastating and deadly alliances. Personal/political performance and the multiple perspectives and declarations of the media are interconnected methodologically through close textual analysis and production research.

Chapter 6 focuses on the ongoing and highly successful drama series *Shameless*. Written, created and executively produced by Abbott, *Shameless* is an outstanding, poignant and philosophical drama focused upon the chaotic intimacies of the Gallagher family. Set on a housing estate on the fringes of Manchester – 'the Chatsworth estate'– *Shameless* represents both the personal and popular departures of Abbott's early life via the interwoven, tragicomic and purposefully amoral orientations of the family members. Again wilfully situating the personal and philosophical musings of the family via opening/closing monologues and the shocking and often beautiful philosophising of Frank – the frequently absent, alcoholic father of nine children – Abbott highlights the significance and politics of perspective in this passionate, non-patronising drama. Interestingly, the opening monologues and personal musings of family members operate to situate and then intelligently undermine generic representations of social realism, characterised by an emphasis on the real difficulties and drabness of working-class life. Instead, Abbott invokes and evokes through such musings an exuberance in the everyday coupled with a fierce lack of shame in order to demonstrate the determination of the Gallagher family to remain together. Threats to the togetherness (in spite of the often violent and excessive shared intimacies and emotions of the family) are presented through the potential for outside agencies (the social services and police) to try to 'improve' or do something about the living conditions and traditional parental breakdown of responsibility and power within the household.

Chapter 7 considers Abbott's production company 'AbbottVision', focusing on the successful sale of several of its creations to the USA and discussing Showtime's development of an American version of *Shameless*, as well as Abbott's recent creation of two dramas (both written by students that Abbott mentored through the AbbottVision writing studio – Danny Brocklehurst and Sean Conway), *Exile* (BBC One, 2012) and *Hit & Miss* (Sky Atlantic, 2012).

Appendix 1 consists of a summary of three specially commissioned

interviews between Paul Abbott and the author. All unattributed quotations from Abbott within the chapters of this book are taken directly from
these interviews. Appendix 2 is a list of Abbott's television programmes
and films.

Notes

1 This and all other unattributed quotations from Abbott are cited from specially
commissioned interviews with the author in 2011 and 2012. Full extracts from the
interviews are given in Appendix 1.

Biographical sketch: Abbott as writer, producer and creator

When I worked on *Coronation Street* and *Children's Ward* first off, I remember spotting what other writers did, and thinking I will never ever be that kind of writer, and being determined not to be someone who just wrote for money. Because people do write for money, and it's the fastest death of any writer. They might get wages, but they're going to lose their writer credentials and just become a typist. Petulance and subversion, I think, are my highest driving forces. Being told I can't makes me, wills me, to pull something off.[1]

Paul Abbott

As noted in the Introduction to this study, one of the key aims of this volume is to evaluate and analyse the televisual output and 'language' of Paul Abbott. Indeed, the stylistic features of Abbott's work are clearly meaningful in that they point to and reflect Abbott's sociopolitical stance and his desires, dissatisfactions and motivations. The purpose of this biographical sketch is to highlight how biographical details can develop a reader's/viewer's understanding of particular aspects of Abbott's craft. Although, as John Gibbs and Douglas Pye (2005: 125) argue, 'as we do in our everyday lives, when we watch [television] we have to rely on accumulated experience of ourselves and others to intuit what might lie behind what we see and hear', it is also important to map the semantic fields of the televisual, considering the inspirations of repeated themes, narrative structures and stylistic techniques employed. The originality of Abbott's televisual auteurism is, in this work, to be associated with what John Caughie (2000: 127) refers to as 'the primacy attached to art as an expression of the self'. While I am fully aware of the potential issues related to the use of the term 'auteur' in television (in particular, the fact that such a term seemingly negates the collaborative realities of contemporary television[2]), Abbott's status as a showrunner demarcates a tone, sensibility and voice that is so clearly identifiable, so distinct, that his creations, writings and productions express his personality.

In this sense, Abbott's work can be understood to have a 'signature' style that is unique and trusted. As Sarah Cardwell (2005a: 14) points out, 'television that is marked out as "authored" ... denotes "quality" of some kind; it is special by virtue of the fact that a unique, named individual created it'. Indeed, it is Abbott's writing, his distinct intention plus the recurrence of specific themes, that shape the programmes discussed in this study. Analysing works by a named author has also, as David Lavery (2002: 2) points out, 'become prominent in the way we think and write about the medium [of television]'. In essence, Abbott's work is unmistakable; original in concept, affecting in terms of its frequently non-conventional points of view, socially conscious, politically engaging, complex, multi-layered and unafraid to tackle controversial themes. Thematically, Abbott's focus on families and, in Andrew Klevan's (2000) words, the 'disclosures of the everyday', translates and assimilates itself throughout his oeuvre in the repeated tropes of parent/child role-reversals, working-class and underclass struggles and the ideological resistance and political activism of his characters. Yet, while clearly invested and interested in drama, Abbott does not present his material as overtly dramatic, but rather as what Klevan (2000: 1–2) nominates as 'visually eloquent, ... interested in life experiences based around the routine or repetitive, the apparently banal or mundane, and the uneventful'. Unsurprisingly, then, Abbott's work is most frequently situated in the locus of the domestic and concerns the revelation or transformation of the ordinary as, or into, the extraordinary. However, it also seems important to state at this point that, while Abbott's work clearly showcases sociopolitical issues (issues that can be traced in each of his texts), his characters are not what Cardwell (2005a: 189) refers to as 'mouthpieces for his own views'. Rather, they are bold, distinct and involved in as well as changed by and through the experiences and communities in which they live and work.

Biographical sketch

Paul Abbott was born in 1960 in Burnley, Lancashire, a dominantly working-class town in the north of England and a place that, he notes, 'still regularly causes him to vomit as he crosses the border'.[3] The seventh of eight children abandoned by both parents, Abbott acknowledges that he was a small and, in his own words, 'weird' kid, who realised early on in his life that if he were to survive the difficulties of his childhood, he would need to 'go his own way'. Brought up by his pregnant teenage sister in a chaotic house filled wall to wall with people yet lacking in money (his father refused to relinquish child benefit, despite being mostly absent from their lives), Abbott, like his siblings, worked at various jobs to ensure that he brought in enough money to pay the bills and thus prevent social services from discovering the Abbott family situation.

Without a television set (for more than a day at a time), but with speakers wired up so that the family could 'listen' to television, Abbott developed an exquisite ear for dialogue as well as a love of writing. Writing was, in Abbott's own words, both an escape and a means of 'arguing without contradiction'. Noting that, in the early days of his family life, 'if you wanted to hold a pen you were called a poof', Abbott remembers using his writing to air his frustrations. After having his nose broken by his brother, for example, he penned the words: 'Look at you, you greasy fat cunt!' His brother was unable to read and thus had no understanding of Abbott's defiant slight, but for Paul, the act of resistance through writing, of being able to voice his own opinion, was realised. Over time, Abbott notes that his writing gained in length, soon developing naturally into stories. However, the chaos of the everyday continued, and took a horrific further turn when, aged 11, Abbott was brutally raped. He told no one for fear of the police and social services separating the family, fell into depression, attempted to commit suicide twice and four years later was sectioned. In the 'bin', Abbott says that he quickly realised he could, with help, be 'fixed'. Talking and writing were part of that process and synthesising his writing, his frequency, into stories became, and remains, Abbott's work of resistance.

The catharsis of writing was not only personally poignant – Abbott's saviour, perhaps – but it was also noticed in his community when he entered and won a fiction-writing competition at the Lancaster Festival. Told he had to read out his story as part of the competition criteria, Abbott read in '9–inch docs [Dr Martens boots] and a T-shirt covered in shit'. He won the competition and recalls that his photograph was put in the local paper, much to the shock of his family, who asked, 'what the fuck he had been up to'. Soon after, Abbott was fostered out of his family at his own request – not, as he notes, because he didn't want to be part of it, but because he needed his own space to recover. Abbott joined Burnley Writers' Circle, and later, interested in psychology due in part to his own experiences of psychological breakdown, took up a place at Manchester University to study this subject. While still at university, Abbott first married at the age of 19, but was divorced by 21. Frustrated but still writing, in 1982 he wrote a radio play for a BBC Radio 4 competition – a play he managed to persuade Alan Bennett to sponsor. Telling Bennett that 'he knew where he lived and that he had a great script', Bennett's response was to tell Abbott that the 'play was very good but not the masterpiece he thought it was'. Bennett did, however, sponsor the play, invited Abbott to his home for scones and rice pudding, and told him to continue honing his linguistic composition skills. Abbott did not win the radio competition, but his play was commissioned regardless and, on the back of it, he was quickly asked to write another, then another. It was then, Abbott says, he recognised that he was a writer:

> When I realised I could pay my rent from writing plays, I realised I'd become a writer and I never planned it. Clearly, subconsciously I was doing it from 15. I was a punk with green hair and I had docs and a razor blade round my neck and I'd go to the Burnley Writers' Circle which was full of 60– and 70–year-old women writing for the *People's Friend*. I knew exactly what to get from it and it was an absolutely intractable compulsion to become a writer and I didn't even know that the job existed.

In essence, Abbott became a writer 'behind his own back'. Very quickly, his writing abilities were promoted and he was put up for a storyline editor job (a member of the team who edits stories to ensure that they work suitably as screenplays) on the television soap opera *Coronation Street* (ITV, 1960–). Abbott got the job. Arguably, this early engagement with the genre of soap opera was central to the lifelong formation of Abbott's preoccupations with and continued focus on the familial and the everyday. As Henri Lefebvre (1991: 31) notes in his discussion of the term 'everyday life', the everyday is complex, contradictory and frequently a site of alienation: 'there is a certain obscurity in the very concept. Where is it to be found? In work or in leisure? In family life and in moments "lived" outside of culture? ... Everyday life involves all three elements. It is their unity and their totality, and it determines the concrete individual.' Abbott's ability to write strong female characters (for example, Linda Green in *Linda Green*, Trudy Graham and Yvonne Kolakowski in *Clocking Off* and Fiona Gallagher in *Shameless*) and engage convincingly in modes of discussion regarding the vast sphere of personal relationships marked out what Lez Cooke (2003: 154) (paraphrasing Christine Geraghty), noted to be a 'shift from the previous focus on "the personal" to an increased engagement with social issues'. While such a focus may indeed have reflected the changing political trends of the period (Thatcher's Britain), Abbott's soap schooling, while not always pleasant, has remained seminally important to his socially conscious ethos.

Coronation Street (ITV, 1960–)

Aged 23, Abbott was taken on by Granada as a story editor on *Coronation Street*. Moving quickly from his position as story editor to that of script-writer, Abbott became the youngest scriptwriter on the *Street*, penning no fewer than 53 episodes of the soap. Speaking of his time there, Abbott recalls both the pleasures and frustrations of his writing life. The natu-rally circular structure of the soap (the importance of getting charac-ters back to where they started at the end of each story) was a process that, Abbott notes, he approached with passion, insisting upon tight, comedic and intelligent storylines. Yet Abbott was also, he recalls, often treated badly because of his youth – in his own words, 'twatted for being about twenty years younger than anybody else'. Discussing the reticence of many writers to share their expertise on the soap, Abbott notes that 'many of the other writers were consistently selfish, refusing to share their knowledge or skill'. Despite this partially negative experience, however, such a closing-off of expertise inspired Abbott to approach his work differently; indeed, his experience at *Coronation Street* is one of the reasons that he now insists upon talking so much to new writers: 'I know stuff that other writers can learn in a day and I love passing it on because I want to work with better writers, writers that can write three layers into one scene.' Rather than being threatened by the skill or domi-nance of others, Abbott has, he notes, always used it as a drive to become better at his job. Laziness is something he detests (a defining charac-teristic of his father he acknowledges), and something Abbott actively rallies against. On *Coronation Street* he admits he 'wrote his tits off' as a reaction to being constantly blocked by more established writers on the soap and, as a way of sneaking round their consistent 'robbing of the substance of his episodes'. One of Abbott's episodes was nominated for a BAFTA and his bravery and determination to be the best was visible in the breadth and depth of his writing.

According to Abbott, scriptwriting on *Coronation Street* also taught him to synthesise his voice more clearly and more delicately – a skill he persistently practised every day and every night during these early times. The writing needed, in Abbott's own word, to 'fly', and charac-ters required their own voices and motivations. But despite the need to create well-rounded and realistic characters and worlds, Abbott notes that 'writing a soap script isn't like writing real life – it's a lie, exqui-sitely told if done well, so that it smells real'. Realism is, of course, a complex issue in television, an issue commonly associated with the connection of character to environment. As John Hill (1997: 57) notes of the term, 'there is probably no critical term with a more unruly or confusing lineage than that of realism. ... Amidst th[e] plurality of uses, one consistent implication does appear to survive: that the distinctive characteristic of realism resides in the ambition to, in some way, approximate reality, to show "things as they really are."[4] Of course, in terms of aesthetics, realistic portrayals and visuals are inherently bound up with temporal conventions. What appeared realistic on 1960s television may today be considered unrealistic, obvious and melodramatic. The tensions of realism are not, however, limited to the look of television, but as Hill (1997: 59) argues, relate to *what* is being revealed rather than only to *how* something is revealed. In terms of television, the conventions of realism are, as Marion Jordan (1981: 28) argues, connected with characters and the expectation that they 'should be credibly accounted for in terms of the "ordinariness" of their homes; ... that the time should be "the present"; that the style should be such as to suggest an unmediated, unprejudiced and complete view of reality'. In addition, landscapes should not only be visually convincing but socially determining, becoming what Caughie (2000: 95) designates as 'a material force within the drama, setting the limits and pressures on action and psychology'. Considering the complex realism of soap and its engagement with northern working-class life on the *Street*, Abbott seemingly concurs with Caughie, noting that

> *Coronation Street* was made to feel like the absolute apex of what working-class life should be depicted as and you think 'you're a liar!' On the street she goes in to the shop and buys a packet of fags and a newspaper every day. Ridiculous. She couldn't afford a packet of fags! So, it's more interesting to see how she affords a packet of fags and a newspaper, if that is what she is going to do. It might be by gall, stealth or favour, but if you let the audience see that you are taking care of that, you get away with murder.

Murder, blood and gall literally became explicit themes in Abbott's work, themes that ran into his next three projects; the scripting of an original two-part drama called *Butterfly Collectors* (Granada, April 1999), the creation of a new drama series entitled *Children's Ward* (ITV, 1989–2000) and later, the production of the second series of *Cracker* (ITV, 1993–96), as well as the writing of three episodes of the third series. The first of these projects to be broadcast was *Children's Ward*.

Children's Ward (ITV, 1989–2000)

When he originally conceived *Children's Ward* as a drama set in a children's home, Abbott was advised by the future executive producer of the series, David Liddiment, to change the landscape of the drama as there

Figure 1.1 *Children's Ward*, ITV (Granada) 1989–2000: various cast members, including Tim Vincent, Jenny Luckcraft and Ken Parry

was a competing series on Thames Television (1985–86) called *Dodger, Bonzo and the Rest*. Realising his idea anew and setting his creation in a children's hospital ward (a ward similar to one Abbott had worked on during his psychology degree training), he worked 'like a train'; something that he admits was an 'escape mechanism from his own child landscape'. After a pilot episode of the newly envisaged *Children's Ward* had been commissioned, Abbott told his team that they would not be making it as the script had initially indicated, as he had been forced to 'put lots of stuff in the script for lazy fuckers so it would be commissioned'. Instead, Abbott wanted to make the drama series more political, more radical and more intelligent, to match the social awareness of his intended child audience. Filmed at Bolton General Hospital, the first series consisted of 13 25–minute episodes and was considered a landmark series in children's television drama. As Dave Rolinson (4 July 2011) noted, the series was 'a great drama ..., a quality soap opera, packed with continuing storylines, threads to resolve, dramatic conflict and some potent cliffhanger endings'. *Children's Ward* went on to attain critical acclaim, continuing for 11 years and winning a Royal Television Society Award in 1995 for Best Children's Drama and being nominated for a BAFTA in the category of Best Children's Programme in 1993 and 1996.

The first episode of Series 1 launched with a chaotic sequence, displaying narrative excellence and demonstrating the quick-paced multi-layered style and emotional complexity that were later to become some of Abbott's writing hallmarks. Specifically, the opening sequence of Episode 1 begins with the hard-hitting heavy-metal music lyric – 'Can I Play With Madness' (Iron Maiden, EMI, 1998) shouting out from the screen before fast-paced pans interspersed with close-up shots of various band posters reveal what appears to be a disorganised and chaotic teenage bedroom. The soundscape, whip pan and staccato shot combination gives a youthful, resistant and frenetic energy to the scene; however, the loud aesthetic is soon interrupted as the camera comes to a five-second halt on a framed photograph of a teenage girl dressed in school uniform sitting next to her mother on a park bench, surrounded by leafy green trees. As the camera zooms in on the photograph, the smiling faces of the young girl and her mother are brought to the fore. The camera then pans right, revealing more late 1980s band posters (with a distinct emphasis on boy bands) before again coming to a halt, this time in front of the teenage girl's mirror reflection. Sitting at a messy dressing table and surrounded by palettes of luridly coloured eye make-up, nail varnish, green hair gel and dirty cotton-wool swabs interspersed with a fluffy pink rabbit and *Garfield* soft toys, the girl moves a bright red lipstick over her already overly made-up lips. Adorned in a green sweater dress, large green hoop earrings, permed and back-combed hair and bright pink eyeshadow, the girl is clearly framed here as a typical 1980s rebellious teenager. The music is, we understand, diegetic, and is her chosen battle cry of adolescence.

A cut then reveals that the music being played in the bedroom can also be clearly heard by the girl's mother, who looks up from the garden towards the bedroom window before bowing her head in frustration and entering the house. Walking into the kitchen, the brown checked décor again confirms the contemporary (when it was first screened) nature of the story. Upstairs, the girl changes her music from Iron Maiden to a classical track (seemingly in the hope that her mother won't find this offensive and come up to her room) before picking up her handbag, exiting the room and quietly shutting her bedroom door behind her. Sneaking down the stairs, the girl rushes for the front door, where her mother confronts her with an angry 'Don't you dare, young lady! I've told you – if you want to go to this concert then I'll take you, but you're not going all the way to Birmingham on your own.' Rejecting her mother's offer, the girl shouts that her friends are going so she won't be on her own, finishing her angry response by noting that none of her friends' mothers are accompanying them. As the girl is ordered upstairs and her mother retreats into the kitchen, we see the girl raising her eyes defiantly, her lips pursed, before running down the stairs and out of the door. As the door slams behind her, her mother shouts her name, Fiona (Rebecca Sowden).

Then we cut to outside where Fiona is seen in a long shot desperately running down the garden path and into the road. The aggressive and prolonged sound of a car horn interrupts the scene and a quick shot change shows the audience two successive close-ups; the first of a pair of male hands hitting the horn of a car and the second revealing a suited man's feet hitting car brakes. The tightness of these close-up shots punctuates and reiterates the crisis of the moment. Fiona is then seen in an extreme close-up, screaming, her eyes wide open with terror. Back to a long shot, Fiona is seen being flung over the bonnet of the car, her head pressed against the windscreen. The car screeches to a halt and Fiona falls from the bonnet on to the tarmacked and leaf-strewn road. The driver's face remains hidden; however, we see his hands open the driver's door, the back of his head surveying the scene before he closes the door and speeds off down the road and away from the accident. As Fiona's mother runs down the path, the sound of the speeding car can clearly be heard in the diegesis. Seeing Fiona's lifeless body in the road, she screams Fiona's name before clasping her hand over her mouth. The shot then freezes, becoming a still. The trauma is momentarily frozen in time and the audience is asked to contemplate the horror of what has just occurred. Non-diegetic electronic beats are then introduced and the opening title-card written in bold black-and-white font appears on the right-hand side of the screen, declaring: 'Children's Ward – by Paul Abbott and Kay Mellor'.

As demonstrated above, Children's Ward starts dramatically, concerning itself with familial and generational disputes, resistant ideologies and the possibility of traumatic, heartbreaking consequences. Indeed, as the episode continues, the initially domestic setting changes and the family home is replaced by the fractured structure of the ward at South Park General Hospital. Yet, because the ward is one specifically designated for children, the focus on the domestic is not lost. Rather, the ward is seen to stand in for or take the place of the home. The children sleep there and have access to sweets, magazines, music and play areas and their own clothes. Despite this domestic leaning, however, the hospital space is also clearly sanctioned as a sociopolitical one, with band posters in Fiona's home being exchanged for explicitly political ones, proclaiming, for example that 'AIDS IS EVERYONE'S PROBLEM. / In 1991 AIDS claimed 400 deaths a month and a quarter of a million people were infected.' This clear showcasing of the political and in particular the magnitude of the AIDS crisis in the early 1990s is telling. While it is of course possible to argue that the prominent placement of the posters is declamatory and didactic – in essence, over-assertive – I would argue that such an inclusion of an adult topic points to the deferential ways in which Abbott addresses his child audience. In addition, the placement of such posters within the frame also highlights a hallmark of Abbott in that he brings difficult and complex issues to the screen and leaves them hanging by not suggesting a quick fix, but rather, by asking the audience to recognise the issues and think about them for themselves. As the episode continues, other difficult problems and issues are highlighted, such as child alcoholism and abandonment via the character Billy (Tim Vincent) who, we learn, fell off a roof at a party while intoxicated and Keely (Jenny Luckcraft), who is treated for hepatitis after having an illegal tattoo of her boyfriend's name – humorously, 'Grim' – cut into her body. Telling a fellow patient that she was unable to walk when she was admitted and was segregated on a different ward due to her infection, the results of children's misguided decisions are, like Fiona's, cast as life-threatening.

Co-created with Kay Mellor and employing Russell T. Davies as both a writer and series producer from 1992 to 1995, the drama continued throughout its run to tackle difficult social issues such as child neglect, drug use and sexual abuse. Abbott's respect for his audience was visible in the complexity of the series content and, on reflection, he notes that 'even with the crude skills I had then, I knew you couldn't have a scene with just one thing happening. It's important to have multiple layers, multiple voices and never, ever write with depleted respect for your viewer.' Abbott's skill was commented upon by Davies in a 2011 article in the *Guardian* written by Vicky Frost. Nominating Abbott as his 'TV Hero', Davies noted that

> I noticed his name before I knew him. Because if you watched a *Coronation Street* that was really good, where Deidre suddenly had a sex life or Liz had a party at the back of the Rovers, that was Paul Abbott. He put that salt into *Coronation Street*. Something real comes out of his characters ... I think he's simply the best writer in the world ... If Paul writes a scene in an office and if a secretary walks in, or someone with two lines, he makes that person cross, or angry, and you realise that even the smallest character has so much going on. The last few years have been glorious because I've seen a lot of him. He kind of inspires you personally because his standards are so high, and he has such a massive work ethos. You have a cup of tea with him and come out with five insights into people. You will find yourself writing at 2 am and remember something he said to you. If you were starting out as a writer today, I'd say just get his entire body of work. I've read his scripts and I've watched his shows and I do hope to emulate it – but, really, it's beyond emulation.

Cracker (ITV, 1993–96)

Abbott's involvement in the highly influential television series *Cracker* was offered to him on the back of Granada liking his *Butterfly Collectors* script (a dark, two-part crime drama broadcast by ITV in 1999); a script in which Abbott told the story of a police officer, John McKeown (played by Pete Postlethwaite), jaded by his job, and a 17–year-old boy, Dex Lister (played by Jamie Draven), a young man bringing up his two younger siblings alone. Like *Butterfly Collectors*, *Cracker* was a psychological drama and a series that exuded darkness in its emotional twists and aphotic narrative. Concentrated around a larger-than-life criminal psychologist, Fitz (played by Robbie Coltrane), *Cracker* was a cerebral series, an emotional series and, despite its darkness, a distinctive 'hit' for ITV. Engaging with what Mark Duguid (2009: 3) nominates as the 'social conscience' of 1990s Britain, ugly issues such as the crisis of masculinity, madness, grief, poverty, unemployment and the seeming abandonment of the working-class (in particular the white working-class) were rendered visible, if not explicit, as motivators of fear, anger and violence in the series. The first series reached viewing figures of almost 12 million (Duguid 2009: 28) and it was on the back of this success that Abbott was asked to produce the second series and deliver the quality that its audience demanded.

With no previous production experience, Abbott was, nevertheless, hugely excited at the opportunity. In Abbott's own words, he was 'shitting himself' about the producing role, was lambasted by other experienced producers who had wanted the job and was simultaneously elated and determined to do it 'bloody right'. Looking back, Abbott avers that Granada needed someone 'a bit mad' to work alongside Jimmy McGovern, as he was sending in dark, socially repellent but exceptionally original scripts. They must, Abbott notes, have recognised him as both 'a bit twisted and respectful of audiences'. Liddiment (the executive producer on *Children's Ward*), who offered Abbott the job, knew that Abbott could produce the dark *Cracker* scripts that McGovern was writing and would 'take the blame' for such wretched stories if it was so apportioned. It was not. The series was both a huge learning curve for Abbott and a veritable success, ending with viewing figures averaging 15.2 million (Duguid 2009: 28).

The production of *Cracker* was, Abbott notes, a new but terrifying experience in that he had to 'learn the whole film thing'. Having been used to working on multi-camera tape drama, Abbott took a 75 per cent pay cut and worked 18–hour days to 'get it right'. His passion for learning new skills took him to the next level, a level where he learnt to 'speak from his spleen'. Abbott didn't, he admits, have 'a producer's voice', but he was also unaware that, in fact, he had displayed production skills on *Children's Ward* by constantly being on set and 'making sure everything was all right'. Abbott worked to exhaustion producing the second series, despite a busy home life. In the midst of one of the biggest *Cracker* shoots, Abbott's baby girl was born and he was allowed 12 hours off. The year 1994 was Abbott's terrifying but fulfilling producing year. Reflecting upon it, he notes:

> There was so much I didn't know – like stuff about neg checks. I thought neg checks were checking the negatives and I was like, 'haven't we got an Avid camera now?' The scripts were also in a different format. We used to write [in *Coronation Street*] on one half of the page because the camera direction went on the left. Working with a new voice was so exciting, but I was scared stiff. But I'm so proud that I was scared and admitted that I didn't always know what I was doing. I did know why I was doing it, though.

Abbott also notably learned from the writing of McGovern, a writer he says is 'brutally honest', and was asked to write the third series of the drama.

Scripting penetrating episodes such as 'Best Boys', 'True Romance' and 'White Ghost', Abbott's writing on Series 3 of *Cracker* displayed a different track to McGovern's, frequently focusing on child abandonment and the psychological implications of distorted or absent parental love. 'Best Boys' deals explicitly with such issues. Opening with a manic and raucous sequence (foregrounding the industrial spaces and stories of Abbott's later series *Clocking Off*), the episode showcases a chase on foot inside a factory and follows a young John Simm (playing new factory boy Bill Nash) being forcibly stripped by a group of high-energy female machinists desperate to remove his trousers. As the scene is witnessed and subsequently disbanded by factory foreman Stuart Grady (played by Liam Cunningham), Nash is told to 'run faster or think faster'. Highlighting the issue of personal responsibility from the off, the complexities of such a seemingly simplistic statement are brought to bear as the episode continues. Nash, a teenager living in a halfway house, works purposefully late at the factory, misses his 'home' curfew and is kicked out. Breaking into the factory in order to find a place to sleep, the perceived innocence of Nash's action is soon revealed to be more purposeful and calculated. Questioned by Grady as to why he broke in when he knew the building was alarmed, Nash retorts, 'I knew you had the keys. You'd have to come and get me.'

The notion of an older male having to 'come and get' a teenage boy demarcates the beginnings of a strange parent/child relationship between the two characters, a relationship that is later explicitly played out and performed to a police officer. The dialogue also, and more subtly at this stage, stresses the curious father/son relationship that the pair take on. After Grady agrees that Nash can sleep on his sofa, Grady is awoken as Nash is tapping a chisel against a sculpture of a wooden bird. Demanding to know what he is doing and removing the chisel from Nash's hand, telling him, 'Don't touch that', Grady clearly enacts the role of parental protector. Further, when Nash asks, 'What kind of bird is it?' Grady replies by telling him that it is a Lanner Falcon, before silently giving him a bird book to look at. While the details of the book remain outside the screen frame, the potential significance of and both men's attraction to the Lanner Falcon is clearly signalled as important. The Lanner Falcon is, most obviously, a bird of prey and is, furthermore, a bird that both hunts by horizontal pursuit and mainly takes birds in flight. The resonance of such a creature is pertinent in foregrounding the unfolding of the narrative and its clear significance can be reread in the aesthetics of the screen. For example, considering an earlier sequence in which Nash decides not to clock off at the end of his shift, and tells Grady that he will work overtime, despite Grady's protestations that Nash has finished for the day, Nash's clear, fixed, horizontal gaze at Grady can be understood as acutely meaningful. While told by Grady to go home, Nash continues staring directly at his boss, ignoring Grady's orders and continuing his work and his determined and silent observation of Grady. Though Grady is clearly the older of the two, and the more physically, powerfully and vocally established of the men, he is not the hunter but rather, is hunted by Nash. Such a sentiment is clearly echoed in Nash's later cry when, referring to his relationship with Grady, he shouts, 'I picked him! I picked him!' Towards the conclusion of the episode, the fact that Grady was already a 'man in flight' (in Fitz's words, running away from his wife, child and the army) when he met Nash, is exposed.

Yet the father/son parallel is not straightforward. The continual exposure of Nash and Grady's half-naked bodies[5] in intimate domestic spaces belies a strong, unspoken erotic tension between the men. While not physically acted out through sex, the intimacy and desire of each man for the other compels and drives the burgeoning relationship. Confronted about their relationship by Grady's landlady, Mrs Franklin (Jackie Downey), Nash is accused of being Grady's rent boy. Filmed in close-up and with a facial expression of disgust, cross-cuts between a shirtless Nash, an agitated Grady and a return to Mrs Franklin result in her stating, 'Get that whore back where it belongs. I don't like this at all. Shirtlifters under my roof! ... I'll call the police.' As her diatribe continues, a close-up shot of a wooden box filled with chisels dominates the screen. Quickly followed by a medium shot, Nash is shown mindlessly picking up one of the tools and twirling it between his fingers. Next, Mrs Franklin storms off, telling Grady to 'be out of here in two minutes'. As Grady follows her and places his hand on her shoulder the camera tracks him briefly, before showing Mrs Franklin turn, slap Grady in the face and call him a pervert. It is at this point in the narrative that Nash, incensed by her bigoted (and partially unfounded) assumptions, confronts her: 'Who do you think you're talking to, you silly old cow? We've done nowt wrong!' As Mrs Franklin raises her arm to slap Nash, Nash lifts his hand to protect himself. Nash's face is then seen in a rapid close-up before a replacement of the original medium shot occurs, revealing the bleeding arm of Mrs Franklin, the shocked face of Grady, and the confused expression of Nash. The quick insertion of Nash's rapid close-up works here to demonstrate his shock, while the intercutting between the three indicates the ways in which the characters are now bound together by this traumatic and avoidable tragedy. Despite this, Mrs Franklin clearly has not learned her lesson. Telling Nash that he is a 'little shit' and that the police will 'have you now', the camera continues its focus on Nash's face. From the left, Mrs Franklin's hands can be seen to enter the frame and attempt to close around Nash's throat. As Nash's eyes refocus, he grunts loudly and his body and that of Mrs Franklin jolt, indicating that he has stabbed her. A long shot then shows the three characters in the confined space of the hall. On the far right-hand side of the screen, Grady looks on. In the middle of the screen, Nash is seen to be pinned against a wall, with the now heavily bleeding Mrs Franklin clinging to him before slowly losing her grip and sliding to the ground. A return to a close-up shot then shows Nash's mouth whispering the words, 'Oh, God' before looking pleadingly towards Grady. Mrs Franklin is next seen in a bird's-eye-view shot (indicating her new vulnerability), and then a long shot, crawling away from the men and towards the telephone, presumably to call the police.

In the next long shot, Nash begs Grady for help, holding up the chisel. Grady takes it, walks towards Mrs Franklin and stabs her forcefully twice in the back. Interestingly, the stabbing is not actually seen on-screen. Rather, Grady is seen walking purposefully towards Mrs Franklin and placing a steadying hand on her back before the shot cuts to a slightly low-angled close-up of Nash looking on. Two loud grunts are heard, followed by a close-up of Mrs Franklin's body falling flat on the ground, and a close-up of the bloodied chisel.

Packing his clothes into a bin bag in the next scene, Nash tells Grady that he can't bear to go back to the children's home. As the narrative continues and Grady and Nash go on the run, Nash confides in Grady

Figure 1.2 *Cracker*, ITV (Granada), 1993–96: Mrs Franklin (Jackie Downey), Bill Nash (John Simm) and Stuart Grady (Liam Cunningham)

that he is an orphan, and when he was 7 years old (and after being fostered countless times) a couple, Diane and Brian Nash, agreed to adopt him. As the adoption process proper was beginning, Diane (as Nash calls her his 'nearly-mum') became pregnant and the adoption was cancelled or, as Fitz later notes to Diane, 'Age seven. You cancelled William [Nash].' Confronting Diane, Brian and their two boys after seeing them in a shopping centre, Nash and Grady follow the family home. Nash watches the children from the garden before entering the house. Spotting him, Diane telephones his social worker, McVerry (Paul Barber), who comes to remove Nash from the house. Outside, clearly having waited for him, Grady tells Nash that he doesn't have to go back, intimating that he will look after him. Angry at what he infers to be Nash's subsequent refusal to go back to the children's home with him, McVerry gives up on Nash, saying, 'I'm washing my hands of you. I'll call the police.' This secondary abandonment sends Nash over the edge. Getting into Grady's car, Nash and Grady follow the social worker, driving him off the road before murdering him in a deserted car park.

Murder as the end point of emotional extremis is a trope continued when the identities of Nash and Grady are discovered by Fitz. While Grady is captured, Nash goes on the run, taking Grady's gun and taking Diane and Brian's eldest son, the child they swapped him for, hostage. As Grady is interviewed by Fitz, it is revealed that psychologically, the reason that Grady murdered Mrs Franklin is because her bigotry towards homosexuality may have subconsciously reminded Grady of the attitude of his own mother, who he was desperate not to let down. While the relationship between Grady and Nash did not become sexual,

Figure 1.3 *Cracker*, ITV (Granada), 1993–96: Fitz (Robbie Coltrane), DCI Charlie Wise (Ricky Tomlinson), DS Jane Penhaligon (Geraldine Somerville) and Stuart Grady (Liam Cunningham)

it is further revealed that the only reason for this was Grady's weakness rather than his strength. As Fitz asserts: 'That's the waste. You never did it. You never said it. Bill Nash offered you the best-ever chance of making all this mean something. Your legs went. Your stomach went. You could hardly breathe. It's tragic that you should do all this, that you should feel all this and not say it. You love him.'

Indeed, Grady does, and when Nash takes Diane and Brian's eldest son, Steven, hostage with Grady's gun at a summer fair, Grady, accompanied by Fitz, goes to him and begs him to let go of the boy and put the gun down. Crying, Grady pleads with Nash, admitting finally: 'I love you. I love you more than I ... Please put down the gun. If you don't put the gun down I'll never be able to tell you again.' Scared, Grady persuades Nash to hand the gun to him, and immediately after doing so, Nash is shot by police marksmen and dies in Grady's arms.

Such a narrative echoes the academic arguments of Duguid (2009: 122), who notes that an idiosyncrasy of Abbott's writing on *Cracker* can be seen and is at times flaunted via the coda of an 'altogether more hyperbolic melodramatic mode' than that employed by previous writer and series creator, McGovern. Employing a generic mode that moved, in part, away from the gritty realism of McGovern's scripts, Abbott's writing, and in particular his dialogue, frequently showcased and grounded the fantasies and psychological desires of his characters. Indeed, the painful and, in Fitz's own words, 'heartbreaking' pitch of emotion evidenced in 'Best Boys' (as well as 'True Romance' and 'White Ghost') is a dramatic trait that can be seen to continue into Abbott's post-*Cracker* projects – a four-part soap opera entitled *Springhill* (BSkyB, 1997), a six-part crime drama broadcast on ITV in 1997 called *Touching Evil* and a beautiful six-part drama starring Robson Green and Francesca Annis, telling a story of love and deceit, entitled *Reckless* (ITV, 1997).

Notes

1 This and all other unattributed quotations from Abbott are cited from specially commissioned interviews with the author in 2011 and 2012. Full extracts from the interviews are available in Appendix 1.
2 For discussions on TV auteurism see, for example, John Caughie, ed. (1981), *Theories of Authorship: A Reader* (London and New York: Routledge); Bishetta D. Merritt (1991), 'Bill Cosby: TV Auteur?', *Journal of Popular Culture* 24:4, 89–102; Roberta Pearson (2005), 'The Writer/Producer in American Television', in *The Contemporary Television Series*, ed. Michael Hammond and Lucy Mazdon (Edinburgh: Edinburgh University Press), pp. 11–26; David Lavery (2002), '"A Religion in Narrative": Joss Whedon and Television Creativity', paper given at the *Blood, Text and Fears* conference, Norwich, England, available at www.slayageonline.com/PDF/lavery2.pdf (accessed 12/06/2012).

3 Paul Abbott, cited from a specially commissioned interview with the author.

4 As John Hill goes on to note, 'such an understanding of the term "realism" does not, however, "resolve the critical difficulties" of the term. Part of the problem here derives from the very definition of reality itself.' Hill also notes the significance of 'conventions' of realism. *Sex, Class and Realism: British Cinema 1956–1963* (London: British Film Institute, 1997), p. 57.

5 As Mark Duguid notes, Dick Dodd's camera is 'repeatedly drawn to Bill's hairless chest' in this episode. *Cracker: BFI TV Classics* (Basingstoke: Palgrave Macmillan, 2009), p. 127.

For me, *Reckless* was about losing control. Unconditional love for somebody is really complicated because you can't stop thinking about them.
It's really hard to hide. I wrote *Reckless* because I wanted to write a version
of a younger man/older woman [relationship] because my second wife
was 13 years older than me and we were together nearly 10 years. In
my opinion, it only fell apart because she felt that I was bound to go
for somebody younger. It got racked with suspicion. I've never had an
affair in my life but, the less energy you have to fight back, the more
it looks like they're right because you've got no answer. The power of
suspicion tells you that people don't know how to ask questions. You've
got to ground stuff in real life but, I didn't want to write about my experience directly, but to use the younger man/older woman and put some
bite into it. I wanted to write a romantic comedy with teeth. It shouldn't
just be dark stuff that attracts good writers.[1]

Paul Abbott

Inspired, in part, by Paul Abbott's second marriage to an older woman
and broadcast for the first time on ITV on 6 February 1997, *Reckless*
was a serial drama in six hour-long parts. Created by Abbott, produced
by Sita Williams and executively produced by Carolyn Reynolds, the
BAFTA-winning drama tells a story of love, obsession, infidelity, heartbreak and desire. Set in Manchester and starring Robson Green as
Dr Owen Springer, Francesca Annis as the object of his desire, Anna
Fairley, and Michael Kitchen as Dr Richard Crane (Anna's unfaithful
husband and Owen's boss), the narrative brings to the forefront the
disruption of domestic life by the extraordinary emotions and intersections of love. Mapping the recklessness of love, the cartography of
the serial lays bare the tumultuous emotions and consequences associated with the breaking down and building up of passionate sexual
relationships. While hailed by Maggie Brown (1997) in the *Guardian*
as a 'drama without murder, psychopaths or psychiatrists stealing the
scene, just people flinging their clothes off and going with the flow

of messy passions', *Reckless* is, while focused in part on sexual desire, more, I contend, a story of romantic love. Though often utilised as a staple theme of mainstream television drama, love is not treated by Abbott in a light-hearted way, but rather as an experience, a process of self-knowledge and transformation that is frequently agonising, arduous and painful. Love, in essence, is framed by Abbott in *Reckless* as a test, a process of testing or, in more literal terms, a personality assessment.

The notion of testing relationships and an abandonment to love is where *Reckless* first kicks off. Against the backdrop of non-diegetic electric guitar music and amidst traffic noise, the serial opens with the youthful Geordie, Dr Owen Springer, running with abandon out of a hospital building and through the grounds towards the main road. He is wearing a suit and has a brown leather holdall slung over his shoulder. Owen's desire to travel is framed by both the traffic noise and the increasing diegetic rumble of an Inter City train. Running across

Figure 2.1 *Reckless*, ITV (Granada), 1997: Dr Owen Springer (Robson Green) and Anna Fairley (Francesca Annis)

a main road and barely missed by a car whose horn seems to echo a crescendo to Owen's emergency, he manages to hail a cab. The next shot, from the air, shows a fast-paced train heading speedily along its tracks. Owen cannot be seen in shot but his voice is heard. Audibly hyper, Owen asks passengers if he can borrow a mobile telephone. Confronted with several refusals (Owen is clearly out of place, signalled by his accent and his lack of ownership of a mobile telephone), Owen nominates his situation as an 'emergency'. Suddenly, as the view inside the train is revealed, we hear Owen continue on his quest to borrow a telephone, but we do not initially see him. Instead, the camera focuses on an attractive mid-forties woman sitting in a First-Class seat, watching events unfold. As Owen is told to 'sod off' by a posh male passenger, the woman looks directly at Owen and, as he comes into shot, she holds out her mobile telephone to him: 'Here, use mine.' Thanking her, Owen makes his urgent call.

While the voice on the other end of the line cannot be heard, Owen's own dialogue is tellingly familial and domestic in its focus: 'Elma, its Owen. What's going on? I've just got the message.' Obviously listening to Elma on the other end of the line, indicated by his pause in dialogue, Owen responds by asking, 'Has the GP seen him?' Cross-cuts between Owen talking on the telephone and the woman whose telephone he has borrowed dominate the sequence. While the woman is clearly watching Owen (with concern rather than suspicion), he himself is engrossed in the telephone conversation. Becoming more animated as the conversation continues, Owen angrily asserts into the telephone: 'Elma, you listen to me. You ring him back and you ask what he thinks emergency means. If he's not there in fifteen minutes you call an ambulance and take my Dad straight to Casualty. I'm coming up to Stockport so I'll be there in half an hour.' The difficulty of family attachments, love and fear of loss thus set the scene, clearly demonstrating Owen's love for his father and his desire to be closer to him geographically. As the camera again moves to a high-angled shot of the train from above, non-diegetic guitar music is introduced. Shots of the train powering up the tracks from different angles are then intercut in rapid succession before being faded out. Fading in is a sprawling soft red cityscape at dusk – Manchester. The opening credits roll as Owen is seen in the back of a cab on a terraced street in the city, a cab that soon comes to a halt, signalling that Owen is 'home'.

Parent/child role reversal

Once he is home, the strength of Owen's familial and loving ties to his father are highlighted. Rushing up the stairs to his father's bedroom, Owen enters to find his father asleep in bed, being injected with glucagon by his doctor. After Owen tells the doctor that he is Arnold's son and also a doctor, as well as outlining his father's history of angina, the doctor calmly tells Owen that his father is diabetic. As Owen reels at the news, the doctor leaves the room, leaving Owen sitting on his father's bed. As his father sleeps, Owen looks at him with tenderness and this scene specifically is clearly constructed as a parent/child role reversal. Downstairs, the doctor tells Owen that his father's poor health is due to his lifestyle. In a tragicomic speech he notes:

> We call it 'Logan's Run'. Friday morning, as soon as they get their pension, they're straight out of the post office into the White Lion. Five pints of Guinness and enough Scotch to remake *Whisky Galore!* He's diabetic because of the booze. Circulation's lousy on account of the fags and his heart's usually racing faster than the horse he backed at dinner. He talks about you a lot. He's very proud of you.

As the GP leaves the house, Owen surveys the décor, looking intently at a framed photograph of his (clearly younger) father and mother seated in a pub, holding pints of beer and grinning. A close-up shows Owen smiling before looking away and moving into the half-light of the lounge, scanning his father's many bottles of pills placed on a side table. A cut then takes us to the next morning. In a medium shot, Owen is making breakfast for his father – two slices of brown toast, a bowl of cereal bran and a glass of orange juice. Quickly joined by Arnold, Owen's father looks at the breakfast, noting, 'It's not for me. I have bacon and eggs.' In response, Owen says, 'Not any more.' The tone of the scene here is interesting. While the dialogue pitches the father and son at loggerheads, the tone of their disagreement lacks any aggression, but rather is relayed with concern and love. Asking his father why he didn't follow the diet that Owen had sent him, Arnold responds that it tasted like cardboard. Equally, when Owen attempts to talk to his father about his excessive drinking, Arnold avers: 'That's the trouble with you lot [doctors]. A bloke can't fart without it on his file!' While Arnold showcases the petulance and frequent humour of a teenager (simultaneously perhaps attempting to point to the seriousness of political oppression or the 'nanny state'), Owen clearly enacts the frustrated but loving role of a parent. In essence, Owen and Arnold's relationship here exemplifies Máire Messenger Davies's (2005: 136) notion of 'children rescuing adults from themselves', whatever the age of those children, and as such, can be considered as subversive. Even in these exchanges, however, the tender intimacy of their relationship is audible and visible on the screen. While Owen reprimands his father for his rebellious behaviour as if he is a naughty child, Owen's love for his father unquestionably underpins his behaviour.

The reversal of parent/child roles in *Reckless* outlined above is a theme that continues to dominate and frame the parent/child roles represented in the rest of the serial. Later in Episode 1, we are privy to Arnold searching in the back of a kitchen cupboard for a stashed bottle of whisky. Finding it, he pulls it out and a close-up reveals a handwritten note stuck to the bottle and penned by Owen. It reads: 'I've marked it. PTO.' As Arnold turns the scrap of paper over, another close-up of the other side reveals Owen's PTO: 'And I've wee'd in it.' The playful banter here marks both a continuation of parent/child role reversals but also hints at Owen's insistence that his father change his lifestyle. Owen's clear desire to care for his father (or, more crudely, keep an eye on him) is again highlighted later in the episode when Owen is seen attending an interview at the local hospital, St Gregory's Infirmary. He is there, we learn, for a surgical registrar post. Admitting to his interviewer and potential boss, Richard Crane, that he wants the post (a post which involves a drop in salary and means that Owen will leave a more prestigious job in London under one of the UK's top surgeons) to be closer to his father, the parent/child role reversal is set. Later in the episode, Owen receives a letter from St Gregory's inviting him to attend a second-stage interview – a personality assessment. Ringing the despotic Surgical Business Manager at the hospital, Viv Reid (Daniela Nardini), to ask what the assessment involves, the dialogue between the two demonstrates a distinct difference of philosophy:

OWEN: I've got this letter asking me to go for a management assessment. Just wondered what it was all about?

VIV: Two crucial words there, doctor. 'Management' and 'Assessment'. I have a call waiting.

OWEN: Why do I need assessing if I've already been interviewed? Assessed for what?

VIV: Personality. Independent Assessment is this particular hospital's policy to minimise errors in staff appointments. We don't want to encourage people who wouldn't naturally fit into a highly dependent team system.

OWEN: Whoah! Hang on – this is crazy. Let me get this straight – a management consultant decides whether I'm a fit candidate for a surgical post?

VIV: No. Your personality opens that little door. Seems reasonable enough to me.

OWEN: Do the BMA know about this?
VIV: The only ones who have asked are the ones who have failed the assessment. Bye.

Owen, of course, attends the assessment. Displaying his disdain for the process, however, he is filmed sarcastically answering a series of questions. Shown on the screen within the frame of the assessment camera, Owen visibly begins to perform, shifting from asserting frustrated responses to acting purposefully perky. Indeed, the performative irony of being placed in front of a camera, essentially being screen-tested, is not lost on him. As Sarah Cardwell (2005a: 40) notes, such a scene also perhaps draws attention to the author's [Abbott's] interest in 'playing roles, and the limitations of the roles which we are forced to play in social situations, and which are determined by factors such as age, gender and class'. Owen's perfect personality is something he clearly plays at here, but is not committed to. Importantly, this double framing is also significant to the meaning of the scene, as it helps the audience to register both the multiple aspects of Owen's personality and points to a distinction between the romantic or heroic roles that actor Robson Green had played previously, and his present role. Speaking of this disparity, Abbott notes: 'Robson had a reputation as a housewives' favourite, but to convince in his role as Owen, we didn't need him twinkling. We wanted to subvert that – show him ripping his own guts out, terrified of his feelings for Anna.' Of course, as the show continues, Owen does just that, but, at this early stage in the first episode, when asked to describe his personality, he grins broadly at the camera before stating: 'Young, sexy, bright, ambitious, tasty, adventurous, sexual, oh, and put funny – I'm very funny – and touching and moving and passionate and compassionate. Successful, charming, clean – very clean. I'm tough, fit, sharp, quick to learn, quick to unlearn, truthful when necessary, born liar when necessary ... .' A cut then shows Owen's filmed assessment being viewed by a male office worker. As he looks on in disgust, Anna walks into the office. Transfixed by Owen on-screen (the man to whom she lent her telephone on the train), she listens to his responses before turning to her colleague and noting: 'He's taking the piss.' With this, Anna turns off the screen (indicating her status as the boss), and walks away.

Owen fails his personality assessment, or, does so at least in the eyes of Anna. While the assessment obviously acts as connective tissue in the episode further linking the intertwining of Anna and Owen's lives, it is also significant that Owen initially fails to fit into either Anna's categorisation of a suitable match or what Viv earlier nominated as a 'highly dependent team system'. The team into which Owen's failure to 'fit' occurs is a team that, unbeknownst to Owen, is run by Anna's husband, Richard Crane. As the episode progresses, Owen discovers that Anna heads up the management assessment consultancy, has watched the tape of his personality assessment and has found him 'unsuitable'. Angrily confronting her, Owen admits that he 'took the piss' in his personality assessment but adds that he is the best person for the job (and having found Anna's notes regarding all of the other interviewees is, by her own admission, the most suitably qualified). In addition, Owen's appeal to Anna is personal – he needs the job in order to care for his father. The confrontation ends badly and the potential for the suitability of the pair (a potential intimacy played out on the train) seems to have come to the end of the line. That is, until Owen is informed by letter that his job application has been successful.

While this narrative track seems to connect only tenuously in the first instance with the issue of parent/child role reversals, it is in fact when Anna visits her sick mother at St Gregory's later that month that the theme is clearly brought back into focus. Leaving his rounds to speak with her, Anna tells Owen that her mother is suffering from Alzheimer's, to which Owen responds that Anna is wasting her money paying for a private room in the hospital. This clearly touches a raw nerve, and Anna responds by looking Owen directly in the eye and asking: 'Who the hell asked you to make moral judgements about the way that people spend their money?' Again, the purpose of this sequence contains multiple layers of meaning. First, Anna's reaction serves to demonstrate that, if we were in any doubt, she is a wealthy woman. Secondly, Anna is shown to be a woman clearly in charge of her own mind and actions. Thirdly, the sequence leads to an important dialogue between Owen and Anna in which Anna points out the similarities between them:

> Your father is clearly very important to you. It's where we came in. You were travelling north to be with him because he was sick. Presumably you dropped everything – it would have come at any cost ... She [my mother] was in a nursing home before this, the best we could buy. Constructive care Monday to Friday, fantasy tea parties where we would rig the questions so that the responses would make sense. You made me feel a bit odd about of all that. I pay £400 a week just to see the back of her because she soils her sheets.

In response to Anna's admission and her obvious guilt about not caring for her mother personally, Owen plans a surprise in which he collects Anna's mother, Myrtle (Margery Mason), from the hospital in his car, and drives to Anna's place of work in order that they should have some quality time together. Initially angry, Anna decides to go along with the trip as her mother, for once lucid, seems so excited by the prospect. The trip is a success, and as Owen encourages Myrtle to remember her past, Myrtle takes Anna and Owen to the place where Anna was conceived. There, Myrtle reveals the intimacies of her relationship with Anna's late father. Myrtle's confession to Anna that 'I loved him so much it hurt' is also telling. Injecting both romance and the pain of love into the narrative, the themes set the scene for Owen's developing but as of yet unspoken love for Anna.

Testing love and romantic fantasy

Myrtle's confession regarding the pain of love speaks to a dialogue of anguish discussed by Lynne Pearce in her important text *Reading Romance*. Speaking of romantic love, Pearce (2007: 2) argues that '"falling in love" and "being in love" are, by definition, so confused, contradictory and perverse as to render them inchoate ... As an emotion that is best understood as a heady cocktail of psychic drives, cultural discourses and social constraints, it is experienced by its subjects as a traumatic "impossibility" that is worse than irrational.' Such an expression of love – love as confusing, consuming and disorientating – seems to mark out and more properly explicate the turbulent and increasingly reckless path of Owen's burgeoning feelings for Anna. Finding out that Anna is married and, moreover, married to his own boss, Owen is unable to prevent himself from behaving recklessly in front of her. Outside the hospital, however, Owen's first confession of his love for Anna is framed as both classically romantic and melodramatic. Shown standing in the rain, Owen confesses that he thinks that he is love with Anna before clarifying, as she walks away in shock: 'Mrs Crane. I am. Definitely. I'm in love with you.' Combinations of close-up shots here reveal and reinforce Anna's unblemished elegance, her perfect make-up and bouncy shining hair unspoiled by the pouring rain. In contrast, Owen is drenched. With rain pouring off his nose and running down his face as if awash with tears, the sequence foretells the heartbreak, difficulty and pain of Owen and Anna's relationship. Visually coded as classical romance, the sequence also perhaps foretells a story of pride and prejudice echoed in Joe Wright's 2005 filmic adaptation of Austen's novel of that name.[2] As Elizabeth rejects Darcy in *Pride and Prejudice*, Anna rejects Owen in *Reckless*. The agony of love is thus introduced to the narrative and works to undercut the orchestrally accompanied declaration of Owen's feelings. Prejudiced against Owen's declaration and later in Episode 1:2 noting that she doesn't believe him, Anna asks Owen what he finds so attractive about older women. Again, Owen's reply is figured as romantic: 'I don't go for older women. I'm just in love with you.' Having clearly convinced herself that Owen's feelings are part of a fantasy, Anna stares at him incredulously as he sits powerless, rejected, breathless and out of control. Revealing the reality of his love for her, Owen then declares:

> I swear I've never felt like this about anyone in my life, Anna. When I saw you this morning in the car, I nearly died. I couldn't breathe. I started sweating. My fingers, they went numb. I had to go for a walk up Oxford Road because the woman standing next to me in the lift said I should see a doctor.

ANNA: What about my husband? Your boss?

OWEN: I don't want to talk about him.

ANNA: Oh. But you'd have to. In the given scenario you would have to. The man I love wouldn't evaporate. The man who loves me isn't going to stand aside for your convenience ... This is where you come unstuck. It isn't even a respectable fantasy if you can't see past the obstacles.

The nomination by Anna of her husband as an 'obstacle' is interesting here in that it plays into a narrative structure of romance specified in Janice Radway's *Reading the Romance* (1984) – a text that both follows and adapts Vladimir Propp's seminal *Morphology of the Folktale* (1986[1928]) in which he argues that all characters can be positioned in seven 'spheres of action': the villain; the donor; the helper; the princess; the dispatcher; the hero; the false hero. In Radway's text, she, like Pearce, speaks of love as a transformative experience and prescribes a new 'Narrative logic of Romance' thus:

1. The heroine's social identity is destroyed.
2. The heroine reacts antagonistically to an aristocratic male.
3. The aristocratic male responds ambiguously to the heroine.
4. The heroine interprets the hero's behaviour as evidence of a purely sexual interest in her.
5. The heroine responds to the hero's behaviour with anger or coldness.
6. The hero retaliates by punishing the heroine.
7. The hero and heroine are physically and/or emotionally separated.
8. The hero treats the heroine tenderly.
9. The heroine responds warmly to the hero's act of tenderness.
10. The heroine reinterprets the hero's ambiguous behaviour as the result of a previous hurt.
11. The hero proposes/openly declares his love for the heroine with a supreme act of tenderness.
12. The heroine responds sexually and emotionally.
13. The heroine's identity is restored.

While of course the heroine and aristocratic male of which Radway speaks are reversed in terms of social class in *Reckless* (an issue to be discussed presently), the structure or 'logic' of romantic love is envisaged similarly. Indeed, Anna's prejudice that Owen's desire for her is 'evidence of a purely sexual interest in her' is conveyed through her questioning of his 'older women' fantasies. Although according to the structure of Radway's logic Owen's next step is to punish the heroine, Anna, Owen's next move is not coded as straight punishment but rather as a selfish act. Finding out that Anna's husband is engaging in an extramarital affair with fellow employee Viv, Owen tricks him into confessing his infidelity to Anna. Reflecting on his actions, Owen then goes into his father's bathroom and amidst the intimacy of the dated and ugly space admits: 'I've just done something really terrible, Dad.'

Although the content of Owen's confession to his father is not figured explicitly on-screen, the repercussions of his actions are. Anna, her eyes brimming with tears, sits in shock listening to her husband's telephone confession of his affair at their home. Upset, then angry, Anna has the locks to their house changed and goes to a hotel, where she telephones Owen. On his arrival, she asks him to remove his clothes. The emotional distance between Anna and Owen is clearly placed in the frame here, with Anna standing on the opposite side of the room to Owen. In response to Anna's request, Owen says: 'Anna, we don't need to do this. I just want to talk.' In response, Anna replies: 'What if I don't want to listen?' As Anna and Owen sit on the bed, both clearly nervous, Anna covers Owen's neck with tiny butterfly kisses before asking: 'Do I seem vulnerable to you?' Owen's answer is both tender and honest: 'I think you've picked a really bad time to ask.' Following Radway's logic of romance, then, this sequence moves through to point 12, with Anna responding both emotionally and sexually to Owen. As their coupling is revealed on-screen, the tropes of television romance again come to the fore. In shallow focus and backed by a non-diegetic romantic soundscape, Owen and Anna make love in the half-light, kissing tenderly before being overtaken with sexual passion.

Place and space

It is at this point in the narrative that the importance and meanings of both place and space are explicitly highlighted. In the neat, sexy and neutral space of the hotel, Anna and Owen make love. The next morning, however (as figured in the opening of 1:3), Owen wakes to find an empty space next to him. Where Anna should be, Owen finds a note:

'Had to go.' As Owen clutches the note to his chest, Anna is revealed in a tracking shot re-entering her marital home. As the camera pans away from Anna crossing the threshold, her husband, Richard, is seen to be asleep on the back seat of his car, having been locked out of 'their' space. In the next shot, Anna is seated inside the marital bedroom, drying her hair in front of a three-part mirror. While such a prop is not unusual in the mise-en-scène of a bedroom, the three distinct yet interlinked sections of the mirror are telling here. Anna stares into the central section of the mirror, leaving a half-reflection of herself on the two outer sections, which could be interpreted as the two men now in her life – Richard and Owen. Later in the episode, Anna's mother is taken ill. Owen operates on Myrtle; however, the operation is interrupted by Richard, who takes over as lead surgeon after praising Owen's work. Afterwards, Anna thanks Richard for his contribution and gives him a key to the newly-changed locks of their house. Later as Richard sits in their neat and expensively decorated lounge, Anna arrives home. Walking straight up the stairs, she grabs her toothbrush and takes the pillow from her side of the bed before shutting herself in another room. As Richard follows her, she slams the door in his face, shouting, 'Don't you bloody dare come in. Don't you dare!' before dissolving into loud, contracted sobs, slumped against the inner door in the darkness. The camera then cuts to an establishing shot of the outside of the house. Self-contained within its own grounds, the large white house's symmetry makes it appear idyllic as soft light pours from within through the large sash windows, and yet the sound of Anna's muffled sobs can still be heard penetrating the walls as the trees sway and throw shadows across the exterior before the screen cuts to black.

The foreboding blackness of this formerly idyllic space is discussed directly by Anna in a later meeting with Owen. Sitting with him in a pub, she tells him that she is moving into her mother's house, stating that her marital home 'feels so weird I feel like an intruder'. Though the space of Anna's mother's house is initially rendered neutral and safe by Anna, the notion of the past intruding upon the future is brought aesthetically front and centre via the mise-en-scène of the following sequence. Initially appearing on-screen as an abstract, blue-lit image akin to some sort of X-ray, the blue light turns to black before natural light is allowed to reveal the shadows and facets of the white-sheeted space; a living-room floor on which Anna and Owen sleep. Indeed, the very fabric of this space (Myrtle's home) reveals blankness and dislocation in that Myrtle is no longer well enough to reside there and Anna's father is dead. The fact that Anna and Owen sleep on the floor rather than in a bed clearly marks a further element of unbelonging.

Simultaneously, however, the space can be understood as a romantic sanctuary or fantasy space in which Anna and Owen can be together. The multiple tones alluded to here demonstrate the reflexive nature of the drama. In addition, the emphasis on visual display, on the ways in which spaces are mapped and styled in *Reckless*, promotes a link between location and identity. Going back to Radway's 'logic of romance', it is thus interesting to note that her last point – point 13 – is 'the heroine's identity is restored'. While in Episode 3 of 6 it is, of course, much too soon for a complete restoration of Anna's identity, the mapping of Anna's emotions onto the blank white space of her mother's house is key to understanding the significance of such a space to Anna's new identity as a youthful lover rather than a middle-aged wife. Living unknown in her mother's house, Anna and Owen are allowed to build the space around them into their own. Yet, while Anna is intricately connected to Owen, she is not yet officially separated (divorced) from Richard. Again, the space and texture of her former marital home (a home which, Anna notes, she and Richard lived in for 15 years) pulls her back to commitments of old.

In 1:4, Anna tells Owen: 'it won't always be this easy', and, indeed, her words come to fruition as she moves her belongings out of her former marital home and into her mother's. Visiting her mother at the hospital, Myrtle notes and reinforces Anna's fears about her relationship with Owen. As Anna reveals that they got drunk together her mother responds by saying: 'I love it when that happens ... 'cos it doesn't last very long, does it?' The fantasy of Anna and Owen in a safe, romantic space is unsurprisingly compromised when Richard finds out that it is Owen with whom Anna is now having a relationship. Punching him on the nose at work before being restrained by his former lover, Vivien Reid, and other medical staff, Owen leaves the hospital bloody and angry and goes to the sanctuary of Myrtle's house. Unfortunately for Owen, Anna also directs Richard there so that they can talk. As both men realise that they are occupying the same space, a fight breaks out. Framed as both comedic – via the dialogue – yet bitter – via the violence in which they engage – the haunting repetition of such a fight over a woman is clearly rendered in the language and intertextual reference made by the attending policeman. As Owen and Richard verbally abuse each other, with Owen saying, 'I didn't take your wife. You gave her away, you stupid bastard', the attending officer remarks: 'Bloody hell! It's Alan Bates and Oliver Reed.'

The reference to the film *Women in Love* (dir. Ken Russell, 1969), telling the story of a relationship between two men and two women, is of course poignant here, holding up a mirror to the events occurring

Figure 2.2 *Reckless*, ITV (Granada), 1997: Dr Owen Springer (Robson Green) and Richard Crane (Michael Kitchen)

in *Reckless* as well as transforming the tragic consequences of Richard's infidelity into momentary comedy (as Richard and Owen begin to wrestle on the floor akin to the infamous nude wrestling scene between actors Bates and Reed in Russell's film).

As in *Women in Love*, however, the role of the women in the narrative – Anna and Vivien – (the source, alongside male egotism, of the fight) are given increasingly more space and power. In 1:5, as an inquiry is launched at the hospital regarding Richard and Owen's fight, it is Anna and Vivien who manage to both control the men's subsequent behaviour and shape events, leading to both men keeping their jobs. While Richard in particular is seen to be losing control of the space and place of his rapidly disintegrating marriage, he is able to command control over his workspace and Owen's within the hospital. Ordering Owen to work 'on call for a month' (to prevent him spending time with Anna), Richard designates Owen as a constant performer in his surgical theatre of revenge. In response to Owen's situation, it is Anna who shows her control by telling Richard that his actions have led to her filing for divorce. Directly after Anna's announcement, the next shot cuts to Richard at the marital home. Having opened the front door to be informed that Anna has booked a team to redecorate the lounge, it is clear that Anna is literally painting over her and Richard's past. While Anna is in control of the situation, both Owen and Richard appear to be floundering. In theatre, Owen's patient suffers a rupture and dies on the operating table. At home, alone, Richard drinks and laments his loss – both that of his wife and the impending loss of the house, which, Anna informs him, she is 'putting on the market'. The next day, Richard turns up at Anna's workplace and informs her he is moving out of the house: 'It feels like somebody died in there.' Indeed, more accurately, in this statement Richard is conveying to Anna acknowledgement of his acceptance of and grief at the death of their marriage. Anna says nothing but wordlessly understands.

Feeling sad and, perhaps, we infer, a little guilty about her new relationship with Owen, Anna arranges to meet Richard at their former home to talk through the breakdown of their marriage. Knocking at the door of her former home, Richard invites Anna in and thanks her for agreeing to come. The strangeness or strained nature of these gestures denotes the tension between Anna and Richard and past and present that is keyed into the very space of the home that they had built together. As Anna and Richard enter the lounge space, the mise-en-scène highlights the breaking down of the past; lamps have their shades missing, the shelves are bereft of books and paintings are propped up against the walls rather than hanging on them. As Anna tells Richard that she had to 'wait twenty years for him to stop looking at his doctor's badge and look at her, only to find that [he] was sharing his success with a piece of middle-management', Richard responds with a cutting truth:

> You weren't waiting for me, you liar; you were waiting for yourself to get your bloody finger out. The further I went the more jealous you got. All that waiting and then, then you start your own business – when there was this much gap left in our life for a family. A baby. A son. A daughter. A family.

Richard's assertion here, his truth about the shortcomings of their marriage and about his own late desire for children that he couldn't push because he had made Anna (by his own admission) wait ten years, is both ultimately disruptive in terms of causing Anna to reconsider her own role in the disintegration of the relationship and interrupted by a loud repeated knock at the door. On being allowed entry by Richard, Owen insists that Anna admit to her husband that she loves Owen and will go through with the divorce. Though this is clearly demanded at the wrong time and in the wrong space, Anna complies. In response, Richard delivers his final blow, forcing Owen to tell Anna that it was he who forced Richard's confession of infidelity, he who revealed a truth to Anna that hurt her irrevocably. Demanding that both Owen and Richard 'get out', Anna is left standing alone amidst the wreck of the room that was once warm and alive. The anxious residue of mistrust and lies is clearly suffused within the drama of the marriage breakdown here, in the space that was once, on the surface at least, a perfect, neat and ordered upper-middle-class home. The changed significance of the physical space clearly indicates the reckless destruction of former happiness, and visually implies an uncertainty about the future place of any relationship for Anna.

Mapping the romance of cross-class relationships

The issue of social class and in particular, cross-class romantic relationships is acknowledged in Radway's 'logic of romance' as noted above. Indeed, the space between Owen and Anna is figured not only in their age gap, but also in their distinctly different social positions. The difference in their class status is mapped onto the social spaces of the text itself in *Reckless* and is thus worthy of note here. In their very first fateful meeting on the train heading north, Owen's requests to borrow a mobile telephone take place not in the standard-class carriage, but in the First-Class one. As mentioned at the beginning of this chapter, Owen is heard before he is seen in the diegesis of this sequence. His first line is figured as a polite request: 'Excuse me. They've no phone cards left at the buffet. Do you mind if I use your phone?' While a seemingly simplistic statement on the surface, Owen's request in fact belies essential information about his social class and identity. First, he does not own a mobile telephone. Secondly, he is not travelling First-Class. Thirdly, this makes him reliant upon the kindness (or not) of others who have the finances to afford such luxuries. Fourthly, he is confident in his ability to interact with members of a higher social class and is not hurt by their condescending responses, but rather is used to such challenges and is able to keep his focus and temper. The many denials that passengers give Owen are also figured as an interesting point of audible difference here. While Owen's accent is clearly Geordie and his language abbreviated, the accents and sentence structures of the First-Class passengers with whom Owen interacts are, without exception, complete, 'posh' and spoken in 'the Queen's English'. Indeed, the many rejections he receives prompt him to say, 'Look, I've got money.' Seemingly, though, no one believes Owen and the refusals continue. Thus, in the 15 seconds during which Owen is heard and not seen here, he is explicitly framed as 'out of place' in this upper-middle-class social space.

Anna, in contrast, is first made visible in *Reckless* seated comfortably in the First-Class carriage. In a close-up shot, her head is framed and is shown resting against an explicit, stitched 'First Class' sign nominating her seat (and thus her own identity). Anna's hair is clearly 'done', her make-up is elegant and her attire (a crisp, cream blouse and red necklace) connotes middle-class finesse. Like her fellow passengers, Anna's accent is received pronunciation, yet her attitude is clearly different as she smiles and holds out her phone for Owen to use. On Owen's arrival 'home', he enters his father's terraced house. While aesthetically pleasing from the outside, inside, the dirty old paintwork and the awful brown 1970s décor, the visible chip pan, mismatched cups and cheap kitchen table and chairs are at once figured as normal and, simultaneously, made strange by Owen's arrival. Dressed in a matching blue blazer, shirt and tie, Owen stands out, and his difference is voiced by the visiting doctor to his father, who notes of Arnold: 'He talks about you a lot. He's very proud of you.' Pride is, from this point in the narrative, a defining feature of Arnold's character and, by extension, Owen's own. The next day, as Owen confronts his father about being 'pissed', Arnold's proud response is: 'Pissed nothing. This is a medical condition. Just because you're a doctor, doesn't give you the right to everyone's business ... I didn't send for you.' Though Arnold is clearly a proud man who refuses (explicitly at least) to be told how to live his life by his son, he does, as earlier indicated by his own doctor, have an immense pride in Owen's achievements, a pride that is filtered through and nominated by his female 'home help', Irma (Kathryn Hunt). Arnold's closest friend and confidante, Irma is not intimidated by Owen's success but clearly proud of the 'boy done good' from a working-class background. When Irma's relatives 'our Gary and Mick' – young lads dressed in vests and baseball caps – come to the house to tip junk, she says to them of Owen, 'He's the Doctor.' Gary and Mick couldn't care less (or, as Abbott puts it in the stage directions for this sequence, '*couldn't give a shit*'). Nevertheless, Irma's pride in Owen (a pride informed by Arnold's own) is clear.

It is not until 1:4 after Owen and Anna's deep love is confirmed that Arnold is actually seen and heard on-screen discussing and confronting the possible difficulties of such a cross-class relationship. After Anna sends a courier to Arnold's house in the middle of the night to deliver a mobile telephone to Owen, Arnold sees Anna standing in the street next to her car. Asking if Owen intends to introduce Anna to him, and, receiving a negative response, Arnold states: 'M reg[istration] Audi. That's not your welfare state, is it? If she loves you, she must be curious about your background. There's only one problem with women like that. If you've taken this long to get this far, and she's married to him and used to better, what have you got once the nookie wears off?' Such a response to Anna and Owen's differing social backgrounds is brought up by various other characters in this episode. After finding out about Anna's relationship with Owen, for example, Anna's husband, Richard Crane, exclaims: 'How could you! With a grubby, underqualified little twat like that! With a pokey-faced, bloody uncultured drone like that! How could you?' Though Richard's derivation of Owen is framed as humorous via Richard's dialogue and his exaggerated and excessive facial and bodily gestures, the sentiment of his verbal and physical assault on Owen is undoubtedly sincere. The sensibility of Owen and Anna's lack of 'fit' together is also more poignantly addressed in 1:5. Meeting Anna by chance for the first time, Arnold takes her to the local pub for a drink, to play bingo and then for takeaway chips. Walking back to the house, Anna asks Arnold to be frank about what he thinks about her and her relationship with Owen. It is at this point in the narrative that both Arnold's pride in Owen and his concern for him (a concern relating to Owen's lower social status) is made explicit. Stopping in the street and speaking gently, Arnold says:

> I think you're gorgeous. A very nice lady. Done well for yourself, and I think our Owen's lucky to have found you. But, this country is still weighted in the favour of your type, not his, so he's had to fight to get this far and, er, well, I'm very proud of him for that, so, I wouldn't want to see him messed about with. You know?

Though Arnold's 'confession' regarding his honest opinion of Anna and Owen's relationship is a trope more commonly found in feminist or, as some argue, 'post-feminist' television texts such as *Sex and the City*, it is also worth noting here that the intimacy of this moment can in fact be read as what Glen Creeber (2004: 151) refers to as 'a dramatic re-examination of "politics" itself, a contemporary dialogue about "choice" that reveals the part we all play in the political nature of ourselves and inevitably, the world around us.' Anna's political responsibility (according to Arnold) is not to abuse – even unintentionally – her higher social status and the luxuries of choice that her high social class has afforded her. While Owen risks losing all that he has worked for and, we intimate, fought for through his continued relationship with Anna, she herself is neither exposed to nor expected to take such risks. Her wealth, her status and her connections are seemingly secure. Despite this, however, Anna is not represented as one-dimensional but as a complex, fallible and at times flawed individual who refuses or at least is fearful of confronting issues that might disturb the middle-class façade of perfection that she and Richard spent 15 years building. It is worth reiterating here that it is only after Anna finds out about Richard's marital indiscretion that she strays from the constraints of her position as a faithful upper-middle-class wife. Socially then, as Arnold points out, Owen is Anna's counterpoint and, indeed, it is this disparity in class status that informs not only the very foundations of the characters' actions and drives, but also the casting of major actors in *Reckless*.

Casting

Robson Green, Francesca Annis and Michael Kitchen, playing the love triangle made up of Owen, Anna and Richard, are startling in their poignant performances of reckless honesty and selfish desires in romance, lust and love. The verisimilitude of painful love and illicit passion is convincing, however, because it is not represented or played in a straightforward way, but is instead framed as a process of becoming, a process in constant flux. At times blackly comic and, at others, gut-wrenchingly melodramatic, the characters' changing feelings for one another create a milieu of anxiety. Such anxiety is performed and rendered visible in relation to the social and political identities of their characters; identities that are often bound up in the existence of the 'other' characters in the serial as well as their other characters – other identities – that exist outside the show. Robson Green, for example, was, according to Abbott, 'fantastic' for the role because of his acting skills, his physicality and his reputation as a hard-working, working-class 'everyday man' (a status cemented in part by his role as Fusilier Dave Tucker in *Soldier, Soldier* (ITV, 1991–97)). In addition, however, Green's various press interviews about his own background undoubtedly added to the believability and intimacy of his public/private identity crossover. In one such interview, Green noted to journalist Frances Hardy (2010): 'I'm a working-class lad who had to struggle to achieve success.'

The similarity, then, between Green's private persona and his public one as Dr Owen Springer – the working-class 'boy done good' in *Reckless* – can also be seen in Owen's romantic counterpoint, Anna Fairley/ Crane, played by Francesca Annis. As an established actress, Annis had a persona described by Tim Auld (2009) of the *Telegraph* as a sophisticated beauty, somewhat 'regal, cold but strangely sensual'. Having had her big break at the age of 16 in *Cleopatra* (starring alongside Elizabeth Taylor and Richard Burton), Annis went on to star in the controversial Roman Polanski film *Macbeth* (1971), as well as taking other lead roles in both film, theatre and television. While her genuine upper-class background and established 'status' are both tropes played on in *Reckless*, another oft-discussed aspect of Annis's interpretation of Anna concerned the similarity between Annis's own well-reported and unfortunately timed love affair with actor Ralph Fiennes, a man 18 years her junior, for whom she had left her husband and father of her three children. While Annis remained for the most part tight-lipped about the seeming conflation of off- and on-screen events, she did note in an interview with Richard Barber of *The Times* in 1998: 'I suppose people must wonder why I'd choose a part where art could seem to be imitating life. But I was contracted to make *Reckless* before all the mayhem of the past two or three years. Looking back, I must have been a publicist's dream.' In terms of publicity, Annis certainly did hit the headlines and in 1998 was voted TV's sexiest woman at the age of 54,[3] something unheard of in previous generations. However, the politics of representation regarding placing on-screen the desires of 'women of a certain age' was a subject Annis and the executive producer of *Reckless*, Sita Williams, embraced in their discussions of the serial. In an interview with the *Independent* (1998) Williams argued that the older women was and remains essential to the diversity of life representations and experiences as represented on television:

> To my mother's generation, 50 was old, but now we've got spending power, we're very aware of our own independence and we have emotional and physical confidence. That's why *Age Concern* used that poster of a beautiful woman in her fifties wearing a bra. More and more women boast about their age because they look and feel terrific. Also, women want to watch women of substance. You can only watch so many young things prancing about.

Indeed, while Annis injects a mature independence, complexity and sexual vibrancy into her role as a forty-something lover, Michael Kitchen – an established and serious English actor – plays out his part as Anna's unfaithful husband in a gorgeous yet simultaneously revolting childish manner. Characterised as a successful wealthy brat of a man, Richard, Kitchen's character, is not, however, without warmth, and in particular his cutting, dry irony, his clear intelligence and his adolescent reaction to Anna's affair are gripping. Indeed, it is Richard/Michael who often has the best lines in the drama and delivers them with superb comic timing. Boasting a hilarious confetti of curse names for Owen, Richard calls him 'a jumped-up, poxy bloody Registrar' and a 'grubby, underqualified, charmless little twat' in 1:4 before moving on to say he is 'a Jacobean genital-waving Tin Tin' in 1:5. Fully aware of his own conceit, when Owen calls him a 'twat' in 1:5, Richard's comic response is a smile, accompanied by the word 'Absolutely.' Unfortunately for Richard, while he succeeds in driving Owen off the road, he loses the ultimate battle for Anna, who, following true 'romantic logic', ends up in the arms of Owen and has her identity restored through her relationship with him.

As a prominent and respected actor, Michael Kitchen's stardom is intrinsically associated with both British theatre and television, primarily through his preference for playing serious roles or roles in serious texts, such as Martin in Dennis Potter's *Brimstone and Treacle*, Peter in Stephen Poliakoff's *Caught on a Train* and Mercutio in *Romeo and Juliet* for the Royal Shakespeare Company at Stratford. In many ways, then, his personification of Richard, a successful upper-class surgeon is, on the face of it, not a great leap. However, the humour that he injects into this role and the performative, adolescent solipsism allow a clear demonstration of his emotional range that plays on his thespian roots yet showcases them in a distinctly melodramatic tele-visual style. In terms of Annis/Anna, the conflation of the serious and sexy also works by playing on the aforementioned blurring between her public persona and private life while clearly, in the words of Julia Hallam (2005: 89–90), registering a shift in the 'representation of women from secondary characters to central roles they now commonly occupy in many prime-time series and serials'. Indeed, Annis/Anna is not merely a love interest but is framed as a strong, confident, talented woman, able and willing to take control over her life. Yet, in *Reckless*, as Anna sometimes finds difficulty in balancing professional decisions and private feelings (for example, in the hiring of Owen after his unsuc-cessful personality assessment), Annis seemingly feels the same in terms of her emotional behaviour, noting in an interview for *Woman's Journal* (1997): 'I am not afraid of change, which is not necessarily a good thing. I expect I am reckless.' As for Robson/Owen, the crossover between the two can be understood in the fact that they both show-case professional success beyond their years. With the issue of social class informing the authenticity of on- and off-screen personas, both are socially symbolic figures of the 1990s, highlighting a shift from the 1970s and 1980s power of what Hallam (2005: 101) refers to as an upper-class 'theatrical heritage' towards the more popular and commercial.

Conclusion

While, as aforementioned, Abbott's goal of creating a 'romantic drama with teeth' can be understood in Richard's own words as 'absolutely' achieved, official confirmation of the drama's success came in the form of a National Television Award win in 1997 for 'Most Popular Television Drama Series', as well as a raft of BAFTA nominations for Abbott himself in the category of 'Best Writer', and Annis and Green for best actress and actor, respectively. Speaking of the cast and the show itself, Abbott reflects on *Reckless* thus:

> I loved that cast and I had a ball making it. After the darkness of *Cracker*, I went home and painted my basement white. I wanted to make a romantic drama. It needed to be unmissably magnetic. Robson was cast, then Francesca went in, then Michael Kitchen went in and we cast around the three of them. You had, as a viewer, to come to terms with the big stuff that is a back story. The characters had to be rounded. The more you like all the characters, the better drama it is, because you don't want to see anybody hurt.[4]

The emotional pull of each of the characters that Abbott discusses here, his insistence on making all of the characters rounded, intelligent, flawed, proud and prejudiced, work to reveal a dramatic tendency in *Reckless* that sways towards an aesthetics of melodrama or perhaps, more specifically, the 'soap opera'. While 'soap' aesthetics are traditionally connected to the personal rather than the political, however, *Reckless* suffuses its drama with and amidst the self-reflexivity of the central characters. Owen is, through his love for Anna, forced to recognise his own strengths and weaknesses, his own tendency to fight to achieve his goals and to confront the disparity in social class between himself and the woman he loves, using his words to persuade her of his genuine status rather than his fists. Anna, in turn, is confronted by her own prejudices in her relationship with Owen. Not only is she forced to learn through her personal liaisons with Owen that she initially 'reads him wrongly', but that, ultimately, he is more honest about his feelings, more willing to lay bare his emotions and desire than Anna or her former husband ever were. As for Richard, faced with his own self-conceit, he recognises that his initial affair came about as a result not of his weakness, but of his arrogance and his secret desire to have a child.

For all of the main characters, then, the personal is rendered political, public, painful and pertinent to their growth, their becoming, their identity. As sociologist Anthony Giddens (1991: 70) notes: 'What to do? How to act? Who to be? These are all focal questions for everyone ... – and ones which, on some level or another, all of us answer, either discursively or through day-to-day behaviour.' The potency of the characters' personal choices are thus mapped onto a much larger political framework, meaning that the politics of the serial grow out of the personal rather than being contrived in a reverse formation. In an auteurial sense, Abbott's tropes of parent/child relationship reversals, cross-class relations and the personal as political are evident, powerful and potent signifiers of his own love triangle. In Abbott's last stage direction on *Reckless*, he noted that '*Owen and Anna should look at each other and connect with a kiss that seals their future.*' On reflection, it seems that in Abbott's work, *Reckless* may well function in the same way.

Notes

1 This and all other unattributed quotations from Abbott are cited from specially commissioned interviews with the author in 2011 and 2012. Full extracts from the interviews are available in Appendix 1.
2 In the film (a tale of love across social class), when Mr Darcy confesses his love to Elizabeth Bennett, they too stand amidst a backdrop of pouring rain as Darcy (Matthew Macfadyen) admits: 'I have struggled in vain and I can bear it no longer ... I had to see you ... I fought against my better judgement ... I ask you to end my agony. I love you, most ardently.'
3 As noted by James Rampton in 'An Actress in her Prime', *Independent*, 10 October 1998, available at: www.independent.co.uk/arts-entertainment/an-actress-in-her-prime-1177415.html (accessed 12/09/2009).
4 See note 1 above.

You've got to dignify every character – even the scummiest. The biggest antagonist in a story wasn't born like that, so we need to know why he became like that. You can't say it literally, you've got to make a smell that he has to have that job and he has to do things a certain way and it's an imperative, not a choice.[1]

Paul Abbott

Clocking Off is an issue-based television drama set in Manchester, England. Broadcast by the BBC in 2000, produced by the Red Production Company and introduced via a vivacious, fast-paced and luridly colourful opening sequence (in the form of industrial-sized rolls of brightly coloured fabric filmed through fluorescent lens filters), the start of the drama determines the expansive, varied and colourful nature of time spent both outside and inside the Mackintosh Textiles company. As the title of the drama indicates, the significance of time and the very nature of temporality are central tropes in Abbott's series. Set in and around the factory, the importance of the temporal is connected strongly with the routines of the everyday, the pace of extra/ordinary information and the dynamic flow and rupture of well-timed or mistimed events. The nominated importance of everyday demands – demands represented through opening scenes of mass early-morning congregation outside the factory in order for the workers to 'clock on' – are, however, indexed by a more significant temporal loop in which *Clocking Off* demonstrates a return to age-old social realist television drama. Providing self-contained stories in each of its episodes, the drama returned, at least in part, to the format of the single play so customary in social realist texts of the 1960s and 1970s. The origins of social realism itself, however, go back further. As Lez Cooke explains (2005: 186–7):

Social Realism has a long history in British culture, dating back to the 1930s documentary film movement and manifesting in different forms at different historical moments. A celebrated moment was that of the

Figure 3.1 *Clocking Off*, BBC One, 2000–3: Driver Stuart Leach (John Simm) standing next to a Mackintosh Textiles lorry

British 'new wave' in the late 1950s and early 1960s, when many plays and films were awarded the dubious accolade of 'kitchen-sink drama'. In television drama this tradition can be seen as early as June 1956 when Ted Willis's *Woman in a Dressing Gown* (Associated Rediffusion) was screened as a Television Playhouse production on ITV ... But it is in the Wednesday Plays and Plays for Today of Tony Garnett and Ken Loach that social realism in television drama achieved its fullest expression as a result of their preference for shooting on film and on location, enabling the 'lived reality' of working-class life to be shown with a documentary verisimilitude.

Indeed, as noted by the executive producer of *Clocking Off*, Nicola Shindler, in the BBC press release for the drama, a focus on social realist television was desired when creating *Clocking Off*: 'The idea that Paul Abbott and I had was to create a modern Play For Today.'[2]

Yet, despite this nomination of a social realist coda in Abbott's drama, *Clocking Off* is notably distinct from the drama of the 1960s in its aesthetic vibrancy, variable tempo, carnivalesque imaging and playful perspectives. As the BBC website notes: '*Clocking Off* is a patchwork of colourful stories.'[3] More than this, however, *Clocking Off* can also be identified as a generic patchwork. Via the multiplicity of editing methods and aesthetic modes employed in the series, the representations of the characters' everyday lives can be seen as extensions of the geographical landscape; a landscape that, while initially appearing serious and grey from the outside, reveals itself as a new, colourful, generic hybrid. *Clocking Off* is a drama that is socially aware, a drama that focuses on the importance of the everyday and a drama that attempts to represent 'real' issues. In addition, however, *Clocking Off* is something more than a standard social realist text. It is frenetic, experimental, colourful and cinematic in its representative techniques: a hybrid. The 'quality' high production values evident in *Clocking Off*'s frequent mosaic montages serve to remind viewers of the growing proximity, the hybridity between cinematic and contemporary televisual texts – a proximity that, Robin Nelson (2007b: 11) notes, 'might be best understood as an enhanced visual style'. Indeed, as Cooke (2005: 192–3) states: '*Clocking Off* differs from [other] contemporary drama series ... in its use of film rather than video. ... Film tends to connote "quality drama" because of the higher production values involved.' The production values include camera and sound quality (no dramatically over-modulated or barely audible sonics), extensive set constructions, lavish budgets and post-production editing. Such convergence is not only significant on a generic level here, but, as the BBC website indicates, on a thematic level too. In representing the everyday personal struggles of a community of workers on-screen, the series foregrounds the significance of the messy spillage between public and private time and space, highlighting its importance.

The erosion of liminality between everyday intimacies concerning private, familial or romantic relationships and everyday public relations and interactions with work colleagues are slippages repetitively foregrounded in the diegetic discourse of *Clocking Off*. Scenes revealing the dismantling of borders between work and leisure include Episode 1:5, where, for example, the factory boss, Mack (Philip Glenister), is called to the work canteen to find his workers have staged an unwanted birthday celebration for him consisting of alcohol, nibbles and the presence of a 'stripogram'. In Episode 1:1, a boozy 'works do' is organised, to take place one evening at a local working men's club, again demonstrating a preoccupation with working-class collectivity. Social arrangements (friendships, romance, casual sex, going out) made between the factory employees are, however, continuously pitched alongside the painful and often unwanted exposure of private emotions in the public working sphere. In 1:1, Sue (Alison Swann), a canteen employee at Mackintosh Textiles, breaks down at work following a private incident in which her missing (presumed dead) husband, Stu (John Simm), a former lorry driver at Mackintosh prior to his disappearance, unexpectedly returns home. Confused, relieved and angry over his lack of an explanation, Sue crumbles while working in the canteen. As twenty or so female machinists go about eating their lunch, Sue tries to ask the girls to 'empty their cartons'. Realising that no one is listening, Sue is shown placing a meal tray on the canteen counter. In the next long shot, she is framed in the background of the image looking down at the floor while the machinists eat obliviously in the foreground. Sue lifts her chin up, attempting to repeat her request, but soon breaks down, her attempted discourse of order punctuated only by loud sobs. Then seen in a medium close-up, Sue's plain gold wedding band is explicitly displayed when she raises her hand to her mouth to muffle her sobs. In the next shot, we see a reverse perspective. The machinists are looking at Sue. Machinist Yvonne (Sarah Lancashire) stands up and walks towards Sue, holding out her arms in a consoling gesture.

Rather than this act being structured as a straightforward act of empathy, however, Yvonne's knowing look at her friend, Julie (Siobhan Finneran) and 'partner in crime' (literally, as is revealed in Episode 1:2) before she rises from the lunch table to comfort Sue indicates that Yvonne has an interest in this situation that surpasses a mere shoulder to cry on. Demonstrating her power amidst the group of machinists, Yvonne snaps her fingers at her friend before indicating a smoking gesture. Cigarettes are brought to Yvonne and she gives one to Sue, sitting her down and ordering one of the other girls to 'shut the door' of the canteen. Standing above Sue, Yvonne fills the silence of the canteen: 'Come on Sue, these are all mates.' The irony of this state-ment is realised when the camera pans round the machinists to reveal them all observing Sue intently. None of the women are shown to be 'real' friends to Sue, but all desire to hear her reveal what has happened in the privacy of her home. The silent anticipation and strained looks of the machinists seen in this shot also indicate that perhaps a rumour mill regarding Stu's recent return has already been at work in the factory. Indeed, it appears that the delay in finding out others' personal information constitutes the ordinary flow of desired knowledge inside the factory. Accordingly, it is the deferral of private knowledge being made public that ensures both its importance and drives the desire for its circulation. Interestingly, it is never revealed to the audience what Sue does or does not say to Yvonne and the other machinists but, significantly, we are shown that the private does not remain private in the public work space. It is this sentiment that is stressed here. Importantly, it must also be noted that as an audience we have already been exposed to the knowledge that the machinists seemingly crave in the opening scene of the episode. The compulsion to repeat and nominate Sue's exact feelings regarding Stu's unexpected return is resisted by Abbott here. Instead, the flow of information inside the factory is shown to function in a similar mode to the textile production line itself. The compulsion to repeat is thus not one that Abbott gives in to in order to clarify Sue's complex emotions. Instead, Abbott allows the audience to see that the dissemination and nomination of information from inside the factory will soon be repeated by its own employees to others both within and outside the factory community. This process is captured in a scene where, we infer, the workers are shown passing on the information to others after they have 'clocked off' and left the factory building.

Working in tandem with the on-screen knowledge flow discussed above, the audience is also asked to consider the ways in which multiplicities of knowledge, private, public and social, are mapped in the series. From the opening of the first episode, multiple narratives come into play, with fast-tempo-cuts between them. In the very first sequence of 1:1 the camera establishes the factory as the hub of the textile town that it dominates. The prominence of the large red-brick building and copious towering chimneys set against a grey sky indicates the central positioning of Mackintosh Textiles amidst its surrounding community. With the audible score of drumbeats in the background, the notion of the factory serving as the heartbeat of the community is made explicit here. Workers arrive en masse, some on buses, some on foot, others in cars. Lorries move in and out of the factory premises, indicating the constant and dynamic movement of goods. The life and movement of the factory are then visually matched in the next shot by a further form of transport: a tram moving up a hill. A straight cut then takes us back to the factory, where a graphic match is made between the tram in the previous shot and an upwardly sloping, moving conveyor belt. A further cut then takes us back to the tram before focusing on a male (a man we later identify as Stuart) looking out of the window. Another cut then takes us back to the factory floor.

After a montage of shots inside the factory, a straight cut reveals Stuart leaving a newsagent's shop and walking casually down an ordinary street before entering his house. Announcing his arrival with the colloquial, 'It's me', Stuart enters the kitchen, switches on the kettle and begins to read the paper. A young boy in school uniform comes into the kitchen slowly, his eyes firmly locked on Stuart. Looking up briefly, Stuart asks the boy, his son, if he is OK. In response, the boy shouts loudly for his mum. Outside, the boy's mum, Sue, is seen pegging washing on a line before hearing her son calling. Running into the house, her reaction to Stuart's arrival is, like her son's, one of shock. Covering her mouth with her hand, she stares at Stuart, mumbling: 'Oh, God. Oh my God.' The next shot then cuts back to the factory, highlighting the multiple yet soon to be intertwined narrative strands. As Nelson (1997) argues, the structure of multiple narrative strands or 'flexi-narratives' in television drama demonstrates a temporal shift from 'single-issue narratives of social realism', and this departure from single narratives can be seen both in the structure of *Clocking Off* and beyond it.

Models of dialogue can also be understood to operate as 'flexi-narratives' in *Clocking Off* in the sense that individual characters' voices, perspectives and spoken expressions are continuously analysed, judged and moved between. The flexibility and heteroglossic nature of socially typifying language and its appropriateness (or not) in the corporate world is highlighted in 1:1 in an exchange between the boss of the textile company, Mack, and his personal assistant, Trudy (Lesley Sharpe). In a glass-fronted office positioned above the factory floor, Mack and Trudy have the following exchange:

MACK: Tell him he's a tight-fisted prick and tell him, from me, tricks like this get around – he's going to be a very lonely guy in two years' time!

TRUDY: Can I answer the phone? *[To caller]* Mackintosh Textiles, Trudy speaking, how can I help you?

[While on the telephone, Trudy picks up a 'swear box' and rattles it at Mack.]

MACK: For what?

[Covering the telephone with her hand (in order that the caller does not hear her), Trudy replies.]

TRUDY: 'Bollocks', twice, and 'prick'!

MACK: 'Prick' isn't a swear word!

TRUDY: *[To caller]* Is this a personal call? Is that Sue? I'm sorry, Sue, he can't take personal calls during work hours, but if it's urgent and he's about then I can take him a note. What's the message, Sue?

[Mack continuously mutters the word 'shit' while putting pound coins into the swear box while Trudy enters into a dialogue with the caller.]

The political evaluation of language as appropriate or, more aptly, inappropriate in this scene, indexes the way in which Abbott accommodates distinct dialogues within the field of public dialogic spaces in *Clocking Off*. Moreover, this scene also highlights a class or power disparity in that while Mack may commonly use coarse lexis to express his anger, Sue, a worker in the factory, is reminded that her voice cannot interrupt other workers on the factory floor. Mack's disaffected profanity is thus heard and performed in opposition to Sue's silent absence. Trudy's ability to multitask and deal with both Mack and Sue's narratives is only interrupted when Sue's message is unexpectedly given precedence and Mack is suddenly shut out of the scene. This breakdown of traditional order and authority is significant in that it reveals that the dominant narrative voice of the series is not fixed in accordance with power relations but is, rather, a dynamic process. In this way, the series and the differing perspectives that episodes take can be understood as a flexible mosaic rather than structured via a fixed narrative focus. Moreover, this very structure also draws attention back to the thematic modes of exchange that are foregrounded amidst daily factory life.

Secrets, lies and exchange value

Friendship operates as a coherent mode of exchange in *Clocking Off*. Represented as a commodity that is highly valuable, support, secrets, lies and home truths are gestured, spoken and accumulated in the series, resulting in a complex web of power shifts. Sharply etched and highly nuanced, speech rhythms, dialect and character postures work to convey both intimacies and differences between characters as well as a close-up view of the pains and pleasures of love. Tragicomic, friendship is positioned in *Clocking Off* as errant, dynamic and ideological; a counterpoint to repetition of the everyday. In 1:2, 'The Fire', for example, friends Yvonne and Julie (Siobhan Finneran) are given primacy in that the programme opens with a black, hazy screen punctuated by brightly coloured dots. As the image is brought into focus, the neon dots are revealed to be Yvonne and Julie, dressed in clown costumes, running down a stretch of tarmacked road. The digital treatment of this opening scene, leading to what Nelson (2007b: 116–17) notes to be 'the capacity for manipulation by visibly playful distortions', challenges televisual naturalism – a naturalism that is at once denounced before being restored in the very next scene. As the camera pulls back, the pair are seen framed by houses on either side of them before breathlessly coming to a halt in a playground. With Yvonne in the centre of the screen, a shot reverse shot reveals her to be looking at a blazing house on the other side of the street.

As this filmic structure is repeated for a second time, Yvonne suddenly sees a light being switched on in the upstairs bedroom. With her face contorted in horror, she addresses her friend: 'Oh my God! Julie, Julie, Julie. That's Mum's car. She's got the kids in there!' Running across the road towards the house, Yvonne and Julie stand terrified, their faces tear-stained with recognition at the tragedy that is unfolding before them, and, as the guilty looks exchanged between the pair also indicate, their own possible involvement in the fire. After Yvonne's mother, young son and 12–year-old daughter escape from the burning property, Yvonne's screams of 'Adele! Where's Adele?' leave the viewer in no doubt that one of Yvonne's children remains in the property. Luckily for Yvonne, a new male neighbour, Jim (Christopher Eccleston), is able to break an upstairs window in the burning house and feed a ladder from his own home to Yvonne's, entering and rescuing her 14–year-old daughter, Adele. Later, after fire crews have put out the fire and boarded up Yvonne's home, she is seen in a state of shock, sitting on Jim's sofa, hugging her children. As a fire officer asks her what happened and if she is sure that 'the front of the house went up before the back', Yvonne breaks down. Jim abruptly cuts off this exchange, asking the officer if the interview can take place the next day and saying that the family will be staying with him.

Later that evening, once the children have gone to bed, Yvonne is seen sitting on the sofa of Jim's house in the dark, smoking a cigarette and silently crying. Jim enters and lights a cigarette himself. Anticipating a confession of sorts from Yvonne, the viewer, like Jim, is made to wait. However, the silence is broken not by Yvonne, but by Jim, stating:

> I told the coppers that I heard the explosion from my bedroom. When I got outside I saw you pulling up with your mate – clown number 2. Which is bollocks, 'cos I saw the pair of you creeping through the garden just before the fire went off. I saw you shoot through the playground just before the first explosion. So, tell 'em what you want, but you better say summat similar or you're in deep shit, aren't you?

Jim's confession that he has 'clocked'[4] the pair of clowns interpolates a response and explanation from Yvonne, aligning the pair in a game of dangerous private honesty. Reinforcing their alignment, the cinematography of the next narrative day ensures that the audience understands both the forced proximity and the separation of Yvonne and Jim. The local newspaper wants to cover the story of the fire, and as such insists on photographing Yvonne and her three children standing outside their burnt-out and boarded-up former home. While the photographer himself is not seen on-screen, his voice enters the diegesis (directing the facial poses of the family), as does the distinct and repetitive click of a camera shutter. In a quick cut, the sound of the camera shutter functions as a sonic bridge to a scene of Jim being photographed at his place of work (the airport), seemingly being interviewed and framed as a local hero for his act of rescue. While publicly, then, the pair are framed and forced to perform social roles of victim and rescuer, in private the truth is certainly not as neat or clear-cut. Indeed, the instability of the public story about the fire is threatened not by the relative unknown character of Jim, but by Yvonne's closest friend, co-worker and partner in crime, Julie.

Julie is a single female in her early thirties who lives with her mum. Her reaction to the fire and, more specifically, to Yvonne's confession to Jim regarding her own and Julie's involvement in it, exposes and belies Julie's deep fear of the truth coming out. Julie's fearful, angry and flustered reaction to Jim's 'real' knowledge of the situation provokes a difficult exchange between the two women in a deserted toilet block at their workplace:

YVONNE: He's not gonna say anything.
JULIE: You don't even know him. I knew, I knew this was gonna go bad. Didn't I say, eh? It were a really nice house and you had to – bloody destroy it! And that's a woman with three kids looking for somewhere to live. You're mental. I'm mental for getting involved. Every time anybody asks me about it I go bright red.
YVONNE: Well, don't! The only people that know about this are you, me and him, and right now, he's the least of my worries.
JULIE: Charming!
YVONNE: Well, look at you!
JULIE: Look at you! You're not even sorry!
YVONNE: Course I am – what? How can I tell my kids sorry if it was meant to be a bloody accident?
JULIE: Sorry to me.

Yvonne pointedly refuses to apologise to Julie, noting that Julie 'knew what she was getting into'. While Yvonne seemingly adopts behaviours coded as traditionally or stereotypically masculine (refusing to apologise or show emotion in public), Julie enacts a social discourse associated with an equally stereotypical femininity (she blushes and is emotionally weak, embarrassed and hurt by Yvonne's behaviour). After several days in which we infer the friendship between the two is severely strained, Julie asks Yvonne to have lunch with her. Exchanging looks and eating Pot Noodles on the deserted top floor of the factory, we are made privy to a conversation between the women about Yvonne's financial difficulties. As an audience, we have already been given knowledge regarding the question of why Yvonne burnt down her home (Yvonne's partner of several years and owner of the now burnt house had tried to beat her, and when she resisted his abuse, had left her for a younger woman and had been about to kick Yvonne and her children out of the house). Revealing to her friend the full story of why she is unable to get a mortgage, Yvonne confesses to Julie that when her husband (and father of her children) died, they had debts, their house was repossessed and she was blacklisted. This new information, after what the audience presumes to be a reasonably long friendship between the women, functions as a clear indicator of Yvonne's pride and her newfound ability to open up to Julie. The looks exchanged between the pair as Yvonne haltingly speaks also mark out the exchange as what Julia Hallam (2005: 88) refers to as 'women's business'. Recognising a new and intimate element in their friendship, Julie's response to Yvonne's dilemma reveals another, previously hidden truth: 'They'd give me one ... we could move in together.' As Yvonne and Julie's eyes lock, recognising the potential magnitude of Julie's confession – that she in fact wants to live with Yvonne and transform their friendship into something much more intimate – silence permeates the scene. Gently breaking the silence, Yvonne replies: 'No offence, Julie, I just can't afford to rely on other people any more.' Yvonne's refusal to become Julie's partner is indexed not only by her proud refusal to 'rely on anyone', but further by her clear heterosexual desire evidenced in the next scene when, after chatting to and drinking wine with Jim, Yvonne asks Jim to have sex with her. He does, they enjoy it, and on the following night they have sex again. With Yvonne and the children set to move out from Jim's house the next day into a rented property, Jim makes it clear to Yvonne that he does not want her to leave. In response to Yvonne's assertion that he is a bachelor with 'more birds than a battery farm', Jim confesses that he wants her and only her and will change his ways. Yvonne's rejection of Jim's offer is explicitly aligned to her rejection of Julie's offer just days before. Yvonne states: 'I don't know how I do it; I must have that sort of face. I can't look at a bloke without him chucking a house at me! Well, not just blokes. I had a girl at work offering me a house and a mortgage the other day. Do I look like I need that much help? Because I don't!'

While Yvonne is seemingly quite prepared to leave her newfound relationship with Jim behind, she is not willing to give up on her fractured friendship with Julie. She asks her out for a drink and we join the women in mid-conversation in the pub. While Yvonne does not refer to Julie's lesbianism explicitly in the diegesis, it is strongly implied that she has done so in the ellipsis between scenes: 'I know what I've heard, and

that's fine, Julie. But I don't want to stop being friends because of it.'
Julie's response is again telling: 'We're not friends. I'm just somebody
you drag behind when it suits you.' Julie's designation of Yvonne 'using
her' when it suits can be understood as a repetition of her earlier demand
that Yvonne apologises to her for asking her to become involved with
the arson on Yvonne's home. The initial ellipsis in the scene, then (the
ellipsis in which we infer Yvonne confronts Julie about her sexuality), is
subtly repeated here. Reading between the lines, Julie seems to be asking
Yvonne to acknowledge that she has manipulated her, knowing that she
was in love with Yvonne and thus would do anything that Yvonne asked.
Yet, Yvonne's response to Julie's earlier demand for an apology is accordingly echoed here in the mind of the audience: 'You knew what you were
getting into.' Yvonne's confrontation of the situation, then, while an
apology of sorts, also operates as a demand that Julie considers her own
culpability in their fragmented relationship and in her own refusal to
reveal the truth to Yvonne at an earlier stage in their friendship. Rather
than moving forward, however, the conversation, while transformative on one level, ends with the women being able to move back into
their former friendship positions, with Julie denying her sexuality and
Yvonne prepared to accept that Julie is not ready to have her truth 'come
out' publicly. Julie's fear of a threat to the social order of her world is,
importantly, a trope that is highlighted throughout the series.

Disruptive possibilities, structures of 'othering' and domestic instability

Order, or more specifically, threats to order imbued in the everyday, are
made visible via a focus on domestic instability in *Clocking Off.* Akin to
the apparatus of television itself, what John Caughie (2000: 136) refers
to as 'the *possibility* of interruption' is positioned as a perverse, struc-
tural coda within the series. That is to say, while the mundane routine
of the everyday – clocking on, clocking off, cooking dinner, and so on
– works to convey the 'ordinary' in the series, the possibility of disruption to that ordinary order is a primary mode of subversion utilised by
Abbott to represent social rupture. Within the series, social problems
are dominantly given a prominent place in the domestic space. Indeed,
it is the potential interruption to domestic spatio-temporal rhythms
that constitutes a dynamic of potential and dramatic upheaval in the
opening scenes of 1:3, 'K.T.'

Showcasing factory boss Mack shaving in front of the bathroom
mirror in his home, a quick cut to a sleeping young blonde woman

in the bedroom of the same property allows the audience to infer that the woman is Mack's wife. This is confirmed when, in the next sequence, Mack enters the bedroom and, after gazing at her, sees her manicured foot exposed at the bottom of the duvet. Mack proceeds to kiss her toes before gently waking Katherine (Christine Tremarco) to tell her that builders are due to arrive at the property. The gentle tempo at which Mack engages with Katherine's body belies a moment of potential intimacy; however, the moment is disrupted by a knock on the door downstairs. In the next scene, Katherine's bare calves are seen to dominate the left half of the screen as she makes her breakfast dressed in a short silk nightdress. To the right of the screen, a workman lies on the floor, looking up towards the kitchen cabinets, as well as Katherine's bare calves and exposed thighs. While Katherine's face is not shown in this shot, the proximity of the voyeuristic workman to Katherine's half-dressed body solicits an unexpected response from her. Rather than moving away from the builder, Katherine moves her right high-heeled foot towards the man, thus parting her legs more widely to seemingly provide him with a better view. A cut then shows Mack silently watching the pair. Staring angrily at the builder, Mack asks him to resume his work after Katherine has finished her breakfast. Rather than confronting Katherine regarding her behaviour, Mack refuses to address it, instead whispering to her: 'Stick some clothes on – you know what they're like!'

While Mack then attempts to prevent disruption in their marriage by refusing to nominate Katherine's inappropriate behaviour, the actions of Katherine herself can be understood as purposefully and wilfully disruptive. This will to disrupt is further indexed by the dominant focus on Katherine's conscious ramping-up of her sexual allure in order to manipulate others and control their gaze and behaviour. Moreover, the camerawork of this scene strongly echoes the way in which femme fatale Phyllis Dietrichson (Barbara Stanwyck) is first seen descending the stairs of her husband's home in the classic film *Double Indemnity* (dir. Billy Wilder, 1944). Both women are adorned in white silk clothing and fluffy high-heeled shoes, and the camera in each text focuses upon the women's legs, fragmenting their wholeness and ensuring that their bodies are transformed (according to Laura Mulvey, 1975: 12) into 'mere spectacle'. Yet, rather than being wholly objectified by male spectators, such scenes demonstrate the ways in which the women's own knowledge of their bodies can be purposefully used to disrupt normal or acceptable social relations. Indeed, Katherine's will to disrupt is given more prominence just a few scenes later when it is revealed that she is having an affair with one of Mack's employees, a naive and socially

inept teenager called K.T. (Andrew Sheridan). In a repetition of exposure of that which should traditionally be kept private, Katherine picks
K.T. up on a busy street in her open-topped car before bringing him
back to her and Mack's home and seducing him in their marital bed.
After placing herself firmly on top, Katherine has sex with K.T. After
they have finished, Katherine plies K.T. with wine, asking him if he has
told any of his friends about 'their secret'. On being told he has not,
Katherine looks disappointed but then proceeds to kiss K.T. passionately
before telling him that 'I thought that was meant to be the fun of it all
... sharing secrets.'

Katherine's clear attempt to manipulate K.T. into telling his friends
about their affair is interesting not only as a clear indicator of her
disruptive will, but also as a reconfirmation of the Mackintosh Textile
factory as a rumour mill. Due to K.T.'s inability to communicate socially,
he does not have an ordinary cohort of friends, but rather his work
colleagues, and in particular, a young male co-worker, Kurt Robinson
or Robbo (Jason Sampson), seemingly fill this obvious gap. The role
of K.T.'s main friend, Robbo, however, seems to be one of protection,
ensuring that K.T. is safeguarded from some of the more aggressive and
less sensitive employees at the factory. Unlike most of the other workers
in the factory, K.T. is not self-aware, but is positioned as woefully shy,
naive and determinedly odd. With a visible disability to his left leg and
a clear nomination of a mental as well as a physical disability by the
factory supervisor Steve (Wil Johnson), K.T. is shown to be bullied both
inside and outside the factory, having cash stolen from his coat pockets
in the street by a gang of teenage boys who are aware that K.T. is unable
to protect himself. Once he has returned home after the attack, it is
revealed that K.T. lives with his elderly grandparents who are themselves inscribed in the routine of the everyday. When they tell him
that he is late and as such that his dinner will be ruined, K.T. bolts to
the kitchen and pulls a plate of food out of the hot oven (burning his
hands) before stuffing his mouth full of chips and leaving the room. His
explicitly unusual behaviour again points to his social difference, and
it is perhaps in an effort to overcome his domination by others that he
chooses to reveal his secret to fellow worker Robbo before deliberately
stepping out into the road in front of Mack's moving car.

While K.T. does not die from his injuries, Katherine's femme-
fatale status is confirmed by K.T.'s endangering of his own and Mack's
lives in the name of misplaced love. The subsequent revelation that
Katherine has had sexual affairs with various other employees at the
factory, nominated as Kev from the cutting room, Pete Donahue, Andy
Cummings and factory foreman, Steve, leads Trudy (the holder of this

knowledge and Mack's secretary and friend) to reveal to Steve that 'She's left two messages at work for you. At work! She expected me to put two and two together and tell Mack. She wants Mack to find out. Why else pick on someone like K.T.?' Indeed, Mack does find out but again, rather than confronting Katherine, he threatens and then pays off K.T. to keep his mouth shut and find new employment. While Katherine is prepared to 'front out' her behaviour in the domestic sphere, in the space of the factory, the disrupting rhythm of Katherine's behaviour cannot be ignored. Waiting outside the factory for Mack to finish work so that they can go to the airport (for an exotic holiday), Trudy tells Katherine to come up to the office and wait. Advising her that she cannot enter through the executive entrance, Trudy purposely leads Katherine through the factory floor, thus insisting that she confront, albeit wordlessly, the countless men that she has 'fucked over' and the others who know about her behaviour. As the men stop their work to watch her walk by, Trudy tells Katherine: 'Watch your step. It can be lethal round here.' This warning obviously has a double function, both reinforcing Katherine's nomination as a lethal woman and serving to demonstrate to Katherine that she herself may become increasingly under threat if she continues her reckless and traditionally immoral behaviour.

The dramatic form of Katherine's humiliation points to a bigger question of innovative form marked in the series by the self-contained stories offered in each episode. As Cooke (2005: 184) points out: 'one of the novelties of *Clocking Off* was the way in which regular characters would also feature as the leading character for an episode while other factory employees played secondary or subsidiary roles'. The primacy of different leading voices and perspectives in *Clocking Off* is important in that its focus is both socially and televisually ordinary and extraordinary. Well-known actors such as Christopher Eccleston, Sarah Lancashire and Lesley Sharp are alternatively given leading and minimal narrative focus. While their voices are certainly recognisable to UK television audiences, Abbott also allows and ensures that the voices of less well-known actors such as Christine Tremarco (Katherine Mackintosh) and Wil Johnson (Steve Robinson) are heard. The differing voices and multiple perspectives represented in the series foreground an aesthetic of realism in that such diversity is more akin to contemporary experiences of everyday working environments. Yet, the stories that *Clocking Off* tells are not simple, easy or necessarily recognisable but rather, are dramatic, complex and confronting, dominantly marked by Abbott's refusal to neatly tie up tales of fragmentation.

The negotiation of fragmentation functions as the very textile on which the series is built. Bits and pieces of fabric are literally split, cut and remapped inside the Mackintosh factory. Similarly, the stability of the characters' lives is continuously fragmented, torn, coloured and reshaped by everyday experiences. The relentlessly slippery fabric surfaces on which the ordinary is built are thus at once figured as beautiful and dangerous. This uneasy tension both highlights the schisms of the commonplace and reinforces an important relationship regarding the difficulties of narrative closure presented in *Clocking Off*. In 1:4, 'Steve's Story', the troubled marriage of Steve (factory supervisor) and Sylvia (Diane Parish) (machinist) is foregrounded. After Steve has cooked Sylvia a special anniversary dinner, she confronts Steve with the knowledge of his affair. Admitting his indiscretion but refusing to name the woman, Steve apologises profusely, promising his wife that it was a 'one-off mistake'. Eventually taking him at his word, Sylvia goes to bed with him and they make love. The restored equality of their partnership symbolised through their lovemaking is indexed by an interesting camera movement in which the on-screen image of Sylvia lying on the bed is turned 90 degrees to the left. As the couple come together, the screen image rotates back to its normal position in a series of repeated fades and superimpositions, perhaps recalling their long history of tenderness which has produced their three children.

The tender, romantic superimpositions accompanied by the diegetic haunting of Annie Lennox's track 'Primitive' function to place the marital bed as a space of negotiation and renewal here. However, after they have fallen asleep, the additional, uninvited third party that has been silently haunting their relationship in previous months is literalised in the form of a violent, knife-wielding burglar. On waking, Steve is ordered to relinquish any money – which he does before chasing the man down the stairs of the house and into the street. Police officers soon attend the house, but, on finding a spliff in the ashtray, become suspicious of Steve. Questioning him regarding whether he has a job, if he is involved in drug dealing and expressing incredulity when Steve notes that the burglar was a 'white male with blue eyes', the issue of racial inequality is brought to bear here. Steve's black skin and his relative wealth demonstrated through his 'nice' home on a 'nice' estate seemingly work as factors which, we infer, point to Steve's potential guilt rather than his innocence in the eyes of the white officers. The implicit nomination of Steve by the police officers as a potential criminal gangster reaffirms Steve's 'difference' within the dominantly white diegetic world. Steve's aggressive yet entirely understandable response to such an implication results in his arrest. When he calls the ethics of the officers into question while in custody, the police reveal they have found additional drugs in Steve's son's bedroom in the form of eight ecstasy tablets. Shocked and stunned, Steve takes responsibility for the tablets in order to protect his teenage son, Robbo, which results in him being charged with drug possession and (temporarily) losing his job.

That is not, however, the end of the story. Steve, remembering the identity of the burglar, realises that it is a disgruntled ex-employee at the factory whom he sacked for stealing. After confronting the thief, Kim Ronstadt (Lee Warburton), at his home and reporting his identity to the police, bricks are thrown through the windows of the Robinson family home, narrowly missing injuring Steve and Sylvia's children. Blaming Steve for the succession of destruction, starting with his affair, the marriage becomes increasingly fractured as Steve refuses to reveal the name of the other woman with whom he was involved. Eventually confessing to Sylvia that the woman was Katherine Mackintosh, Sylvia prepares to leave her husband, telling him: 'I get months dragging on when all you've done for me is make me feel like a parent. I don't feel sexy. I don't feel funny. I don't feel interesting. Not to you.' Steve's response is that the anniversary meal was about celebrating their coupledom as people, not just parents. While this statement seems to appease Sylvia, causing a rethinking and remodelling of their fractured relationship, the next shot reminds the viewer of the resistance to happy endings.

While Sylvia agrees to 'erase' Katherine from the picture of their marriage, Robbo, confused by Kim's vengeance, goes to the estate where Kim lives. Seen, tracked and hunted down by Kim and his gang, Robbo asks Kim why he is persecuting his dad. Robbo's naivety is stressed in this scene as his politeness in the face of the gang, his rejection of violence and his will to talk through the problems with Kim only serve to increase his powerlessness in the hands of a gang who privilege violence over reason. Despite this, Kim's response to Robbo's assertion that his dad had to sack him as he 'had been caught nicking on CCTV and if his dad hadn't, then Mack would have' propels the statement from Kim: 'Mack's one thing. Your dad's an*other*.'[5] The focus on Steve as an 'Other' calls forth the arguments of theorists such as Edward Saïd (1978) in his compelling discussion on *Orientalism* and Richard Dyer on race in his more recent text *White* (1997). Speaking of racial othering, Dyer argues that the West's consistent refusal to see whiteness as a race has allowed for the continuation of clear relations of domination and submission, with white people dominating and non-white people seen as something 'other'. Dyer (1997: 1) notes: 'As long as race is something only applied to non-white peoples, as long as white people are not racially seen and named, they/we function as a human norm. Other people are raced, we are just people.' This recurrent 'othering' of Steve is important here as it sets up and brings front and centre the consciously racist diatribe which forms the fabric of Kim's subjectivity. After being threatened with a knife and subsequently promising Kim that he will persuade his parents to drop their identification of Kim as the violent burglar who entered the family home, Robbo realises that the gang, and in particular, Kim, are not finished with him. Recognising that Kim's knife-wielding hands are purposefully gloved (in order, we infer, to prevent fingerprints and thus avoid any potential evidence of his criminality), Robbo cries out and asks Kim not to hurt him. Restrained by the throat by another member of Kim's all-white gang, Robbo kicks out as Kim approaches him with the knife. The kick results in the knife cutting Kim's arm. With a look of anger on his face, Kim approaches Robbo again. Diegetic police sirens can be heard in the background of the scene and Robbo closes his eyes, waiting to be stabbed. Instead of stabbing Robbo, however, Kim places the knife in Robbo's (ungloved) hand and orders his gang to run before sitting down on the concrete and grasping his bleeding arm in order to enact and perform his victim status to a rapid emergency police response. Robbo, knife in hand, begins to run away from the scene, and in doing so performs a role of guilty implication. As the Annie Lennox track 'Primitive' plays again, Robbo is put in the back of a police van.

The reference to contemporary mediated reports of 'black knife crime' plays a political role here in that the dominance of white power (power attained through the othering of non-whites) is explicitly acknowledged. Moreover, the dominance of white power through othering is seen to operate on two levels in this episode – professionally, through the law enforcers themselves, and, privately, on the street. In a conversation between Steve and the arresting officer in 1:4 after Steve has had the bricks thrown through his windows, the following exchange takes place:

STEVE: So I can stick a knife to somebody's throat and be walking the street in 24 hours – that's the kind of protection we get?

OFFICER: Whether Ronstadt gets bailed or not is nothing to do with me.

STEVE: I want him arresting.

OFFICER: I'll put fifty [pounds] on us not getting fingerprints off that brick.

STEVE: I'm putting in a complaint about you, pal. People like you shouldn't be wearing that [police uniform].

OFFICER: And people like you shouldn't be doing what you do and telling other people what's normal, so we make a right pair don't we? Look. OK. The night I came to your house I got you wrong. You got me wrong, OK? But I didn't arrest you for anything you didn't do. I'm not that kind of bobby. I know your boss – he speaks very highly of you.

STEVE: So I'm OK now because my boss says I am? You're a joke, pal.

The admission by the police officer that he 'didn't arrest Steve for anything he didn't do' is interesting in that, while factually correct, his admittance that he had previously 'got Steve wrong' implies that the officer had made a case based on his prejudice – a case which, luckily for him, came to fruition in the form of the discovery of the ecstasy tablets which Steve's naive son, Robbo, was manipulated into buying for other factory employees. Further, the fact that the officer notes that he is 'not that kind of bobby' belies his unspoken admittance regarding his knowledge that other officers indeed 'set people up', and thus break the law by abusing their dominant and powerful position while pertaining to uphold it. Steve's retort regarding the officer's change of opinion based on Steve's (white) boss's nomination of him as a 'good man' functions to anger Steve further as the officer appears to be blind to his continuing racist actions and assertions.

While it seems that the officer is behaving in an unconsciously racist way, however, Kim Ronstadt is seen as a man who deliberately utilises the stereotyping and frequent real twenty-first-century mediation of a link between black male youth and knife crime to his white advantage.[6] Indeed, as the officer unwittingly notes, Kim knows the law and is aware of how to play the game, so he will have left no trace evidence on the brick he threw through the family's window. While the exchange between the officer and Steve demonstrates Steve's ability to question institutionalised racism on a public level, Ronstadt's exchange with Steve's son, Robbo, demonstrates that Robbo is not yet strong enough to do so and, perhaps, is still too young and too naive to recognise Ronstadt's real racist motives. The negotiation of power in both verbal exchanges cited above punctuates the scenes with real political questions and thus demonstrates a sense of play between the diegesis and the reality of the UK in the twenty-first-century. Yet, in the diegesis, the question of if the power exchanges will end with the continuance of Steve and his family being publicly and privately othered is a narrative tract that is refused closure – it is, after all, too big an issue to be neatly foreclosed. As the episode ends the audience is left not knowing whether Steve and Sylvia will 'drop' their identification of Kim in exchange for what we may infer to be Kim offering to 'drop' the charges against Robbo.

Again, then, modes of possible exchange are highlighted through their ellipsis. Indeed, it is not necessarily what the characters within the series say, but also what they fail to articulate that demands consideration. The notion of reciprocity is highlighted in the scene discussed above and in this case, exchange is not focused on material gain, but rather on a balancing of benefits between parties, however imbalanced the original circumstances may be. Social relations that are intrinsic to and implicit in gift exchange are continuously conveyed through refusals of narrative closure. In each episode of the first series, absolute closure, absolute knowingness, are denied. Conversations are not finished but rather, are interrupted. As Andrew Klevan (2000: 86) argues in *Disclosure of the Everyday*: 'Conversations are ongoing affairs, not overridingly orientated towards goals, and by their nature, they do not have a global inclination towards finality.'

The formal irony of having self-contained episodes which simultaneously deny narrative closure can be understood as a playful and vibrant motif. Social play is also constituted in other ways in the various narratives. One such specificity relates to the employment of everyday humour in order that the diegetic workers can each occupy specific roles or, in other words, play their part in the social arena of the factory. Kev (Jack Deam) is a superb example of a character that beautifully exhibits such humour as a way of demonstrating his role within the factory community. As a material cutter, Kev's manual role is bolstered by his frequent displays of hyper-masculinity. With his conversations and comments to others frequently revolving around sex, his girlfriend Bab's breasts and his self-nominated sexual prowess, Kev's humour often functions to diffuse and give temporary respite from the emotional pull of serious melodrama. For example, in 1:4, after Sylvia (wrongly) accuses Julie of having had an affair with her husband and the pair engage in a physical fight in the factory canteen, fellow workers stand around in shock. In contrast to close-ups of Sylvia and Steve's son, Robbo, hanging his head in confusion and Yvonne's desperate attempts to stop her friend Julie being hurt, Kev responds to the situation with a wide smile, an audible laugh and the words: 'Brilliant! It's given me a hard-on.' Similarly, in 1:2, the day after Yvonne's house has burnt down and all the other workers are having a whip-round for her, Kev, dressed in a sleeveless vest to emphasise his muscle tone, watches her walk past his cutting machine, looks pointedly at her backside and legs and begins shouting the following public monologue: 'Dear Kilroy, I find myself shrugging at the fittest, most attractive bods with the most enormous slonkers. Might I be a lesbian? Call our 0999 number now. Give us your thoughts: straight, lezza, swings like a monkey?' Kev's public assertions are soon cut off, however, as a male colleague whispers in his ear – a communication that, we infer, is to tell him about Yvonne's recent fire and thus, imply his insensitivity.

Kev's hilarious interjections and fantastical projections of his heterosexual desires are employed here, then, not only to make the audience laugh out loud by revealing his lack of social dominance despite his public voice (an irony, considering his monologue was intended to demonstrate that he was 'in the know'), but by perhaps revealing his insecurity. As Kenneth MacKinnon (2003: 63) points out: 'There is an increasing focus on masculinity as troubled and unsure of itself – never more unsure than when it is shouting its self-confidence via exaggeratedly muscular heroes toting modern weaponry.' In addition to underscoring Kev's insecurity, the scene also functions to reinforce the contemporary nature of the series through references to known popular cultural texts and thus UK television presenters such as Kilroy. Alternatively, however, Kev's speech could be understood on a deeper level – as another acknowledgement of the formal modes and codes of contemporary popular culture such as television and radio debates, which often pose serious questions only to collapse into spectacular, stereotypically sexist and racist debates.[7]

Conclusion

Clocking Off reveals a contemporary dialogue that actively confronts the political through the personal. Indeed, the very texture of the series refuses to adhere to what Cooke (2005: 194) nominates as the classic social realist aesthetics so prevalent in the 1960s and 1970s of a factory and working-class community that are grey, downtrodden, bored and limited. Instead, the series presents a world of colour, complexity and style as well as social awareness. The very identity of the series is, then, an identity of significance and self-renewal. As differing characters are given precedence in each episode, so the identities of the workers at Mackintosh Textiles change, grow, metamorphose and continuously self-renew. The notion that the workers in this northern working-class setting may be financially constrained by the 'ordinariness' of their minimum wages is visually rejected, replaced by a distinct variety of housing, transport and work levels as well as the constant motion of the diegetic world seen through changes in homes, cars, kitchens and partners. Such strong visual reminders of the variance between the workers in the series clearly demonstrates that those who inhabit this world frequently and consciously make new lifestyle choices – choices which foster, cause and force the inhabitants to reflect upon their dynamic identities. As Glen Creeber (2004: 121) argues in relation to serial television: 'lifestyle choices become an important component of self-identity, a crucial site of individual freedom that reflects a world in which identity itself is now a matter of continual renewal rather than compulsory inheritance'. Abbott's rejection of traditional working-class identity as a televisual 'compulsory inheritance' of greyness underscores his determination to inject colour and quality into the very veins of twenty-first-century British television.

Equally vibrant and politically potent in terms of its various representations of gender performance, *Clocking Off*, a series so chronically bound up with the significance of the temporal, also demonstrates what could certainly be classified as a fin-de-siècle feminist turn. Refusing the dominant masculinity of 1990s British television drama, characters such as Yvonne Kolakowski, Trudy Graham and Katherine Mackintosh are positioned as strong women who refuse to be defined by men. Akin to the dominant female figures of soap opera, their lives are defined through their everyday routines. Yet, as Anthony Giddens (1991: 81) notes, this does not mean that the freedom to change is restricted, rather: 'the routines followed are reflexively open to change in the light of the mobile nature of self-identity'. On a less positive note, however, *Clocking Off* also highlights the presence and dominance of whiteness – the lack of multicoloured peoples – on British television screens. Via revealing the institutionalised racism of the police force, for example, the drama draws attention to the routinely racist practices of the everyday, making visible the often hidden 'othering' of non-whites. Showcasing such an issue works to challenge the logic of cultural racism, and while the drama does not pretend to offer a solution to such a vast social problem, the highlighting of racism places it firmly under the critical spotlight.

Notes

1 This and all other unattributed quotations from Abbott are cited from specially commissioned interviews with the author in 2011 and 2012. Full extracts from the interviews are available in Appendix 1.
2 *Clocking Off* press release: www.bbc.co.uk/pressoffice/pressreleases/stories/2003/02_february/13/one_drama_clockoff_1.pdf.
3 www.bbc.co.uk/drama/clockingoff/.
4 As Michael Massey notes: 'Clocking is also a slang term for "taking notice of, watching or observing".' *Studying TV Drama* (Leighton Buzzard, Auteur Press, 2010), p. 74.
5 Emphasis added.
6 For an example of such mediation recalling UK Prime Minister Tony Blair's assertions regarding knife crime, see the *Guardian* article at: www.guardian.co.uk/politics/2007/apr/12/ukcrime.race.
7 Robert Kilroy-Silk, an ex-MP and media face, had his television show *Kilroy* axed from the BBC in 2004 following the publication of his article entitled 'We Owe Arabs Nothing' in the *Sunday Express* newspaper.

Linda Green

Linda Green was based on one of my female friends who could drink any bloke under the table. She ransacked three of them in one night and they weren't even thinking about it and didn't know what'd happened until she'd banged them in the toilets. So, I wrote a little postcard to myself in a scrapbook saying, 'fat bird with a pint – and what's wrong with that?'[1]

Paul Abbott

Created by Paul Abbott and produced by the independent production company, Red, the Television and Radio Industries Club award-winning drama series *Linda Green* was broadcast in 2001–2 by the BBC. Classified as a comedy drama, both Series 1 and 2 centred on the everyday life of a vivacious, selfish, sexually confident, pint-loving, working-class white female in her early thirties, Linda Green (Liza Tarbuck). Influenced by American television series such as *Rosanne* (ABC, 1988–97) and *Rhoda* (CBS, 1974–78), *Linda Green*'s blue-collar status was deliberate, as Abbott has noted, describing Linda as a determinedly 'blue-collar Bridget Jones'.[2] Made up of ten half-hour episodes per season written by a combination of talented scriptwriters including Abbott, Russell T. Davies, Catherine Johnson and Danny Brocklehurst (amongst many others), the series was not only renowned for its originality, richly detailed content, humour and female titular lead – a lead Paul Connolly of the *Times* (2001) noted to be 'pretty much perfect as the eponymous heroine' – but also for its 'quality'. Quality television is defined by Robert Thompson (1996: 13–15) as 'what it is not. It is not "regular" TV [but] tends to be literary and writer-based [and] is self-conscious.'

While the term 'quality' television has been most dominantly applied to the original programming of slick American shows such as *The Sopranos, Six Feet Under* and *Sex and the City*, Kim Akass and Janet McCabe (2008: 84) note that other factors of quality can be 'intangible', involving 'prestige, cultural influence and public awareness'. The prestige of the award-winning drama, its will to demonstrate public awareness of gender and class politics in twenty-first-century Britain and its significant place on the BBC (a trust that notes in its mission statement the need to 'inform, educate and entertain') positions the drama as an extra yet markedly 'ordinary' or 'real' quality text. As Jane Tranter (Drama Commissioner for the BBC 2000–6) noted of *Linda Green:*

> We want to give BBC drama a stronger flavour of the way that we live our lives now, a stronger sense of modernity. As far as the subject matter is concerned, this show is an important step forward for the BBC. It is a completely down-to-earth piece of drama, grounded in absolute reality – and that is one of the directions that the BBC is currently moving in. [*Linda Green* represents] the most mainstream way in which this kind of drama/entertainment/comedy crossover has been tackled by the BBC. As far as I'm concerned it has one of the most impressive declarations of intent that you can ever get from a drama series. The characters are very clear; Linda's character is written large from the start.[3]

In line with Akass and McCabe's discussions of quality television, the originality of *Linda Green*, its modernity (and indeed self-referential postmodernity), generic crossovers and culturally significant representations of twenty-first-century social values both evoke and invoke 'quality'. In addition, the quality of the series can be traced back to its US format. As Abbott notes, with *Linda Green* he wanted to get closer to 'the sort of American shows that have singular name title stars', as the format 'allows writers to do anything they like within the lives of their central characters, giving a more flexible approach to storytelling'.[4] Despite the American-inspired narrative flexibility of the series, the comedy drama is not all slick surfaces but is, rather, notably British in its exploration of identity, culture, social class and civilisation. Abbott's consistent use of British guest stars such as Simon Pegg, Christopher Eccleston, David Morrissey, Jane Horrocks, Peter Kay and Meera Syal bolsters the national distinction of the series, allowing for both a humorous and simultaneously frank snapshot of twenty-first-century life, a life that, as Jane Tranter acknowledges, 'most of us can recognise'.[5] This pronounced tendency towards the realistic and recognisable is foregrounded through the aesthetics and idiosyncrasies of the everyday in which Linda's excess or lack of restraint functions as a clear counterpoint to the restrained pacing of the episodes.

Televisual pacing is utilised to communicate the emotional subtext of Linda in *Linda Green*. As a character, Linda is loud and raucous but, pertinently, she keeps quiet regarding her own emotions at times when she is extremely emotionally upset – for example, when her paternity is called into question in 1:9. The consistent measured pacing of the episodes, coupled with a strong employment of medium shots, allows the audience to uncover the 'real' Linda. In line with the measured and predictable pacing of the series, three repeated spaces and three dominant characters are used to demonstrate the stability and sameness of Linda's experience. The three dominant characters are Linda's friend (with sexual benefits), Jimmy (Sean Gallagher); Linda's best friend since school, Michelle (Claire Rushbrook) and Michelle's husband, Darren (Daniel Ryan). The three most frequently repeated sites in the series include Linda's flat, the social club at which she sings on an evening and her friend Michelle's bedroom where Linda and Michelle chat, drink, dance and dress. The steadiness of these three settings belies the ambling nature of Linda's life, her inability to make different choices from those which are the most obvious and her refusal to change her life and attitude in any significant way. For example, offered a promotion in 1:6, Linda admits that she 'would rather be sexually harassed than promoted', and in 1:10, when asked by her friend and lover Jimmy if she ever thinks about children, she replies that she 'think[s] about being invited to a party and not being able to go because of lactating breasts'. Linda is determined to stay as she is, in the community in which she has been brought up, with the friends who she has known from school, doing the same job that she has done since leaving school.

Linda Green/Liza Tarbuck

Liza Tarbuck, the female star at the heart of *Linda Green*, was inspired casting in terms of situating Linda as a believable, sassy, naive and yet wholly convincing character. Having acted in the Granada comedy *Watching* (1987–93), as well as being known for her television-presenting roles on *She's Gotta Have It*, *The Big Breakfast* and *Have I Got News for You*, Liza's credentials as a witty, intelligent and sharp woman – a woman able to give male colleagues a serious run for their money while simultaneously bringing them to their knees with laughter – were established prior to *Linda Green*. The significance of Liza's presenting roles is particularly pertinent in terms of understanding why Liza's casting as Linda was such a good fit. First, Liza's persona as a straight-talking, intelligent and 'up-for-a-laugh' presenter meant that in Liza's screen time she was, effectively, playing herself rather than another character. This notion of audiences being aware of the 'real' Liza was important in her casting as Linda in that Liza's character as a fun, flirty and everyday woman was considered to be authentic rather than a performance. Secondly, Liza's warmth on-screen when interviewing people, a warmth that Sheryl Garratt (2001) refers to as her 'genuine interest in people and not scoring points at their expense', is infectious, believable and refreshing, permeating the barrier of the screen.

Liza's enactment of ordinariness rather than celebrity is even more extraordinary in that while she clearly works to celebrate her normalcy, she is simultaneously considered as part of a British comedy institution in that her father is the famous British comic, Jimmy Tarbuck. Despite this, Liza's hard-won success can be put down to her own sheer hard work, her RADA training and her quick wit. While following her father's 'showbiz' footsteps may have seemed like an obvious thing to do because of his success, Liza, while immensely proud of her father, has noted that his fame was, in the beginning, more of a hindrance than a help. As she discussed in an interview with Garratt: '[At] RADA she considered using her mother's maiden name to avoid the Tarbuck connection.' Reflecting on her decision to go into the world of television, Liza's own determination, her will to be different, can be seen. While her father had been insistent that neither Liza nor her siblings should go into 'the business', it became intriguing. 'When your parents tell you not to do something, you do it.' Indeed, it is Liza's normalcy accompanied by a pointed refusal of 'celebrity' status – a status she nominates as 'bullshit' – that most dominantly comes across in both her professional and personal life.

The parallelism between Liza's well-reported respect for her own family (particularly her father) and her close familial relationship with her fictional father within the *Linda Green* series is certainly interesting, actively promoting a link between Liza and Linda. Indeed, Jimmy Tarbuck's guest-star appearance in Episode 1:9 as Linda's Uncle Vic, or, perhaps, father, further compounds and conflates this crossover. The deliberate physical and gestural resemblance between Linda (Liza) and her Uncle Vic (Jimmy) is purposefully drawn upon in the diegesis of this episode in order to consciously and comedically play up the real/fictional crossover. In employing this purposeful crossover between the real world and the televisual world, the line between the actor and character or private and public persona is blurred. According to Karen Lury (1995/6: 118): 'this is part of the pleasure for the audience, to believe that the actor is (or is at least like) the character he or she plays'. This blurring is particularly important in terms of Linda/Liza. Indeed, Linda's normalcy – her humour, her imperfection, her dirty laugh – can be seen as an extension of Liza's own. As noted in an interview in the *Observer* (2001) prior to the first broadcast of *Linda Green*, Garratt noted: 'Liza is about to take the lead in the BBC's new drama series, a series that will stand or fall depending on whether viewers warm to its central character – a whole series, in other words, relying on Liza's likeability.'

The notion of normalcy does not only apply to Liza's/Linda's actions and gestures but also to her physical appearance. As has been well documented, a study carried out in 2000 and published in the *Independent* newspaper found that the average dress size of a UK woman was a 14.[6] Liza/Linda can be aligned with this average size and this is important in that her role as Linda represents a recognisable reality rather than a size 0 screen-mediated fantasy. The perceived pressure for modern women to adhere to a mostly impossible size 0 has been evidenced in several recent programmes such as *The Truth About Size Zero* (2007, RDF Media), which saw the British singer Louise Redknapp struggle to slim down to a size 0 in order to demonstrate its dangers, and *Super-skinny Me: The Race to Size Double Zero* (2007, Betty TV), in which Kate Spicer, a well-known UK journalist, was prevented from continuing her radical diet owing to serious mental and physical health concerns. Liza herself has spoken out about the pressures on modern women to adhere to a specific vision of perfection, noting that in 2000: 'They [TV shows] were very looks-orientated.' Despite this, Liza goes on, in her straight-talking way, to discuss her normal size and the ways in which it would be useful to reframe the size debate: 'How do I feel not being a size 8? Well, I don't know what it's like to be a size bleeding 8. My legs are size 8. I'm not. I don't get that. Why is somebody better than somebody else because of something like size? Because actually it might mean that the other person's ill' (Garratt, 2001). Liza's noted concern for others and her refusal to utilise body size as a way of measuring quality is important in that it demonstrates that her values are not comparative, but rather, are based on an interior rather than exterior perspective. The contentions between internal and external judgements of others are also highlighted in *Linda Green* in association with gender expectations and romantic ideals.

Moonlight and music and love and romance

The distinctions between Linda's public and private interactions are frequently figured as comic in that while at times the emotions of the public and private match, at others, such parallelisms are signalled as explicitly out of sync. Indeed, this out-of-syncness also extends to Liza's performativity and the casting of Liza. Speaking of Linda's persona, Liza notes on the BBC website[7] that 'There are times when I think I'd tell her to piss off. Times when she's a bit hard. One of the most difficult things for me is to make her warm because she can be very selfish sometimes.' In part, the selfishness that Liza speaks of relates to Linda's constant

Figure 4.1 *Linda Green*, BBC One, 2001–2: Linda Green (Liza Tarbuck) singing on the stage of her local social club

desire to be the centre of attention, something specifically avoided by Liza. As Garratt (2001) notes: 'Liza doesn't really do celebrity. She talks about her love of DIY and her plans to tile her new kitchen, about litter (which annoys her) and dog poo (she scoops hers scrupulously). Sometimes she thinks she's boring, that she should get out more. She doesn't go to showbusiness parties and premières.' This 'normality' seems to jar with contemporary models of celebrity, based upon a desire, much like Linda's, to be recognised as a 'face', to be at every party imaginable. In essence, whereas, despite her fame, Liza expresses a clear desire for normality, Linda is framed as a normal woman who wants to be a celebrity. Indeed, it is disparity between the public and private that is played upon as a deliberate source of comedy in the series.

The dichotomy of the public and private sides of Linda's life are persistently and clearly flagged up as each episode begins its action with tragicomic montages of Linda singing in public in a local social club intercut with earlier (and thus nonlinear) footage of Linda in the privacy of her own home. Episode 1.1, for example, opens with the non-diegetic words 'Linda Green' written in white against a dark background. As the background comes into focus, the back of a woman can be seen in the centre of the shot. In the half-light, diegetic music is suddenly heard and it soon becomes apparent that the woman on-screen (presumably Linda) is singing into a microphone on a dark stage.

The words of the well-known track 'Perfect' fill the diegetic space of the club. The lyrics of this particular track are significant not only in that they are the first words to be heard in the whole of the series but, more importantly, they point to certain characteristics of Linda's personality. 'I don't want to have half-hearted love affairs / I need someone who really cares / Life is too short to play silly games ...'. Interestingly, the final line of the song's verse – 'I've promised myself I won't do that again' – is not heard. Instead, a sudden cut places Linda in a domestic setting, arguing angrily with Neil (Christopher Eccleston) about their imperfect relationship. Joining them in mid-argument, the dialogue exposes the ways in which their desires are clearly out of sync:

LINDA: When have I tried to organise your life?
NEIL: Now!
LINDA: Before that!
NEIL: Monday. 'Neil, meet me at the flat ...'

A quick cut then takes the viewer back to the social club where Linda continues singing. While Linda's voice is certainly reasonable, her clothing, make-up, posture and the tittering of the audience work to establish Linda's status as a club singer rather than a genuine 'star'. Again, the words of her song are telling in that she admits that: 'Young hearts are foolish, they make such mistakes / They're much too eager to give their love away.' Again, the next lines of the verse (the lines that explicitly nominate an intention to change) – 'Well, I have been foolish too many times / Now I'm determined I'm gonna get it right' are cut. In their place, we go back to Linda and Neil continuing their argument. This shot pattern is repeated twice more until Linda finishes her song to applause at the club, and Neil simultaneously packs his bag and leaves Linda.

While on the one hand an explicit parallelism can be seen between Linda's sung desire for a meaningful relationship and her domestic desire for control in and over her relationship with Neil, where she succeeds on stage in public, she notably fails privately. Indeed, this failure is soon concreted not as a one-off, but as a persistent haunting flaw in Linda's character. In the next two scenes in the programme Linda is told by friend Jimmy that she is 'the same every time ... You're too intense ... You try to cram five stages of man into a fortnight. They just burn out.' As with the song that opened the episode, Linda refuses to recognise and take responsibility for her own behaviour and its change, instead asking Jimmy a question about football. Linda's flaws, her quest for perfection in relationships, is also critiqued in the very next scene by her father, Frank (Dave Hill), who, in a play on words regarding his name, tells Linda some home truths about why her relationships fail. He notes:

There are three reasons why you can't hang onto a man, Linda. A) You're scared to death of commitment because you're scared to death it might actually lead to something, i.e. kids, i.e. giving somebody something. B) You pick men (and I've seen you do this) when you've always had just that little bit too much to drink. You're always a little bit pissed and they're always a little bit wrong. So, lay off the booze. You just might surprise yourself. C) You won't grow a fringe ... you had one at twelve and you had a lot more luck then.

While the first two of Frank's points are 'frank', honest and cutting, the close relationship between Frank and his daughter is poignantly addressed in Frank's final point. In essence, Frank's ridiculous memory of the 12–year-old Linda's fringe functions to communicate to Linda and the audience that she is, in the eyes of her father, still his cherished young daughter. While it is unspoken, Linda recognises the love her father has for her as she reciprocates his kiss on her head with a long, childlike cuddle.

Linda's quest for relationship perfection is clearly intertwined with a romantic vision of Mr Right. In this way, the series bears similarities to other quality televisual texts such as *Sex and the City* (HBO 1998–2004). Yet, Linda is simultaneously more realistic in her quest and prepared to put up with (at least temporarily) bad behaviour. The masculine archetype that Neil, for example, represents is very much the 'bad lad' – a man who consciously manipulates, uses and mentally abuses Linda. Neil's masculinity is rendered phallic in that he clearly enacts the role of a 'dick'. Lean, muscular and domineering, Neil's sexual allure to Linda is problematic in that he is both positioned as a 'dick' and a 'dick on legs'. His 'dick on legs' status is explicitly rendered visible by Jimmy, who notes that in her relationship with Neil, Linda's actions followed the protocol of: 'answerphone on, head down, lots of yelping ... only coming up for air when you need the chemist'. Neil is thus positioned as powerfully sexual, a 'great shag', rather than a 'great love'. Love, for Neil, doesn't come into it; rather, it is a matter of power. Linda is attracted to Neil's phallic masculinity.

Similarities can be drawn here between Linda and the behaviour of other leading ladies to 'big men' in recent contemporary television series. While Linda Green is very different from the fashion-conscious, waiflike Carrie Bradshaw of *Sex and the City*, for example, both women's fascination with phallic masculinity can be seen to underlie painful relationship outcomes. Carrie Bradshaw's attraction to Mr Big in *Sex and the City* and Linda's attraction to Neil can thus be thought of comparatively. Linda, like Carrie (Sarah Jessica Parker), is 'intense and unapologetic. Th[e] sexual attraction highlights how powerless Carrie is to Big's phallic masculinity, which works primarily at a libidinal level' (di

Mattia, 2006: 21). While obvious class distinctions are evident between the American upper-class Mr Big and the British working-class Neil, their powerful and selfish statuses within their own diegetic worlds are signalled in both series. Whereas Mr Big's status as a city tycoon is signified by his sharp suits, fat wallet, limousine and domination over Carrie, Neil's power is expressed not only through his domination of Linda, but through a tattoo on his hip. The tattoo exclaims: 'EAT ME', and indeed, we presume that Linda does. The colloquial arrogance of the statement 'EAT ME' also clarifies Neil's self-serving attitude as the everyday understanding of the term is figured as a retort similar to 'whatever', a sign that clearly signals that Neil doesn't care about others, only about himself. While Linda is clearly hurt by Neil, she herself is presented as an equally flawed character within the series. In particular, Linda's selfishness, her traditionally masculine desires and her lack of sympathy towards others at times are not shied away from. Indeed, it is in part these aspects of Linda that make her feel like a 'real' person.

Linda as 'ladette': exploring the sociocultural context

Tapping into the zeitgeist of the late twentieth- and early twenty-first-century 'ladette' culture, *Linda Green* presents an interesting cultural shift in its representation and subversion of gender norms. Rather than being presented as either a girly girl or a tomboy, Linda, the main focus of the series, is explicitly constructed differently. Importantly, Linda is represented as a twenty-first-century 'ladette' in that she is both laddish in her behaviour (her excessive drinking, for example) and heterosexually appealing and desirable. This construction of Linda is important not only in its display of gendered difference, but as a political gesture in that Linda can be read as the epitome of the real working-class white modern woman on whom various powerful institutions attempted to impose shame.

To signal this link more explicitly, it is necessary to define and contextualise the term 'ladette' as one appropriated by the British media in the 1990s in an attempt to nominate as shameful women who refused the traditional confines of feminine behaviour. Indeed, as Angela Smith (2011: 165) notes, the term 'ladette' is 'widely used in British culture ... to describe young women who adopt "laddish" behaviour in terms of boisterous assertiveness, heavy drinking and sexual promiscuity. In Britain it is frequently associated with young working-class women.' Such characteristics – assertive behaviour, boisterousness, promiscuity and heavy drinking – could indeed be levelled at Linda yet, as a seemingly accepted staple of white working-class male identity, such characteristics in Linda are affiliated with excessive, out-of-control and offensive gendered identity. As Ang and Hermes point out, however, 'an individual's gendered subjectivity is constantly in the process of reproduction and transformation' (1991: 316). One of the questions that Linda perpetuates via her behaviour in the series is thus the one Abbott nominates in the quotation which opened this chapter – what's wrong with that? In other words, what, if anything, is 'wrong' with Linda?

Perhaps, according to Justine Ashby (2005: 128), the diagnosis of Linda's 'wrongness' could be related to 'post-feminism in a British context' – that is to say, the ways in which and through which 'girl power' was, in the late 1990s, conflated with both political movements associated with the 'new', moral panics and popular culture in the form of casual and cool Britpop. The ways in which such values – values of girl power, Britpop and ladette freedoms – were appropriated, produced and consumed are integral to understanding Linda's complex emotions, politics, ideologies and everyday choices within the drama. As Smith (2011: 153) argues, the notion of young women presenting a new cultural threat is evidenced in various 1990s newspaper articles which were arguably used to 'represent women as a threat to themselves (on account of the fact that their drinking leaves them more exposed to risks of assault and ill health) and to patriarchy (through the challenges they pose to established norms of female passivity)'. As noted by Abbott in relation to his more recent television series *Shameless,* the frequency of shame is complex in that it can be appropriated not only as a term utilised to name actions that diverge from the traditional or normal but, furthermore, can be understood as a mode reflection – casting the shame back upon its speaker, who says 'shame on you!', highlighting the fact that, as Abbott notes: 'it's a shame that you think "shame on you"'.

Engaging in a myriad of sexual encounters with her 'shag buddies' and strangers and notably refusing to solicit the shame of others' judgements, Linda is represented in the series as a woman who knows what she wants, when she wants it and how she wants it. For Linda, the trappings of romance fail to seduce; she is instead her own woman who desires fun, friendship and lots of satisfying sex. Linda's daytime job as a car saleswoman at Craven Lane Motors sees Linda not intimidated by the male-dominated workforce around her, but rather revelling in it, deliberately flirting with her male co-workers by telling them she is not wearing underwear, for example. Linda's active and deliberate flirtatiousness also signals a breakdown of traditional boundaries of control. Indeed, as Adam Phillips (1994: xvii–xviii) argues:

> Flirtation has always been the saboteur of a cherished vocabulary of commitment ... The generosity of flirtation is in its implicit wish to

sustain the life of desire; and often by blurring, or putting into question, the boundary between sex and sexualisation. Flirting creates the uncertainty it is also trying to control.

Linda's attempts to control the desires of others through her flirting work in line with Linda's general rejection of vocabularies of commitment. When Jimmy mentions that he has enough money set aside for a wedding if she ever fancied it, Linda squarely tells him that marriage and commitment are not for her. Linda does not, however, play up to the feminine stereotype of manipulator of the body perfect, but rather, is shown to genuinely relish her sex even while enacting a performance of gender more associated with the masculine rather than the feminine. Linda eats like a man, jokes like a man, drinks like a man and fucks like a man. Yet, simultaneously, by night, Linda adorns herself in sequins and lipstick and sings at a local club – a 'likely lass' indeed.[8] Like all of Abbott's characters, then, Linda Green is not one-dimensional but is rather a complex, complicated character who, while being 'in your face', is also completely unknown. While Linda has many interesting traits, it is the trait of excess (frequently shown as a form of repetition) by which she is most dominantly defined.

Comic disorder

In the series, Linda's 'excessive' desire for sexual satisfaction is often rendered comic. In fact, the very notion of sex and sexual desire is frequently figured as a comic anchor in the series. In Episode 1:2, for example, Linda offers a temporary home to her old schoolfriend, Pete (David Morrissey), who has been kicked out of his own flat by his dominant girlfriend, Bev. After Linda gets him drunk at the club with Michelle, Michelle's husband, Darren (Daniel Ryan) and Jimmy before taking him back to her flat, Pete discusses his relationship with Bev, and in particular, the significance of sex to Bev. Noting that his own interest has waned so much that he frequently fakes his orgasms, Pete then goes on to compare sexual dissatisfaction to the eating of a Pot Noodle: 'Ejaculation is not the same as orgasm ... An empty Pot Noodle is only evidence that you ate it. It doesn't say that you enjoyed it.' The comedy of Pete's analogy here is achieved through the unexpectedness of such a comparison between eating a Pot Noodle (a snack advertised as sexual in the sense that it is promoted as 'filthy') and sexual desire. Indeed, what makes the analogy even more humorous is the fact that Pete fails to see the humour in his own comparison, continuing his monotone, stony-faced self-pity.

While Pete makes it clear that the difference between his own and Bev's sexual desires (specifically, Bev's desire for noisy, long-lasting sex as opposed to his own desire for quick and quiet sex) has caused him to lose interest, he describes his mechanical regime for pleasuring Bev: '10 minutes licking and touching, 15 minutes oral sex, 15 minutes on the nest. Set your clock – beep, beep, beep – bam.' As Pete's monotone register during his description reinforces his boredom with sex, Linda looks dreamily off-screen, clearly impressed by the idea of any man giving so much attention to a woman's pleasure. Michelle also expresses shock at Pete's revelation, explicitly asking him to clarify his 'skills'. The 'comic one-liners' that follow end in hysterical laughter on-screen:

MICHELLE: You can really do oral sex for 15 minutes?
PETE: Yeah, but you could train a monkey to do that stuff.
LINDA: Wouldn't be the same, though. *Rupture of laughter*

Following Pete's revelation, Linda's friendship with Pete takes a sexual turn as her desire for him, or at least her desire to be the recipient of such sexual skills, grows. The friendship between Linda, Pete, Michelle, Jimmy and Darren is further conflated when Jimmy gets Pete a job at the garage where he and Linda work in order to help him make some money and thus regain his independence. Speaking on the telephone to her friend Michelle, Linda discusses Pete's relationship with Bev, nominating its unsuitability, thus demonstrating a significant change of attitude towards Pete that Michelle quickly recognises. Linda also reveals that she has read Pete's diary. The pattern, we infer, is one which Linda frequently repeats – that of selecting an object of desire that is unsuitable. Linda's desire for Pete is unveiled in this conversation in that Linda makes an undeniably comedic Freudian slip. Dressed more smartly than normal in a red V-neck shirt, beige suit and wearing a silver heart necklace, red lipstick and seductive glittery eye make-up, Pete interrupts Linda's telephone conversation to inform her that there are clients outside asking about 'finance' – Linda's specialism at work. Asking if he should show them in to her office, Linda smiles longingly at Pete before asking him to 'Give us a sex.'

Linda's quest to seduce Pete (much to the dismay of her other friends) is ramped up even further after another night out when Linda tells Pete that if he is uncomfortable on her sofa he is welcome to share her bed. Linda's attempt to control their relationship and to transform it into a sexual one is not entirely understood by Pete, who accepts the offer without recognising Linda's plan. After Pete has gracefully accepted Linda's offer, Linda quickly retires to her bedroom to secretly 'prepare' herself for sex with Steve. Rummaging through her underwear drawer to find a suitable slip, Linda selects a silky green lingerie set, reapplies her make-up, brushes her teeth vigorously, sprays herself with perfume and covers her body in a seductive spray before climbing into her bed, rearranging her breasts in a provocative manner and lying back on her pillows, pretending to be casual. Our perspective of events is not Linda's nor Pete's but rather a privileged one, embedded in the visuals before us. After waiting unsuccessfully for Pete, Linda gets out of bed to tell him that she is 'decent' – effectively, inviting him to join her. Linda then gets back into bed, continuing her wait. Soon, clearly fed up with waiting, Linda gets out of bed again, pretending to visit the bathroom. This is done so that she can place herself in Pete's visual eye-line, reinforcing and reminding him that she is 'ready' for him. Linda's actions – twice getting out of bed to entice and invite Pete – are comedic in their obvious repetition as they work to reveal what she intends to conceal.

Pete doesn't 'come to bed' and a cut shows that he is sitting in Linda's lounge, happily smoking a cigarette, eating chips and gravy and watching a quiz show on television. A cut back to Linda shows her posture becoming increasingly agitated and it is in this deferral of action that humour is achieved. Folding her arms over her body and sighing, Linda's patience is clearly running out. Her controlling ways are, however, signalled again when she momentarily rearranges a silk scarf that she has placed over her bedside lamp to create a seductive mood. The mise-en-scène here provides the audience with information about Linda's own nuances and idiosyncrasies. Turning the lamp off, then on and off again in quick succession, Linda blows the electric fuse in the house. A medium close-up shot of Linda reveals her smiling face, thus signalling to the audience that her intention was indeed to blow the fuse, thus to prevent the television from working and bring Pete to her bed. The importance of such consistent focus on Linda's facial expressions is key to understanding how her mind is operating as her plans to seduce Pete are dominantly unspoken. As David Thornburn (2007: 447) argues in *Television Melodrama*: 'television's matchless respect for the idiosyncratic expressiveness of the ordinary human face and its unique hospitality to the confining spaces of our ordinary world are virtues exploited repeatedly in all the better melodramas'.

Linda's plan fails as Pete manages to get the electricity back on and continues watching the television. When he does eventually join Linda, she is asleep and snoring. The next morning, she wakes to find the house flooded in sunlight and Pete gone. He has, she learns, quit his job and kicked Bev out of his flat, telling her that any future relationship will be on his terms. Linda's disappointment is clear for all to see. Framed later that evening singing at the social club, Linda's emotions are registered and offset through the deliberately downbeat yet hopeful musical numbers that she sings on stage.

Another important indicator of the differing facets of Linda's personality is registered through the lighting employed in the three main televisual sites or spaces of the drama. The lighting of the social club in which Linda sings on an evening is subdued, tinged with a blue filter and frequently obscured by cigarette smoke. As such, the space of the club is rendered as fantastical, representing a site where Linda can enact her imaginary star status as the desired object of the audience. Yet, the ordinariness of the club, the outdated décor, the proximity of the tables, cheap drinks, everyday pint glasses and the constant conversation during her performances highlight the fact that this is not a stage of Hollywood glamour, but a working-class social environment.

In contrast, the lighting in Linda's flat is frequently bright, drawing attention to the fact that Linda is over-exposed in the supposedly private space of her home. In Episode 1:6, for example, Linda's flat is burgled and one of the results of this is that Linda's supposedly private space and life are placed under the spotlight and thus her choices are made visible for public discussion. In 1:9, the overexposure of Linda in her flat is literally put under the spotlight when she takes part in a drunken game-show mock-up regarding the truth of who her biological father really is. This spotlit reference to the television game-show format is, I suggest, both critically important in that it first comedically parodies the faux television postmodern 'show within a show' tendency. Secondly, the reference rewards the audience for their prior knowledge of Liza's show-host status. Thirdly, the reference exposes the increasingly complex and untraditional arrangement of families in the twenty-first century.

The final setting in which Linda is often seen is her best friend Michelle's marital bedroom. Under the normal lighting of this room, Linda frequently exposes her indeterminacy and her oscillation between extreme self-confidence and a total lack of it. Indeed, the repeated shot-pattern of Linda and Michelle's chatting within this room, Linda's self-reflection and Michelle's divided attention (between Linda's concerns and the demands of her own children and husband) points to the existence of an everyday space in which the various aspects of Linda's character can be tried out, rejected or embraced. The size of the room and the proximity of Michelle and Linda in it renders their friendship emotionally and physically intimate. In each of these three sites, despite their obvious distinctions as noted above, we see differing though equally complex sides of Linda.

Framing performance – heterosexuality and lesbianism

Within the series, Linda is framed in multiple ways: as a 'ladette', a loyal friend, a lost soul, a laugh and a loose woman. The epicentre of Linda's identity, however, tends to circle around her heterosexuality and as such, it is important to consider how Linda's heterosexuality is framed in the series as well as considering how Linda's physical frame is used to conflate her belonging and exclusion in differing scenarios. In 1:3, Linda is, as per usual, determined to get her sexual rocks off. Tightly framed, looking at herself in the mirror, Linda, engaging in female camaraderie with her best friend Michelle, notes: 'If I were a bloke, I'd be gagging for some! What do you reckon, Miche? Hard-ons all round?' Here, Linda's unrestrained dialogue functions to set up a clear, central tension in that Linda's self and sexual confidence are played up in order to demonstrate the centrality of her heterosexuality while simultaneously setting up her larger-than-life confidence which, to comic effect, is eroded as the episode continues.

As with each other episode in the series, 1:3 opens with Linda positioned on-stage, singing. Occupying a position of optical and aural centrality, Linda's desire to be seen, noticed and admired is significant in that it belies her determination to put herself in the frame for each and every viewer. Later, amidst the normalcy of the social club, Linda remarks to married Michelle that she wants sex and determines that she 'won't be going home empty-handed: bring on the boys!' At this point the normality of the social club is interrupted by the entrance of six handsome young Greek trainee pilots wearing uniforms and aviator sunglasses. As Linda and Michelle turn to stare at the men who fill the frame of the shot, the speed of shooting is slowed down, thus the sequence is engineered as fantastical, or, more aptly, the fulfilling of Linda's heterosexual fantasy. Purposefully making herself visible and indicating via silent flirtatiousness that she is interested, Linda states to her friend Michelle: 'I'll have the one in the middle. No, I'll have the one at the end. Sod it! I'll have them all!' Linda's 'child in a sweet shop' response to the phallic potency of the men in uniform is comic in that it demonstrates a further reversal of traditional gender roles in that Linda both objectifies the men and also shows her own lack of restraint in wanting 'them all'. Yet, while Linda and her friend are joined by the young men, it is married Michelle in whom the men show interest rather than Linda, despite her making her desire for a 'shag' explicit. Seemingly, it is the explicitness of Linda's desire that puts the men off her, while Michelle's contented indifference to them is a clear draw.

Deflated by her failure to 'pull', Linda announces that she has 'had it with men' and intends to change her life. The constraints of traditional femininity are made clear by Linda when she nominates the changes that she intends to make: 'No more bloody Brazilian waxes and six-week trim and highlights at Toni and Guy. I'm through with fake tan, mascara, kitten heels and I never have to diet again!' While the grooming routines that Linda notes above have not previously been seen on-screen, her naming of them taps into a frequency regarding the expectations of modern women. Furthermore, these beauty routines are not seemingly undertaken for Linda to feel good about herself, but rather, are defined and determined as routines or rituals that have to be undertaken in order for her to attract a man. Akin to *Clocking Off*, the regulation of women's bodies in this discourse of heterosexuality is indeed a political point of consideration here. As Laura Mulvey (1975: 12) argues:

> In a world ordered by sexual imbalance, pleasure in looking has been split between active/male and passive/female. The determining male gaze projects its phantasy on to the female form which is styled accordingly. In their traditional exhibitionist role women are simultaneously looked at and displayed, with their appearance coded for strong visual and erotic impact so that they can be said to connote to-be-looked-at-ness.

One of the interesting cultural character traits of Linda is linked to the fact that rather than resolutely rejecting the notion of being looked at and judged by men, for the most part Linda actively covets her own objectification. Indeed, what is interesting about Linda's denunciation of feminine grooming rituals in this episode is that her actions are coded as a temporary rebellion associated with her failure to 'pull' a man rather than being situated as a political recognition of unequal heterosexual power relations.

As a response to her heterosexual failures, Linda questions her own identity and sexuality. Displaying obvious confusion and insecurity regarding what it is that she actually really desires, Linda oscillates between lamenting that she is no longer sexy to men and declaring her 'new' non-sexual life is her own choice and that as such, she is free from heterosexual politics and policing. Such self-consideration is interesting and, in line with the comments of Glen Creeber (2004: 121), demonstrates that television can 'depict a contemporary landscape in which young people are faced with an increasingly confusing set of choices, where nothing (particularly careers, relationships, gender roles, attitudes/beliefs and even sexual orientation) is secure'. Linda's insecurity does, as Creeber perhaps anticipates, lead Linda to consider alternative orientations. In conversation with her friends Jimmy, Michelle and Darren (1:3), Linda notes that she has given up on men. In response, her friends discuss going away for a hedonistic weekend and ask Linda if she will 'look after the kids'. The following dialogue is interesting in that Linda, in an attempt to reinforce her own identity as a fun-loving young woman, considers lesbianism when challenged by Darren as to what it is she actually wants:

LINDA: I said I was giving up men. I never said I was giving up enjoying myself.

JIMMY: Come on, Linda. How are you going to enjoy yourself without men?

DARREN: Yeah, face it. The first decent bloke to give you half a look and you'll be all over that condom machine.

LINDA: I love the way that you all assume that all I want is a man.

DARREN: So, what do you want? A woman?

LINDA: Well – why not? Maybe I would. Maybe I'm not so bound up with sexual stereotypes as some people. And let's face it. The penis is so last-century.

DARREN: Er, Linda. Can we watch?

First, it is worth noting here that when Darren asks Linda if it is a woman that she wants he is essentially teasing her rather than asking her a serious question. As both a former schoolfriend and the husband of her best friend, Michelle, we can infer that Darren possesses both firsthand and secondhand knowledge of Linda's usually upfront hetero-sexual desires. Indeed, the tone of Darren's voice and his intonation when he speaks to Linda clearly signal that his suggestion is a comedic one. Interestingly, Linda's adolescent attitude to being teased by her former schoolfriend brings out her own adolescent defiance in her overly dramatic gestured response. In a high-pitched register Linda both replies to Darren and shakes her head at him before turning her head purposefully away from him. Linda's dramatic reply can be understood as a specific performance of defiance here – an attempt to demonstrate that she is in control.

Having consistently noted her enjoyment of heterosexual sex up until this point in the series, Linda's sudden dismissal of the penis as 'so last-century' garners a comedic response from all her friends. Linda's employment of twenty-first-century political and cultural debates regarding sexual stereotypes is revealing here, however, despite their comedic framing. Darren's 'Can we watch?' attempts to reposi-tion Linda's sexuality in the heterosexual frame by nominating Linda's possible lesbianism as a heterosexual male fantasy to be watched and enjoyed by straight men. In defiance, Linda decides to follow her plans through and try a singles/mingles night at the comedically-named lesbian club CHUFFS on Canal Street in Manchester. Speaking to her teenage sister, Katy (Jessica Harris), before going out, Linda's motives are questioned and designated as 'not right'. When Linda petulantly tells Katy that she never had her down as 'homophobic', Katy's response is revealing: 'No – you [are the thing that is not right], you knob. You can't just go gay because you can't get a boyfriend.'

Katy's nomination of Linda as a 'knob' is interesting here on various levels. First, by calling Linda a knob (the colloquial name for an idiot), Katy clearly makes a moral judgement about Linda, explicitly rendering her potential lesbian exploration as unethical. Katy's recognition of Linda's apparent behaviour as unethical is all the more poignant because of the age difference between the sisters. Linda, at 30–odd, is supposed to be older and wiser. Instead, her teenage sister clearly has a much firmer grasp on both the ethical status of Linda's potential actions and the fact that the choice has been made by Linda as part of a rebellion (associated with her inability to 'pull' a man) rather than a genuine desire to explore her sexuality.

Secondly, the framing of Linda's potential lesbianism in iconic Canal Street is interesting in that while the street is renowned as an LGTB centre, it is dominantly connected (in televisual terms at least) with male rather than female homosexuality. Indeed, as a writer on *Linda Green*, Russell T. Davis's series *Queer as Folk* (1999–2000, Channel 4, Red Productions), released a year before *Linda Green*, examines gay male urban life in the late 1990s in Manchester and is situated around Canal Street. The dominance of male homosexuality rather than female homosexuality in this geographical space is potentially significant in that it draws attention back to Linda's own 'masculinised' active desire to pull men.

Thirdly, by addressing Linda as a 'knob', Katy gives Linda some sort of phallic potency, a potency aligned with a type of active heterosexual masculinity. Linda's performance of active female masculinity is rendered explicit in the next scene in which, getting ready to go to CHUFFS, she dresses in black leather, thus framing herself as 'butch' rather than pretty. Again, tightly framed in the mirror in her friend Michelle's bedroom, Linda looks at herself before asking: 'Is it too leather dyke?' Michelle's response that surely 'that is the point' is counteracted by Linda's own expression of the fact that she doesn't know how she wants to be framed. In addition, by airing such concerns, Linda is also made to confront her own behaviour in that she recognises that the subjective judgements that she makes about herself are potentially also going to be judgements made by other women about her:

> I don't know if I want a pretty girlfriend or if I want to *be* a pretty girlfriend. What worries me about women is that they always notice the little things. They judge you by your shoes. They don't expect you to be perfect, but they always notice when you've put weight on, or done

something funny with your hair ... . I'm not bloody going, Michelle.

Persuading Michelle to come with her by manipulating Darren's clear desire to fantasise about his wife's own fleeting lesbianism, Linda and Michelle go to the club. When Linda complains that nobody has made a move on her, Michelle reminds her that 'It's not like blokes. Maybe you're expected to make the first move.' While Michelle's own calmness or, lack of desperation to 'pull' results in her attracting the attention of two female admirers, Linda is left empty-handed. A 'turn' in the form of a sexy female stripper then interrupts the flow of the night and as the stripper stares directly at Linda while undressing, Linda's facial expression seems to oscillate between confusion and pleasure. When the stripper later appears at the bar next to Linda, Linda, looking over at Michelle's success, determines to chat the woman up. As with her earlier unsuccessful attempts to chat up men, however, Linda fails when the woman notes: 'I'm sorry and all, but you're not really my type. I don't go for butch girls.'

Here, not only is Linda's framing of herself as 'leather dyke' seen to be wrong (for this woman at least), but the stripper's nomination of Linda as 'butch' draws attention to Linda's physical frame. Having earlier mentioned that 'giving up on men' means that she will never have to diet again, the comments of the stripper serve to prove here that judgements regarding idealised female bodies are not necessarily only judgements by men but, perhaps, judgements by women about women. As Philippa Willetts (2010) notes in her blog *The F Word: Contemporary UK Feminism*: 'Criticising other women's bodies goes counter to everything that feminism should stand for. It is hurtful to other women, and it is hurtful to ourselves. And it is irrelevant to any other criticisms of a person, be it their politics, their acting skills, their singing ability, or, frankly, anything at all.' Willetts's argument is remarkably similar to Liza's own regarding the contemporary employment of female weight as a measure of quality, control, attractiveness and ability. Indeed, Linda's fleeting lesbianism causes her to confront directly the judgements of other women regarding the ways in which women are most frequently framed in contemporary society.

Conclusion

While Linda's later admittance to the female stripper that she is 'straight' essentially closes off the narrative of Linda's exploration of fleeting lesbianism, the exploration of sexuality and body image in the series nonetheless opens up ideological debates about gay/straight labels, norms and bodily expectations in contemporary society. The engagement of the series with feminist debates offers its viewers an account of the tensions bound up in foregrounding the issues of contemporary women and the ways in which the unhinging of traditional 'passive' femininity affects formulations of normality and moral acceptability. Indeed, as noted by Robin Nelson (2007b: 147), 'despite narrative closure, the ideological debate is left open for viewers to take up if they wish'.

The series explicitly points to the fact that for Linda, desire, sexual activity and seduction are active rather than passive processes. As such, Linda constitutes a challenge to traditional heterosexual discourses in which, as Lynne Segal (1994: 266) notes, '"sex" is something "done" by active men to passive women, not something women do'. On the contrary, Linda is dominantly represented as an active 'doer'. The strategies and aesthetics invoked to express Linda's agency are, ironically, frequently demonstrated through her aggressive heterosexuality, a heterosexuality that could be read on a surface level as anti-feminist. Instead, however, the thematic and continual focus on Linda's desires to pull are so active, so excessive, pushed so much to the centre that the viewer is forced to search for hidden depths – to interpret and negotiate the meanings beyond the surface of the screen.

The aesthetics of the series such as the focus on the parameters of Linda's environment, the recurrent framing of Linda as an object of her own gaze, the paradoxes between Linda's public and private personas and the fact that Linda is continuously caught in the crossfire of her own nominated in/authenticity further demonstrate that *Linda Green* employs a new rhetoric of conflict to speak about the contemporary complexities of womanhood.

Notes

1 This and all other unattributed quotations from Abbott are cited from specially commissioned interviews with the author in 2011 and 2012. Full extracts from the interviews are available in Appendix 1.

2 Cited at www.liza-tarbuck.co.uk/articles/article_21.html (accessed 13/03/2011).

3 Cited from the *Red Production Company* website, 'Linda Green': www.redproductioncompany.com/pastproductions.asp?menuid=67 (accessed 18/03/2011).

4 Cited from the *Red Production Company* website, 'Linda Green': www.redproductioncompany.com/pastproductions.asp?menuid=67 (accessed 18/03/2011).

5 Cited from the *Red Production Company* website, 'Linda Green': www.redproductioncompany.com/pastproductions.asp?menuid=67 (accessed 18/03/2011).

6 Study carried out by Dave Rowlinson, cited in the *Independent*, 26 June 2000: www.independent.co.uk/news/uk/this-britain/average-dress-size-of-women-increases-to-14-715277.html (accessed 02/02/2011).

7 www.bbc.co.uk/drama/lindagreen/.

8 In an article published in the *Observer* newspaper on 14 October 2000, the headline used to describe Liza Tarbuck and her role in *Linda Green* was 'The likely lass'.

State of Play

There was a critic in *The Daily Telegraph*, James Walton, and the only reason I wrote *State of Play* was because he called me a warrior of white sliced bread, meaning I could only write working-class, and I was like 'right, you fucker, I'm going to write something posh and you'll have to retract that'. After the first episode he said that it was really good but that I'd got five hours left to fuck it up – basically that was his summary and I was like, 'ha ha ha, I'm just going to wipe the floor with you now'. I wrote *Shameless* and *State of Play* in the same year to show I can do both things – don't pin me down.[1]

Paul Abbott

The fact that *State of Play* was created in response to a journalistic critique regarding the limits of Paul Abbott's ability (a critique in which Abbott's professional abilities were seemingly aligned with the perceived limits of his own working-class/underclass upbringing) is a valuable insight into the contemporary power of the British press to telegraph, shape and control public opinion. Indeed, it is a similar issue that arguably takes up position at the centre of Abbott's six-part television drama, *State of Play* (BBC One, 2003). Originally shown on BBC One from 18 May until 22 June 2003, *State of Play* starred various respected actors such as Bill Nighy (as Cameron Foster, editor of the *Herald* newspaper), John Simm (as *Herald* journalist Cal McCaffrey), David Morrissey (as Labour MP Stephen Collins), Kelly Macdonald (as journalist Della Smith) and James McAvoy (as reporter Dan Foster). Based primarily in a London newspaper office, the *Herald*, the series engages – via the investigations, stories and ethics of key news journalists, politicians and corporate heavyweights – with the complex language of 'spin', persuasion and political and personal exposé. Focusing initially on the mobilisation of a murder mystery, the story soon opens up to reveal secretive interrelations between corporate, governmental and domestic worlds. Following on from a tradition of award-winning British political dramas concerned with the 'state of the nation' such as *Edge of Darkness* (BBC Two, 1985) – a drama that focused on the shifting global landscape of the 1980s, specifically addressing the zeitgeist of nuclear warfare and power – and *A Very British Coup* (Channel 4, 1998) – a drama that focused on secrecy, conspiracy and the power of secret State surveillance – *State of Play*'s focus upon the shadowy interrelations between the government, press and multinational oil companies under a late 1990s/early twenty-first-century Labour government brought the state-of-the-nation conspiracy thriller up to date.

Plot

As the plot of *State of Play* is not self-contained within episodes, the complexity and multifaceted specifics of the series are important to sketch out here for clarity. As such, publicity material produced by the BBC is cited directly and in full below:

> When Sonia Baker, a young political researcher, is killed on the Tube, her high-profile Labour MP boss, Stephen Collins (David Morrissey), is devastated. The press smell blood and questions are asked about the nature of his relationship with Sonia. The story is pursued by the Herald, its editor Cameron Foster (Bill Nighy) and its reporter, Cal McCaffrey (John Simm), who was Stephen's former campaign manager. Cal is uncomfortable with pursuing what amounts to a domestic scandal until his colleague Della (Kelly Macdonald) discovers a surprising link between Sonia's death and the murder of black teenager, Kelvin Stagg.

> Kelvin had stolen a silver briefcase that contained photos of Stephen and Sonia and a gun. A courier shot at the same time as Kelvin is recovering in hospital when DI Brown, who is in charge of the case, visits him, as does Della. The hospital fire alarm is set off and as they are moving the patient a marksman takes aim at him but misses and kills DI Brown. After the murder of DI Brown, DCI Bell (Philip Glenister) is put on the investigation. He knows Della is withholding information and is determined to find out what she and Cal know.

> Meanwhile, Stephen Collins' story becomes more complicated when an anonymous fax reveals that his affair with Sonia was far from being a superficial thing – Stephen was going to leave his wife Anne (Polly Walker) for her. This doesn't go down well with the party's spin doctor, Andrew Wilson (Michael Feast), who is trying to keep Stephen's reputation intact. Della realises she is being followed and that her life is in danger.

> DCI Bell and Cal collude in a plan to smoke out the hit man. Meanwhile, his team pin the author of the anonymous letters to a City wideboy

named Dominic Foy (Marc Warren). The discovery that he had a sexual history with Sonia leads the team to suspect that he's guilty. Stephen may also be hiding something as Sonia knew she had the job in his office a month before her interview.

Meanwhile, Cal's personal and professional life gets hopelessly tangled when he embarks on a love affair with Anne Collins. This leads Stephen to tell Andrew Wilson to leak the information to the press and ruin Cal's reputation. His only supporter now is the energy minister, George Fergus, who wills him to succeed.

Cal and his team corner Dominic Foy, who is edgy and obstructive and constantly changes his story. They discover a connection between Foy and lobbyists for the oil industry.

Stephen's defence over the hiring protocol of Sonia leads Cal to interrogate his obtuse assistant Greer (Deborah Findlay), who finally admits to being influenced by an unexpected source. When the UK's largest oil company gets wind of where the Herald's investigation is heading, Cameron finds himself under pressure from his board and makes a startling decision.

Sensing that his team is close to snaring their prey, Cal invites Stephen to listen in to an interview with Dominic Foy, hoping that with a few well-aimed questions, the increasingly paranoid Foy will crack. He's right – Foy's confession is a goldmine, but it sends Stephen over the edge and Foy to casualty.

On the morning Cameron's explosive headlines hit the newsstands, Cal travels to Manchester to see Anne. He is disturbed to find her supportive of Stephen when he reveals that Sonia had been planted in his office.

Stephen is now single-minded in his obsession – who in the government knew Sonia was a plant? And why are they protecting George Fergus? His anger at the scale of the deception leads him to Cal once more. But the paper's executive editor puts the brakes on the story, leading Cal and Cameron to hatch a plan to print it. With the stakes at the highest, their story takes one final, gut-wrenching turn.[2]

Multiple genres. Multiple perspectives.

While classified most dominantly as a complex political thriller, *State of Play* is also a series that refuses to be 'pinned down' in adherence to any one generic convention. This versatility and ability to negotiate and interweave different generic characteristics is certainly a hallmark of Paul Abbott's work. As director of the series David Yates notes in his DVD commentary (2005): 'Paul is an extraordinarily versatile writer because he has the ability to switch between thriller, drama, tender love story and real comedic pathos. That ability to switch makes him a genius in my view.' The mobility of the series ensures such switches are not only presented, but interrelated, thus demanding that the audience read both the sharpness of the screen itself, and the gaps that exist between the lines of the text. This purposeful and determined mashing-up of perspectives presented through the drama is a case in point; a revisioned 'state of play' that both uncovers some aspects of 'truth' while simultaneously pointing out that the murkiness of the world it presents is the mere tip of the iceberg.

Using a cinematic aspect ratio, the stylistic grammar of *State of Play* is also telling in that it points to the dynamic and fast-moving pace of technology, information and people in the modern world. Refusing to stand still, the series demonstrates a frenetic energy in both its characters and the ways in which mobilisation is constantly foregrounded through the aesthetic strategies employed on the series, such as the mise-en-scène. On a literal level, characters in *State of Play* are always on the move – on the Tube, in taxicabs, on trains, running, chasing and consciously critiquing the events of their worlds. Paired with an impressive rhythmic soundtrack, which as Nelson (2007b: 205) notes, 'lend[s the series] an energy', the pulsating drumbeats and offbeat sounds that speak to viewers are reminiscent of filmic rather than typical televisual scores. In particular, the music that features in the opening sequence bears a strong rhythmical resemblance to Iggy Pop's track 'Lust for Life' as featured in the film *Trainspotting* (dir. Danny Boyle, 1996).

The frantic pace of events in the opening scene of *Trainspotting* can also be seen to be mirrored in *State of Play*. Like the lovable rogues Renton (Ewan McGregor) and Spud (Ewen Bremmer), black male teenager Kelvin Stagg (Gregory Poorman) is framed in the opening scene of the series running through the streets of London (after stealing a bag), hotly pursued by another male before being calmly and seemingly inexplicably executed behind a large skip. Seen by a male motorcycle courier, the hit man then attempts to kill the courier, shooting him twice. A cut to a moving London bus followed by a wipe then reveals the jostling population of the city going about their morning business. Next, we see a middle-aged white male dressed in a smart suit (a man we later discover is Labour MP Stephen Collins) rushing towards the Underground before boarding a Tube train. The opening sequence of *State of Play* is telling, then, in that it writes large from the start the world of underground activities in both a metaphorical and literal sense. This opening sequence is pertinent as it offers us, I suggest, a way to read the thematic heart of the show in that the underground deeds and spaces represented function as metaphors for clandestine deals, espionage, personal betrayal and political and corporate wrongdoing. The Tube itself can, like the series, be cartographised as a world of intersecting tracks, stories and converging lines of enquiry – enquiries linked, in the world of *State of Play*, to organised murder.

The opening sequence goes on to show Stephen's journey to work disrupted by an unexpected, unnamed event – an event later exposed as the death of his mistress, Sonia Baker, on the very Tube tracks that Stephen rides. This moment of disruption is pertinent and is referred to later by a journalist who asks Stephen how he felt about having his journey to work interrupted because of the body on the tracks, that of his employee, Sonia. As the series moves forward, the interconnection between Stephen and the death (later revealed to be murder) of his lover complements the very narrative drive of the series, a series which, as Nelson (2007b: 201) notes, can be generically understood as 'a whodunnit'. The whodunnit question is actually a complex one within the diegesis of the series, relating not only to Sonia Baker but to Kelvin Stagg as well. A mapped connection uncovered by journalists determines a further unexpected link *between* the two murder victims. As their supposedly disparate worlds clash, an investigation is set in motion which maps out the underground domains in which Sonia and Stagg briefly lived. The parallel track of the investigation is, however (at least initially), a closely kept secret, guarded by specific journalists working on the fringes of the law at the *Herald* newspaper.

Mapping the intimacy of space

As we have mentioned, it is the brutal intimacy of a stranger that frames the first murderous 'hit' of the series in the form of the unexplained assassination of Kelvin Stagg next to a large metal skip in an East End London back street. The insalubrious location of the hit follows a chase through the more populated and affluent areas of the city. The urban sprawl of the city of London works to both hide and expose Stagg's and his executor's criminal activities. The space of the hit is, however, undoubtedly mapped as a fringe space, likened later to the high-rise home of Stagg and his mother and brother, Sonny (Johann Myers). This traversing between spaces is important. Moving between different spaces (and thus further determining Abbott's refusal to be 'pinned down'), *State of Play* exposes unexpected intersections between seemingly separate and ill-fitting terrains. As Nelson (2007b: 201) notes of the series, it 'moves between the domains of marginalised urban black communities, big business (multinational oil companies), the middle-class environs of the London editorial office of a newspaper (something like *The Guardian*), leafy Manchester suburbs where the drama of a family break-up is played out, and the inner sanctums of the Houses of Parliament'. The bleeding of space and borders between these environs offers a critical insight into the complex and ever-shifting 'state of play' of modern Britain. Indeed, the differing yet bleeding border spaces allow for multiple perspectives, ethics and resonances.

The blurring of disparate spaces is formally punctuated through the complex situation and multiple locations of MP Stephen Collins at the beginning of the series. With a family home in the Manchester suburbs (a home in which his wife, son and daughter live), a place in Sonia Baker's bed and apartment, a seat on the backbenches of parliament as well as a bed in Cal's spare room, the space in which Stephen is at 'home' is clearly unfixed. Moving between all of the above spaces, Stephen is also revealed to have planned to move yet again into a new 'home' with Sonia Baker. While of course this final move does not occur due to Sonia's death, the revelation of it hints at Stephen's dislocation, his alienation in a world of multiple options. Moreover, Stephen's mobility (his desire to move upwards) is explicitly linked to his deception – the deception of both his wife via his infidelity, and his colleagues in parliament via the inappropriate nature of his relationship with Sonia and the subsequent tarnishing of his 'family man' (man of honour, trust and integrity) image. Image is, of course, managed and manipulated by the spin doctors in the government and Stephen's strong desire to rise through the ranks means that image is indeed integral to him and his party. Like the images of the oil companies on which Stephen's job focuses, he must be perceived as trustworthy even if he is not. Stephen's ability to present himself as trustworthy is referenced in explicit dialogue between his friend and former campaign manager (now journalist) Cal McCaffrey and his parliamentary secretary, Greer Thornton. Snippets of dialogue referencing Stephen's success in this regard can be seen in Episode 5, when Cal goes to Greer's home to persuade her to give him information that will help him to clear Stephen's name of involvement in an oil scandal. Cal pleads with Greer thus: 'Nine years ago, when I was Stephen's campaign manager, I got to know him and like him – for all the reasons that you do. Somebody somewhere wants to see him hang for something he hasn't done. Stephen's not bent.' Greer agrees wholeheartedly and in response, gives Cal information that she believes will help Stephen, information that she knows is clearly detrimental to her own future in parliament. Similarly, Cal puts his reputation as an investigative journalist on the line to help Stephen, noting in a conversation with him in Episode 6 that 'People knew you had a line when we were trying to get you into parliament. It made my job ten times easier knowing that people trusted you.'

Such dialogue reveals the extent to which appearances of trust or, at least, straightness, are crucial to the politics, both personal and political, of the narrative. When Stephen apparently finds out that the upper echelons of the government knew about his affair with Sonia (a plant but, importantly, a plant known to the government from U-Ex Oil) long before he was forced to reveal his affair to them, he comments to Cal that while the corruption could be classified as inverted (in that the government knew exactly who Sonia Baker was), 'U-Ex Oil were the only company responding to hostile perceptions of their working practices.' The government and in particular his mentor, George Fergus (James Laurenson), Stephen notes, were 'taking the piss out of me!' The language employed by Stephen and indeed by other characters such as Cal, Cameron and wide boy Dominic Foy (Marc Warren) is crucial to the ways in which deceits, manipulations and confessions are framed and understood in the series. Indeed, Cal's investigative language works to persuade, report and convince, as noted in his relations with Greer above.

Stylistics and the language of noir

The series grounds its representations through the preoccupations of Cal and co. to exist, survive and communicate effectively within these differing spaces. In order to connect the dots, language and the ability to speak in and to different voices and perspectives are hugely significant. In the marginalised black community of the series, language is seen operating in various forms. Speaking, especially to journalists, has a negative value attached to it (at least initially), as Kelvin's mother believes that Cal implicated her son in some sort of underground drug-dealing in a newspaper story following his murder. Kelvin's girlfriend enters into negotiation with Cal both through the arrangement of a protector (Kelvin's brother, Sonny) and with a literal monetary value attached (in that Cal pays her £500 in cash in exchange for both her knowledge regarding Kelvin's activities, a metal briefcase with undisclosed contents and the assurance that the girl's identity will not be exposed). The scene itself in which Cal meets Kelvin's nameless girlfriend is mapped in an interesting way. Getting out of his old-looking blue Ford Escort car, Cal zaps the alarm to ensure the doors of the vehicle are locked. Framed by a concrete urban jungle of high-rise flats and litter, the space is clearly rendered 'shady'. Such shadiness is communicated not only through the setting of the scene but also through small gestures of background artists. For example, after locking his car doors Cal turns to see a man dressed in jeans and a black parka coat looking intently but quickly into his back seat, presumably looking to see if it is worth breaking into. Coupled with a shot of a young black male running anxiously along the pavement (echoing Kelvin's earlier run before he was executed), Cal observes the space with obvious trepidation. Moving towards the designated meeting point – an abandoned car park secured with metal shutters – Cal is given access by a brief pulling-back and then replacement of the security shutters.

Both concealed and obscured from the main road, the space of the car park is cast as noir-ish. Occurring in a distinctive 'lonely place',[3] the melodrama of the scene is painted grammatically through deep shadows and oblique angles, features referred to by Susan Hayward (2000: 129) as the cinematographic components of noir's visual style.[4] As Cal is cast and clearly coded as the typical noir protagonist, his shadowy meeting reveals his anxiety, own moral ambiguity, and solitariness as well as the danger in which he has placed himself in order to solve a crime. In the fringe space of the car park (a space in which the law and its associated discourses clearly operate differently), Cal attempts to shed light on the murderous events of the past. Primarily dank, smoky and littered with occasional derelict cars, the darkness of the car park is penetrated only by shafts of sunlight on the left-hand side of the frame. Guided by Sonny Stagg, the law of this urban jungle is made clear as Cal receives his orders from Sonny: 'She don't live round here and you're never gonna know where she lives and she won't tell you her name, right?' Moving towards a young girl from an oblique angle, Sonny kneels, assuring her of her safety before moving to the side to allow Cal access to her. Framed in a medium shot, we see a woman silently smoking a cigarette against the ice-cold walls and broken windows of the car park, her voice heard speaking reticently to Cal. Telling Cal how she and Kelvin had snatched a bag at the train station before being pursued by the owner of the bag, the girl admits that she jumped on the Tube and went home, noting that 'Kelvin could have been nicked for all I know.' Kelvin wasn't nicked, however. When the bag turns up at her house later on, she admits that 'the bag's not what we thought [it was]'.

As Sonny asks her to show Cal the bag and its contents, Cal wraps a dark handkerchief over his hand before delving into the bag and pulling out a professional execution pistol. Replacing it, Cal then leafs through a notebook filled not with words, but with photographs of Sonia Baker and Stephen Collins together. Visibly unnerved by the revelation and confirmation of Sonia's murder and the fact that her death somehow intersected and was obviously connected with Kelvin's own, Cal questions the girl about how contact was re-established between the owner of the bag and Kelvin. Admitting that she and Kelvin had charged a mobile telephone found in the bag, the girl reveals that the owner contacted them, threatening them with their murder and the murders of their families. Recognising that the owner did not know who they were as, the girl reveals, Kelvin's dad died of an overdose the previous year, she goes on to ask Cal for the agreed money. Ordered by Sonny to give the agreed amount to her, Cal does so before walking back towards the shimmering metallic case and slamming the lid shut. Accompanied by an audible strong and fast non-diegetic beat, the scene then changes. Bright lights fill the screen as the camera pans upward and forward from a low-angled shot. Now in the spotlight himself, Cal is seen parking up and looking anxiously around before removing the stolen case from his car and taking it inside the *Herald* newspaper offices.

The cinematic and cinematographic echoing of noir stylistics has resonance on many levels here. The closing down, elusive and obscure framing and lyrical abstractions of space in the sequence work not only to build mood, but to render darkly acute, both abruptly and graphically, the unbearable proximity of Cal, Sonny and the girl to the murderous events. The noir motifs employed for this purpose can thus be read as tropes of official systematic distortion in that while they seemingly repeat the essential components of noir, they also function to offer the audience a different perspective on the underground space they represent. Indeed, as Alison Peirse (2010: 191) reminds us, referencing Andrew Spicer: 'any attempt at defining film noir solely through its "essential" formal components is reductive ... because film noir, as the French critics asserted from the beginning, also involves a sensibility, a particular way of looking at the world'. In terms of the noir elements of the sequence, the generic positioning of *State of Play* is played up in that, as Hayward (2000: 128) argues, noir is 'often referred to as a sub-genre of the crime thriller'. The importance of contextualising the series this way thus speaks not only to the larger-than-life world of cinema (the series after all employs a wide-screen aspect ratio of 16:9), but also to the grammar of collision, crossover, conflict and quality.

Designated as a political thriller by Jane Rackham in the *Radio Times*, the series expands the parameters of journalistic strategies of investigation, demonstrating how invasive and investigative language is used not only in the designated domains of journalese, but also on a day-to-day basis as a mode of exchange. The dynamic worlds of news-breaking, policy-making and reporting are codified through discourses of anxiety,

Figure 5.1 *State of Play*, BBC One, 2003: Stephen Collins (David Morrissey) and Cal McCaffrey (John Simm) in front of the House of Commons

discourses that are pivotal to the hyperactive aesthetic of the series. The dominant power structures seen to operate in *State of Play* are both problematised and awarded legitimacy in oscillating swings of mood and metatext. The use of Abbott's series (itself a text) to comment on and decode other political and mediated texts is pertinent here in that, as Nelson (2007b: 201–11) notes:

> *State of Play* is a consummate political thriller, sustaining something of the political critique associated with the British social realist tradition ... It blurs fact and fiction, taking the temperature of the times in terms of its dominant metaphor of the seat of government depicted as a world dominated by spin and a lack of sincerity. [T]he murder mystery plot, which allows the finger of suspicion to be pointed at multinational oil companies and the inner cabinet of the government as well as individuals, allows a sense of institutional, and ultimately social, malaise to be conveyed, inviting viewers to reflect upon contemporary society.

The invitation to actively read and reflect on contemporary society in the real world as well as the fictional world of the series demonstrates not only the sophistication and multiple layering of the narrative, but also the driving compulsion that individuals and institutions assume accountability for their actions or inactions. As such, the issue of responsibility looms large in the series.

Ethics and ideologies

Ethical questions regarding responsibility are bound up in the multiple ideologies offered in *State of Play*. As Michael Massey (2010: 84–5) notes, while the series 'positions the audience in support of Cal McCaffrey's campaign to expose the corruption at the heart of the Government's handling of a scandal involving one of its rising stars, ... the central issue is the thorny question of the freedom of the press'. Indeed, this issue is not only dealt with implicitly in the series (through, for example, Sonny's refusal to give up the identity of Kelvin's girlfriend and Cal's source), but also explicitly in an explosive argument between Stephen and Cal at Cal's home. A former campaign manager and friend of Collins, Cal offers his house as a temporary sanctuary to Collins after his wife throws him out of his home on discovering his affair with Sonia Baker. Becoming frustrated with one another regarding their different world-views and perceptions of the freedoms of the press and the protection of individuals, the exchange between the men follows thus:

CAL: Piss off! You screw your life up and it's the first I hear from you in months.

STEPHEN: Well, I was busy.

CAL: Yeah. Having an affair that was gonna screw your life up, which, by the way, you might have told me about.

STEPHEN: Like I would.

CAL: Or, I would have guessed, in which case it would've chucked me a cue to say Stephen, stop being such a prick and get your life sorted out!

STEPHEN: Yeah? How well do you think you know me, Cal?

CAL: A lot better than I think you would admit to, Stephen.

STEPHEN: Yeah, well, you'd have to say that in your job, wouldn't you!

CAL: Oh. OK. And what's wrong with my job? ...

STEPHEN: You know, I laughed when I saw they'd given you that 'Journalist of the Year' [award]. Jesus.

CAL: Great mate you are – rooting through my personal stuff. I tell you what. If you don't like my job ... *[interrupted]*

STEPHEN: It's not a job! It's a waste product ... You know, people like you, you can't move until someone spoon-feeds you shit, or misery, or gossip.

CAL: Somebody like you, you mean. When you're pioneering the new dawn of democracy? Piss off!

STEPHEN: That's exactly what I do.

CAL: You arrogant bastard. You've been greasing your own arse since they gave you that shining-star badge.

STEPHEN: In a vote for Chairman of the Energy Committee the closest contender was fifty votes behind me and that was a cross-party vote!

CAL: What have *you* done for your constituency in the last two years?

STEPHEN: Nothing a ligger like you would be interested in.

CAL: You believe what you're told.

STEPHEN: I earn my living.

CAL: Yeah? And you're earning my living, the way that you're going about your private life, so thanks for that.

STEPHEN: Stick your spare room up your arse, Cal.

Such dialogue makes explicit the complexities, multiple viewpoints and ideological contours of social relations in the series. Crossing over from a former public relationship (Cal worked as Stephen's campaign manager years before) to a private friendship, the differences between the men are mapped emotionally in terms of a distinctive gap, not in knowledge content, but in knowledge form and perspective. The worlds of Cal and Stephen do intersect in various ways, but fraught exchanges such as those above show how vectors of change (Stephen's position as chair of the Energy Committee and Cal's award) both colour their shared past and unsettle their future. Such oppositional discourses function to dislodge the reliability of personal accounts and bring to light the dual bias and philosophies of the characters. While on the one hand Cal is clearly positioned as a 'pursuer of truth' (Nelson 2007b: 202), he simultaneously demonstrates his own ability to engage in illegality when he feels that the official structures of the law compromise his own investigations and his ultimate pursuit of truth.

One such example of Cal's criminality is signalled clearly in his arrest at the close of Episode 2. After police officers flood the *Herald* offices looking for the briefcase Cal bought from Kelvin's girlfriend, newspaper editor Cameron Foster looks on in dismay before stating: 'Call the goblins off. What you're looking for is in here.' Shot from a high angle, Cameron goes into his own office, retrieves the case from his safe, carefully places it on his desk and unwraps it for the police detective. Demanding to know where the case has come from, the detective confronts Cal. Refusing to respond to the officer's piercing gaze and determined and angry 'where?' Cal notes: 'The contact is anonymous on the grounds that his or her life may be in jeopardy.' Recognising that Cal is the only person with knowledge of the contact, the detective looks down, then turns to one side, looking anxious, before informing Cal he is to be arrested on suspicion of perverting the course of justice. Ordering his fellow officers to 'cuff him', Cal is led away by police officers through the busy newspaper office. With his walk set to an undulating and increasingly fast non-diegetic drumbeat, the episode closes as the screen suddenly fades to black.

The framing of Cal on both a literal and metaphorical level is interesting in this sequence. Forced to take responsibility for his own criminal actions (withholding evidence from the police), Cal is positioned as
an obstructor, yet his obstructions are clearly coded and framed as part
of a pursuit for a higher truth. Cal's protection of his contact is, we are
led to believe, an ethical choice affiliated to his belief in the freedom of
the press. The protection and safety of sources is integral to this belief
yet, in order to demonstrate the authenticity of his ideology, Cal has to
pay a price. While, then, Cal's submission to arrest functions to frame
Cal as honest, even in his dishonest actions, the sequence also, via the
complex emotions of the arresting detective (who believes that one of his
colleagues was shot as a direct result of Cal's withholding of evidence),
is shown to draw out questions regarding the audience's own ethical
integrity. Indeed, in supporting Cal's actions, the audience is forced to
confront their own collusion with illegal practices. This reflection can
be recognised as a form of ironic double-framing in that the audience is
framed by their identification with Cal to accept his criminality because
he works in pursuit of the truth. Yet, is there just one truth? Can the
press ever be anything but biased? Robin Nelson (2007b: 202) argues
that these questions are indeed central to the politics of the series: 'A
central irony of *State of Play* is that the young investigative journalists, contrary to a dominant discourse of media bias and the somewhat
arbitrary construction of news, doggedly pursue the truth.' While, as
Nelson argues, the notion of pursuing truth is integral to the series, it
is, I suggest, the very versatility of Abbott to turn expected formats and
formulas of television detection and investigation on their head that
unsettles regular rhythms of expectation.

The comic framing of Foy

One way in which Abbott does this, I suggest, is by injecting humour
into the terrain of the detective process. Specifically, in *State of Play* the
introduction of the character Dominic Foy (Marc Warren) functions
to emphasise the comedic aspects of deception or, at least, attempted
deception. A key character in revealing the depth of the relationship
between Stephen Collins and Sonia Baker, Foy, it is revealed, is responsible for anonymously faxing a document to the *Mail* newspaper in
Episode 2 which proves that Stephen was intending to leave his wife and
move in with Sonia. After Stephen leaks the fax to Cal, the identity of
Foy comes under strong investigation from new freelance recruit Dan
Foster (Cameron's estranged son), Cal and Della. With Dan tracing the

fax back to a local business franchise, his description of Foy (a description Dan extracts from the male manager of the franchise by flirting with him) is telling: 'Male. Blond hair. 5 foot 10. Slim build. Black/navy suit. White shirt – Prada? Black suede shoes – Armani? He's used the fax bureau once or twice before and works somewhere in the Apex building.' Foy's nominated liking for designer clothing is seen again when he walks the streets of London wearing a long, brown fur coat followed by Dan and other journalists. Rather than blending into his urban environment, Foy distinctly sticks out, signalling via his clothing his desired status as a wide boy. When confronted about his knowledge regarding Sonia Baker, he runs from the Apex building, escaping via some back stairs before jetting off to Spain.

Foy's return at the end of Episode 3 again sees him adorned in a comedic costume of pink sunglasses (worn indoors), a purple silk shirt, a silver necklace and his trademark fur. Confronted by Cal, Della and Dan at his car at Heathrow airport, Dominic agrees to speak to them at the news office. In Cameron's office, against a backdrop of moving cars, he is questioned about a sexual relationship with Sonia Baker. At first he rejects such an occurrence before being confronted by additional information in response to which he changes his story. The intersection of differing information and stories has two functions here. First, it provides the diegetic world with depth in that it demonstrates that information cannot simply be contained but exists and affects a larger story and world. As the cars outside Cameron's window run on oil, so the significance of Foy's knowledge (knowledge concerning an explicit link between Sonia and U-Ex Oil) garners depth. As director of the series, David Yates notes in relation to the setting of Cameron's office: 'Depth was always so important in the newsroom. In Cameron's office, you can see outside the windows so there is a constant rumble of traffic. I think a lot of television dramas usually (because of budget) try and close everything down into corners and you never feel you're part of a bigger, broader world.' The second function of Foy's multiple stories here is to establish a character pattern for Foy, a pattern of denial, followed by revelation. This staple of Foy's character is frequently treated comedically, as Foy is always outwitted by the journalists he engages with. As his clothing is unconvincing of his supposed professionalism, so is his dialogue.

In both Foy's performance and dialogue, the vulgarity of his character is shown to be shaped around the nexus of greed. Indicating to the journalists that he has information that he is prepared to share with them for a price (literally monetary, as well as the promise that his name will be kept out of the papers), Foy is duped into giving Dan his bags and personal documents. As part of a journalistic tactic, Dan, Cal and Della agree to put Foy up at a local hotel so that he can evade the police. Seen in the hotel lobby buying a copy of the gay magazine *Attitude*, Foy unwittingly reveals his sexuality and thus exposes himself as a liar regarding his earlier confession of a sexual relationship between himself and Sonia Baker. In addition, it is revealed that Foy has received three payments of £25,000 from Warner Schloss, a company who lobby for U-Ex Oil. From there it is deduced that Foy was employing Sonia.

In Episode 4, Foy, suited and booted as usual, walks towards his bright red BMW M3 private-plated car (undoubtedly a phallic symbol) to find a large bird excretion on the front windscreen. Symbolic of Foy being 'in the shit', he soon realises that he is being followed by another vehicle. With the tailing of Foy being continued into Episode 5, Foy's paranoia and anxiety reach an all-time high. Going voluntarily into the police station, Foy rants and raves, demanding to know 'What's all the shit about? ... Why are you following me?' Informed by DCI Bell (Phillip Glenister) that the police are not following him, the visit ends up unnerving Foy rather than calming him. DCI Bell tips off Della, who is aware that the vehicle following Foy has been set up by Cal. Meeting Foy at the station, Della tells Foy that she can help to protect him and persuades him to return to the hotel where he had previously been questioned by Dan and Cal. Bringing Stephen to the hotel, Cal reveals to Stephen that George Fergus recommended Sonia for the job in his office and tells him that it is important that the journalistic team find out what Foy knows about Sonia working as a plant for U-Ex Oil. With Stephen wired up in the hotel room adjoining Foy's, he is able to speak to Della through her earpiece and thus lead the questioning of Foy without Foy's knowledge.

Demanding additional cash from the journalistic team, Foy is seen in three rapidly edited shots repeating his demand for 'money'. The repetition of 'money, money, money' is framed as comedic in that it references the well-known musical track by ABBA in which the singer dreams about finding a wealthy man. Indicating Foy's own fantasy, the following sequence reveals how Foy's fantasy has crumbled. Noting that: 'the shit hit the fan when Sonia stopped filing back [to U-Ex]', Foy reports that he was visited by Paul Channing (Warner Schloss/U-Ex Oil) who told him to persuade Sonia to continue her job. Visiting Sonia after Paul's visit, Foy then reveals to Cal and Della that Sonia was 'inconsolable [because] she'd fallen in love with Collins, and gotten herself pregnant to him. She said that if he ever found out how she had landed in that office with him, she would rather die than face him with that.' We cut to a shot of Stephen listening and silently crying in the next room, and he is seen to clasp his hands together and visibly shake from shock. Back in the adjoining hotel room, Foy continues his confession without recognising or knowing the magnitude of the revelations or the fact that Stephen is privy to them. As Cal turns to face the window (an action that is assumed to be a moment of reflection and sadness for his friend, Stephen Collins), Della continues her face-to-face with Foy. As Foy starts shouting about the stress of keeping Sonia's secret, Stephen angrily leaves the adjoining hotel room and begins loudly beating on the door of the room containing Cal, Della and Foy.

While the sequence that follows is dramatically intense, it is also partially comic. Foy locks himself in the bathroom and Stephen soon kicks down the door. In fear, Foy moves backwards and falls into the bath/shower. As the shower switches on, drenching Foy with water, Stephen runs towards him, drags him out of the bath and punches him repeatedly in the face. With Cal and Dan attempting to separate the men, Foy slips on the wet floor and is kicked in the stomach by Collins, who calls him a 'user' before fleeing from the hotel. In the next sequence Foy is seen being transported from the hotel on a para-medic trolley. Wearing a comedic neck brace, Cal attempts to explain away Foy's injuries, noting to the paramedics that Foy fell. The ironic reply from one of the paramedics is telling of Foy's injuries: 'Fell? From where? A trapeze?'

Fusing grief and anger, the sequence in which Foy is beaten by Stephen invites simultaneous sympathy for and disgust in Foy. The comedic aspect to the dramatic storyline is continued and reaffirmed as the paramedics attempt to exit the hotel lobby with Foy on a trolley. Getting repetitively stuck in the rotating doors of the hotel, Della, who moments before had been horrified by Foy's injuries, looks on before smiling at Cal, acknowledging the obvious humour in the vision. Clearly bruised, still in his neck brace and with two fat lips, Della speaks to Foy as he sits in a wheelchair at the hospital. His voice clearly distorted, Foy claims that U-Ex Oil can't deny knowledge of him on paper, before being wheeled away into X-Ray. In Episode 6, Foy's imminent revela-tions regarding Sonia Baker are presaged in the opening sequence – a slow-motion reprise of Foy and Sonia larking about on a previous holiday in Spain. Set to the earthy non-diegetic sound of a didgeridoo, the haunting tone of the score serves to remind audiences of the ghost of Sonia Baker. As Foy is revealed in a hospital bed with a polystyrene dish under his chin to catch the copious amount of dribble and spit he is producing, Della and Dan make a deal with him based on money. They agree to pay Foy £10,000 in exchange for an email that, in Della's words, 'links one of the top brass at U-Ex, Richard Zeigler, to Paul Channing at

Warner Schloss, to Sonia Baker'. For once, Dominic delivers, though, as Dan avers, 'I think the money helped.' Looking up as if in recognition of the deal he has just made, Dominic sees a toy aeroplane suspended from the ceiling. With his eyes fixed on this prop, Dominic's desire to escape is visibly and comically signalled. Sadly for Dominic, however, Della tips off DCI Bell about his impending escape. Adorned in his fur, though still in a neck brace, Foy's wired jaw sets off the metal detector at the airport and it is here that he is arrested on suspicion of perverting the course of justice. Seeming to concede defeat initially, Dominic closes his eyes before suddenly darting forward. Dominic's attempted escape is again framed as tragiccomic. Looking, as director Yates notes, like a 'wounded animal', Dominic is seen in slow motion half-running, half-limping away from police officers. With his grunts of pain loudly superimposed over the scene, Dominic runs towards a wall, clearly outnumbered and without a chance of escape. Waving his hand in front of his face to signal the officers to stop, he lifts his mobile phone to his ear and begins to scream loudly and incoherently into it. A cut shows Della on the other end of the phone holding her own mobile telephone away from her ear. In a final insult, Dominic is cuffed and an officer says to him: 'Come on, Dominic. Save your breath until we get you a speech therapist.'

From comedy to tragedy

In the very next sequence the comedic atmosphere immediately ceases as Cal talks to Della, revealing for the first time a suspicion that his friend Stephen may well be involved in arranging the murder of Sonia Baker. This ability to shift or mobilise from one register to another is signalled via the aesthetics as well as the dialogue of the text. Aesthetically, this mobility between registers is frequently made visible in both the constant movement of the camera, the jump-cuts employed on the series and the expressive rhythm of the score. Episode 6 is a case in point. After Stephen agrees to expose the corruption of the government to Cal for publication in the *Herald*, he is seen at Cal's home speaking to Cal's colleagues Della and Helen Preger (Amelia Bullmore). Set to the beat of oil drums (a signature sound for the series, as devised by composer Nick Hooper), the lighting of the scene drops. As Della and Helen sit taking notes, Stephen relays his knowledge of inside dealings. Constantly moving in and out of shadow as he strides through the kitchen, the sequence invokes continuous movement and pace, not only from the movements of key character Stephen, but from the continuous movement of the camera itself. Employing jump-cuts to produce a continuation of both energy and adrenaline (and thus clearly signal to the audience the importance of the scene and Stephen's revelations), the mobility of the narrative is brought to a crescendo when Stephen sits at the table explicitly revealing and recording the wrongdoing of his governmental colleague George Fergus. Commenting on the scene, Yates notes that 'the way that the camera moves is absolutely expressive in terms of the drama and conflict of the scene and the dynamic of Stephen's revelation'.

This sequence stands in marked and interesting contrast to what is later revealed to be the reality of Stephen's knowledge and truth. Situated in the final episode of the series at night, in the grounds of Alexandra Palace, the beautiful and wide-ranging panoptic vantage point over London is half-lit. On the building's steps, shot from behind, sit Cal and Stephen, wearing dark jackets; the 360–degree view offered by the location acts as a metaphor for both Cal and Stephen's new and full recognition of truth. It is in this space that Stephen is forced by Cal to admit his responsibility in having had Sonia Baker killed. As series producer Hilary Bevan Jones notes, with Stephen being forced to confront the fact that he had 'written his own truth', a mis-truth, the musical score functions to convey the emotion of the scene. Underplayed but also, in Yates's words, 'epic in its signalling the end of a long journey', the score functions to delicately express the horror regarding Sonia and Kelvin's pointless murders (both, we learn, undertaken at Stephen's request by Stephen's 'hit man'). Indeed, this horror is explicitly signalled by Cal in a parting shot in which he says to Stephen: 'Tell me this, 'cos I won't get it. What did you think you could ever have achieved, however high you went, that was worth demolishing all those families?' Forced to confront the brutal intimacy of Stephen's deception (of both Sonia, his wife and himself), Cal goes back to the newsroom. Filmed in slow motion through a blue-tinted lens, Cal's internal conflict is expressed externally through the aesthetics of the scene. With his head down and drumbeats underscoring his walk through the office, Cal is seen to have conflict etched on his face. Unwilling to respond to Cameron's questions, Cal wipes a tear away from his eye before walking into a corner and breaking down. Della, in real time, then speaks clearly to Cal: 'Yes or no?' Cal nods. 'On tape?' Della follows. Cal, in slow motion, nods. As Cal lifts the tape from his pocket, Della and Cameron listen to Cal's recording (of Stephen's confession) in the isolated space of the gents toilets. In the next shot, the newsroom is reframed, now filled with noise and clamour. The story is, we see, going to be published. As the sequence and series draw to a close, a cross-cut shows Collins getting into the back of a police car. Rather than ending the story here, however, the last scene for the audience focuses on Cal, our narrative guide. In the print room, Cal watches hundreds of newspapers containing the story coming off the press. Framed in long shots interspersed with close-ups of headlines reading 'The Killer', 'The Politician', 'The Wife', 'The Victim' and 'The First Clue' (a story about Stagg), Cal allows the sound of the machines to fill his auditory senses. The screen cuts to black and the credits roll.

Conclusion

As indicated by Abbott in the opening quotation of this chapter, *State of Play* was originally created to prove a valuable point. Both professional and personal, Abbott's refusal to accept the fixity of a status as a 'worrier of white sliced bread' speaks to the agency and urgency of Abbott's multiple talents, registers, texts and voices. Abbott's ability to juxtapose the dynamic rhythms of detection drama (as achieved through the breadth of the world that he paints, coupled with adrenalised cuts and quick pacing) are set in counterpoint to the slow-paced unravelling of multiple disparate and intersecting lines of enquiry. The series' density and complexity accord it credibility – a credible responsibility that is also demanded of its culturally competent viewers in metatext. Frequently undercutting solemnity with sardonic wit, *State of Play* nonetheless functions to both shock and disturb. The uneasy tension between tragedy and comedy in the series is made visible through aesthetic and stylistic accomplishments. For example, the expressive employment of sound evoking the ebb and flow of information (and the value of it as a currency in terms of life, death, oil and blood) points to the ever-shifting parameters of truth and perspective in both political and personal worlds. The highly coded urban landscape of *State of Play* indexes a cultural condition in which progressive politics are determined as not only the responsibility of the government and large capitalist corporations such as U-Ex Oil, but of the individual also. As Nelson (2007b: 211) argues: 'Rather than hang the death of Sonia Baker on U-Ex Oil, the complex unfolding of the plot seems to leave everybody implicated.' The collective implication or culpability of viewers is not, however, assumed to be a passive process, but rather, an active one. Whereas the controlling discourses of big business and government institutions are positioned underground and askew via the haunting death of Sonia Baker, the fact that her death occurs off-screen points to discernible gaps in knowledge which must be pursued not only at the highest level, but at the lowest too.

The strapline for the series addresses this notion explicitly, articulating: 'Sometimes you have to read between the lines.' The nuances of the story particularly as expressed through both the different forms of shooting (forms employed, according to Yates, to express the differing 'heartbeats of the scenes'), coupled with the delicate and urbane gestures of actors, allow for such a reading. As Yates notes in his commentary on Episode 1, Abbott's script both 'had a frenetic pace and energy yet was lean and precise'. This leanness of which Yates speaks is again telling in terms of the fact that Abbott respects and expects the intelligence of the viewer – asking them to read between the lines. Yates also reflects on the integrity of the series, noting that the 'newsroom background artists were all shown footage of journalists at work, given their own desk and role and trained'. As Abbott notes, 'background is rarely directed in the UK ... If you don't spend on the extras it won't work.' This concern with integrity and verisimilitude is seen in the very pattern and constantly shifting rhythms of the series. As Yates goes on to argue, UK audiences tend to be presented with a 'mathematical pattern of similarity'. This pattern is something that Abbott's work aims to move away from but, he avers, it's not always easy to explain to actors: 'You're not doing telly acting today. You've got to be a film actor.' Indeed, it is Abbott's filmic intent, the integrity of his scripts and the high quality of the directors, producers, editors and actors that Abbott employs that culminate in extraordinary, BAFTA-winning television. The aesthetics and style of *State of Play* speak then, of a new rhythm, a new formula of delicate, dynamic storytelling. Insisting upon such quality also speaks to the repeated theme of performativity in Abbott's oeuvre. In *State of Play*, this explicit address is revealed in the way in which the series foregrounds concerns regarding deceptive appearances, lying and spin. As Mark Duguid notes on BFI Screenonline,[5] tapping into the zeitgeist of suspicion surrounding the re-election of New Labour in 2001, *State of Play* highlights the 'ritual and intrigue of Parliamentary life, with its committees, spin-doctors, three-line whips and backroom deals, the power of the oil multinationals and the shadowy world of industrial public relations'. In the series, things, people, seeming truths are not what they seem. Like *Clocking Off*'s personal explorations regarding how well workers actually know their neighbours, *State of Play* explores the public as well as private face of deceptive performance.

Notes

1 This and all other unattributed quotations from Abbott are cited from specially commissioned interviews with the author in 2011 and 2012. Full extracts from the interviews are available in Appendix 1.

2 Publicity material cited in full from the BBC web source: www.bbc.co.uk/drama/stateofplay/ (accessed 02/03/2011).

3 Referencing the seminal noir filmic text *In a Lonely Place* (dir. Nicholas Ray, 1950).

4 In describing the style of noir, Susan Hayward continues to note that 'The essential ingredients of a film noir are its specific location or setting, its high-contrast lighting as well as its low-key lighting, a particular kind of psychology associated with the protagonist, and a sense of social malaise, pessimism, suspicion and gloom. The setting is city-bound and generally a composite of rain-washed streets and interiors (both dimly lit), tightly framed shots often with extreme camera angles – all reminiscent of German Expressionism. The cityscape is fraught with danger and corruption, the shadowy, ill-lit streets reflecting the blurred moral and intellectual values as well as the difficulty in discerning truth. Characters are similarly unclear, as is evidenced by the way their bodies are lit and framed: half in the shadows, fragmented. The net effect is one of claustrophobia, underscoring the sense of malaise and tension. The protagonist (according to classic canons the "hero" is a male) is often side-lighted to enhance the profile from one side and leaving the other half of the face in the dark, thus pointing to the moral ambiguity of this main character' (*Key Concepts in Cinema Studies*, 2nd edn, London: Routledge, 2000, pp. 128–9).
Such a reading of the 'hero' fits with Cal's ambiguous morality.

5 Mark Duguid writing on *State of Play* cited online: www.screenonline.org.uk/tv/id/1049820/index.html (accessed 20/01/2009).

Shameless 6

I hung on to the title *Shameless* for its irony, the kind of accusation outsiders would have chucked at my family back in the seventies. To observers, we were a chaotic bunch of kids trying to bring ourselves up after both parents had walked. We were a mess. But how were we to know that? Ignorance being bliss was our most treasured human asset. We were loud, aggressive, primitive and anarchic. But I never once recall us feeling shameless.[1]

Paul Abbott

As Kara McKechnie (2007: 53) points out, the desires of audiences to link the hallmarks of auteurism to a writer's actual background is 'an established way of reading', a way to 'measure the life against the work and seek connections'. Abbott's voice, his televisual expression of a 'world [he] knows exists',[2] is illustrated exquisitely through the critically acclaimed British drama series *Shameless* (C4, 2004–). In a partially personal and purposefully amoral representation of family life, levity and love set on the 'Chatsworth', Abbott merges social realism with melodrama, situating the series in a 'sink' estate on the outskirts of modern-day Manchester. Delineating the emotional specificity of the everyday, *Shameless* offers up, through our engagement with the Gallagher family, thematic and ideological notions of the personal, the biographical, the honest, the pleasurable and the painful recourse of 'ordinary life'. Indeed, *Shameless* is, as indicated in the opening quotation, based loosely on Abbott's own experience of youth as part of a large and chaotic Burnley family brought up in the 1970s. As Alex Games (2004), writer for the *Independent* confirms: '[Abbott] freely admits that every character is based on someone he knew from his own upbringing.' Yet, in various interviews Abbott muddies the simplistic notion that the Gallaghers *are* his family. It is, Abbott says, much more complex than that. Speaking to Decca Aitkenhead of the *Guardian* in 2008, he alluded to the impossibility of a purely autobiographical adaptation: 'If

I exaggerated my family it would be unwatchable. My dad was never Frank Gallagher ... I show Frank as a derelict dipsomaniac drug addict who nicks his kids' money and breaks their noses – but my dad abandoned his kids and let them starve!'

While Abbott's authorship of *Shameless* could be branded as extremely personal – metaphorically as an AbbottVision project – in reality, Abbott is honest about the authorial collaborations that occur within the various series. In Series 1, the episodes are written predominantly by Abbott alone; however, both Danny Brocklehurst and Carmel Morgan contribute to Episodes 3 and 5, respectively. Moving forward through the various series, writers including Amanda Coe, Phil Nodding, John

Figure 6.1 *Shameless*, Channel 4, 2004–: the Gallagher family (*left to right*): Lip (Jody Latham), Fiona (Anne-Marie Duff), Frank (David Threlfall), Liam (Joseph Furnace), Ian (Gerard Kearns), Carl (Luke Tittensor/ Elliot Tittensor) and Debbie (Rebecca Ryan)

Griffin and Emma Frost – to name but a few – assume writing responsibility for distinct episodes. As Robin Nelson (2007b: 45) notes: '[Abbott] seems to be comfortable with the idea of a collaborative creative process, even to the point of devolving the writing, once the vehicle is established.' Indeed, while such collaborations can undoubtedly be linked to Abbott's background credentials in collaborative soap writing, the loss of a single writer's voice can also be attributed to the centralisation of contemporary British televisual commissioning. As Mark Duguid (2009: 6–7) argues, the luxury of employing a single writer in order to produce a television programme with a 'confident authorial voice' is one that has regrettably been lost due to an 'aggressively commercialised new broadcasting climate marked in the 1990s by the centralisation of commissioning'. While pointedly personal, then, *Shameless* is not a visual approximation of Abbott's own upbringing as the seventh of eight children who were later to be abandoned by both parents. Instead, the series exists as a composite of the real and the performed, truth and fiction, the individual and the collective *Shameless* team. Moreover, Abbott's politics and emotions regarding his formative experiences are relayed in the series through his ability to draw on his memories indirectly, reimagine, reflect and refurbish his history and renounce authorial control over its appropriation.

Subjectivity, realism and *Shameless*

Shameless can be considered as an annex of Abbott's young life, a televisual series that keys out explicitly the significance of temporal development, reflection and change while simultaneously being underlined, infected and shaped by the author's past experiences. The characters that inhabit the diegetic world carry through those thematic passions – developing, transforming and growing before us as they engage with others, undergo new experiences and become acquainted with the ebb and flow of shame. Moreover, the characters' inability to 'stay still' works to invoke referentiality and encourage our acceptance of multiple identities and truths. As Frank Gallagher (David Threlfall) notes of the character Steve (James McAvoy) in the opening monologue credits of Series 1 and 2: 'Steve: Fiona's boyfriend – the truth is out there – not!' The audience must then work to engage actively with the milieu of implicit and explicit changes in characterisation, plot, structure and style. The eclectic frisson of *Shameless* challenges and disrupts the audience's reliability on the speech of the characters alone. Consciously, Abbott makes visible the multiplicity of the creative process. No one truth is absolute and no one perspective is entirely reliable. The subtlety of televisual grammar, the tone, style and implicit gestures expressed, thus function to encourage an understanding of the non-verbal as well as the verbal.

Assorted subjectivities are purposefully made visible by Abbott, who explicitly underscores both the unreliability of the spoken word and the divergent 'readings' the audience can construct as a result of what is frequently left unsaid in the diegesis. For example, while Frank may tell us one 'truth' about his efforts to 'be a good father', Fiona (Anne-Marie Duff), Lip (Jody Latham), Ian (Gerard Kearns), Debbie (Rebecca Ryan), Carl (Luke Tittensor/Elliot Tittensor) and Liam (originally played by Joseph Furnace) often propagate alternate 'truths'. Indeed, in such instances the camera itself arguably operates as the most reliable narrator through a mise-en-scènic focus on character movements, perceptions and gestures. As Brian McFarlane (1996: 112) argues: 'The way actors look, move, gesture, or are costumed, or the ways in which they are positioned in a scene or how they are photographed: in these ways the camera may catch a "truth".' The term 'may' is significant here in that it points to a further complexity. The narrative voices and experiences of 'truth' that are presented to the audience in *Shameless* (particularly in opening single-perspective monologues) are consciously biased and, moreover, constructed in contradistinction to one another. That is to say, we are encouraged to 'consider for ourselves' the truth of a particular character perspective through positioning their narrative version of truth against the presentation of events, interactions and dialogue offered. As such, we begin to 'know' the characters only in relation to other characters. Frank, for example, is, as mentioned above, dominantly coded as a self-seeking, egocentric, unreliable father. Audience perceptions of him are, in part, created via televisual editing which situates (via cross-cutting) shots of his lack of paternal duty, empathy and intimacy with his children directly against, for example, Fiona's maternal duties towards the family. In Episode 1:1 for example, we see Frank sitting at the bottom of the family staircase haplessly trying to tie his shoelaces. A close-up of his hand determinedly attempting to secure his shoes evokes Frank's childlike status. When one of his laces snaps, the camera follows Frank's hand as he reaches for one of his children's school shoes and steals a lace before quickly exiting the house. This scene is punctuated and intercut with images of Frank's daughter, Fiona, washing up in the kitchen and fulfilling the domestic and parental role in Frank's absence. As such, Frank's action – his selfish truth – is positioned as all the more desolate because of Abbott's simultaneous showing of Fiona's selflessness. Frank's transgressions are thus amplified by his contradistinction to Fiona who, unlike the lamenting Frank, is 'getting on' with family life in order to provide some stability for the rest of the Gallagher siblings.

The camera's mediation of space in this scene (establishing the proximity of Frank and Fiona graphically while simultaneously pointing to the 'real' and metaphorical distance between their characters) further aids the provision of intimate thematic tropes, positioning the scene as one of revelation. The ordinariness and commonality of the actions described (Frank tying his laces and Fiona washing up), however, also serve to encourage a realist and invariably domestic reading of the scene. Bearing in mind Abbott's background as a writer for *Coronation Street*, such an invocation of realist aesthetics is hardly surprising. As Marion Jordan (1981: 28) noted in 'Realism and Convention', conventions of realism in soap opera expect that [characters] 'should be credibly accounted for in terms of the "ordinariness" of their homes ... that the time should be "the present"; that the style should be such as to suggest an unmediated, unprejudiced and complete view of reality'. However, critical thought concerning televisual 'realism' stretches beyond conventions of recognition and reflection. As Jonathan Bignell (2004: 190) argues: 'realism ... depends not only on construction and form within television genre but also on the discourses generated around them'.

The *Guardian*, *Manchester Evening News* and *Radio Times* have promoted, mused over and castigated *Shameless* in equal measure, often inviting public debate through consciously subjective articles. In 2008, Aitkenhead wrote of Abbott's originality, noting that 'when *Shameless* came out in 2004, it was so unlike anything we'd seen before that Abbott is widely talked of as a genius. His series ... defies every genre or convention of contemporary television – yet commands equal enthusiasm in media boardrooms and Mancunian council estates.' With the 2010 opening of the seventh series of the programme, bloggers responding to a *Guardian* article relayed their feedback to an unflattering review based purely on the journalist Julia Raeside's (2010) account of *Shameless* Episode 1 alone. Raeside noted that, for her, 'the fire has gone out'. The discourse generated in response to the article was huge – 121 responses in the first five hours of publication alone. One blogger, Ian Clover (2010), arguing for the national significance of the programme, wrote:

> [*Shameless*] lifts the lid on some of England's social problems. What other nations ever write dramas, comedies or movies based upon real suffering, sink estates and ugly people? Can't think of any – even the US' 'gritty' dramas are still populated with beautiful people and set in semi-romantic landscapes. And as for their comedies, the closest they've ever

got is the mini-fight the Fresh Prince of Bel-Air finds himself in before being packed off to LA during the opening credits.

For this respondent, then, the discourse of suffering, sink estates and ugliness in *Shameless* adds to a canon of British social realist television. It communicates social concerns through scopic impact – through its instance on showing that which is ugly and agonising. As Lez Cooke (2004: 183) points out, British television (particularly drama shown on the BBC in the 1960s, 1980s and in 2000) has long been associated with: 'issue-based drama, from *Up the Junction* (BBC 1965) and *Cathy Come Home* (1966) to *Boys from the Blackstuff* (BBC 1982) [and] *Clocking Off* (BBC 2000)'. While Glen Creeber (2009: 432) follows Cooke by convincingly sketching out the similarities between *Shameless* and the aforementioned social realist texts, he also acknowledges the 'stylistic flourishes' of *Shameless*, such as the 'drama's elaborate use of freeze frame, whip pans, surreal flashbacks, still images, and fantasy sequences that draw an audience's attention to the artificial construction of the narrative on offer'. Furthermore, Creeber argues that such aesthetic detail functions to move the series away from a documentary coda by subverting classic realist tendencies: 'These stylistic flourishes ... offer the audience a heightened view of the real that undermines its authority as a piece of realism.' Arguably, then, the series employs such dramatic modes of expression to relay the agency of dynamic, generic paradigms. While the hardship of sink-estate life is made visible, so is the black comedy of its orgiastic excess.

Frank Gallagher's Christmas speech and the politics of perspective

In spite of the series' representation of the ugly and agonising, *Shameless* is not one-dimensional in its presentation of suffering, nor does it attempt to oversimplify or solve the political problems it posits. Both aesthetically and in narrative terms, the series unashamedly celebrates the comical chaos of working-class life while at the same time shamelessly mocking over-sensitivity in relation to serious issues via a wilful rejection of the 'politically correct'. The popularity of such a rejection of the 'PC' (undoubtedly a contemporary hot topic in the UK) is made explicit in an alternate (and, notably banned) Christmas message spoken by Frank Gallagher in 2007. In a beer-soaked monologue which rivals the Queen's annual speech, Frank waxes lyrical about the 'elderly British community'. Pint in hand, he notes his disgust at the state of the British economy, attributing the economic slump to the extended life expectancy of the elderly:

Our elderly needs reminding before it's too late that honestly – they weren't supposed to live this fucking long at our expense ... They are bringing this country's economy to its total fucking knees ... literally, taking the food from the mouths of their children's children et al.! ... Next, they're down the Arndale wearing lippie, spending money meant for us on Thornton's fudge and slippers made by raspberries and hair you would not wish on a minger's minge. For what? ... They need stopping or topping![3]

The irony of Frank's outrageous accusations are emphasised via his agitated and animated tone, his blatant inebriation and his positioning in the Jockey pub – spending money on alcohol and drugs, 'literally' taking food from the mouths of his own children. Frank's slurred speech, his direct address to camera (followed swiftly by a willingness to concede that what he is saying is rubbish when his elderly drug-dealer enters the pub), further aid our understanding of Frank as an unreliable and self-deluded antihero. As a non-realist convention, direct address is a distinctive style choice. Intimate yet compelling, such a technique complicates the aforementioned comparison with soap opera. Instead, direct address is overtly performative and theatrical. As Cardwell (2005a: 151) argues, in witnessing direct address, 'we are asked to question not just words but actions, even the smallest details of performance; this alters the way in which we relate to the character'. Ironically, however, Frank's elderly dealer, attired in an expensive-looking tracksuit and reams of gold chains, wearing full make-up and sporting a sleek if tasteless hairdo, proceeds to rip Frank off, overcharging him for his fix. Simultaneously, then, the scene invokes both comedy (via Frank's animation, stupidity and exasperation) and tragedy (via Frank's addiction, inebriation and self-delusion). Frank has, we see in this scene, no shame. Indeed, Frank's warped perspectives (often preached loudly to an unconvinced audience) function in part to expose his own self-interest to the audience for comic effect. Yet, considering the political content of his frequent addresses, it is interesting to note that Frank does not appear to be making a 'call for arms'; a demand for political mobilisation in regard to the 'real' problems he posits. In contrast, Frank's perspective can in fact be understood to dislocate social realist traditions which demand action and change. His inebriated speech, refusal to venture outside the Jockey pub, in short, his own refusal to mobilise, are screened in order to show a poignant and polemic lack of desire for real change or, at least, the sort of external political mobilisation for change that might take place outside the Chatsworth boundaries. Frank, like the rest of his neighbours, is situated inside, looking in. As Creeber (2009: 434) notes, this internal position is highly significant:

Rather than treating working-class life as a position from which an individual would inevitably long to escape or rise above, the series attempts
to create a portrayal of social class that conceives it from a primarily
internal and subjective perspective. From their point of view, their life
does not need political or social intervention and they refuse to feel the
'shame' placed on them by the discourses of class issued from either
government bodies, social workers, or even middle-class boyfriends.

As such, the series can be understood as indirectly political in that it
reimagines the experience of society on the sink estate from a different
and more democratic perspective.

Rather than attempting to solve the complex issues the series
addresses, Abbott and the series writers arguably attempt to present
the communities focused upon from an internal perspective and, as
such, Abbott's creation can be seen as emotionally honest. Instinctual,
honed and practised as well as reactionary, Abbott's partially biographical series is demonstrative of a trust in British television audiences
and in the dignity and recognition of honest television. While acknowledging the power and horror of his past experiences, experiences which
include, as Creeber (2009: 422) reminds us, 'his mother and father
having both left home by the time he was 11 years old ... a failed suicide
attempt, hospitalisation, a foster home, and a place studying psychology
at Manchester University', Abbott's address of his writing inspiration
and his journey from a Burnley sink estate to world-class television
writer/creator/producer is equally honest. Speaking to Aitkenhead in
2008, Abbott explicated his response to the accusation that his talent
for writing springs merely from his intimate experience of and engagement with pain and damage:

> That's one of the most offensive things anyone could ever say. What, you
> can only get good from damage? ... It's the fact they started making like
> a piece of shit, and laughing at how trashy it was ... We can all do crap
> police series, and London's Yawning-type stuff ... But we know the audi-
> ence is brighter than that, and we've never attended to it ... It's derelict.
> It's fucking derelict.

Arguably the ambition of the series was, then, to go beyond such lazy
televisual productions and engagements and instead to explore and
make visible the shady gaps and tensions that exist in the unsaid and
unseen. As James Walters (2006: 97) argues in his article 'Saving Face',
Shameless '[has an] ongoing interest in probing tensions ... explor[ing]
the gap between characters' inner perceptions of themselves and the
outer perceptions of others'. Abbott's refusal to 'fill in the gaps' – to spell
out every detail for his television audiences – is key to the intelligent,
populist, politically aware success of *Shameless* and the cult following

of *Shameless* audiences. *Shameless* defies generic classification in terms of the fact that it exists in contradistinction to more typical working-class expressions of dramatic, deprived and dilapidated dignities. Dry, ludic, evocative, traumatic and deeply humorous, *Shameless* also bleeds with warmth. Daily life, its dirtiness, its disarray, its discipline, dogged-ness and dynamic embroidery are positioned as dialogues of intimacy that inhabit the screen, making manifest the intricacy of colloquial cohabitation.

Shameless demonstrates an explicit invocation of what I have previously referred to as 'politics of perspective'. That is to say, Abbott purposefully focuses each episode of *Shameless* on the internal social and emotional perspective of an individual character – on their 'way of seeing', their 'way of experiencing' the everyday. Via opening mono-logues, a character in each episode is given their own multidimensional space to communicate personal sensibilities and put forward their perspectives, truths and experiences. Separated yet tied to the 'family', such personal visions are decentred, beguiling and yet peculiarly situ-ated in order to reveal the unity of diffusion. It is in and through the experience of others that the self appears to be located, lost, found and changed in these monologues. Each bearing a distinct rhythm and temporality, such monologues operate to simultaneously segment the different episodes of *Shameless* and establish a continuity; a 'flow' of sequentiality. In addition, it is important to note that most of the opening monologues in *Shameless* are positioned within the domestic space of the Gallagher household. As such, the televisual flow is arguably explic-itly connected to what Rick Altman (1986: 44) defines as a 'household flow – the routines and times of everyday living' here. Furthermore, such monologues (and their repetition) work to determine an emotional tone via the continuity of the insight offered up to the audience by estab-lished key characters. The privileging of such perspectives thus encour-ages a temporary alignment with the speaker and this is, of course, furthered through the camera viewpoints. As John Corner (1999: 51) notes: 'By such means, displacements and pseudo-resolutions can be effected without their ideological character being made explicit or recog-nised by the viewer (a character which includes not only what is said and shown but what is *not* being said and shown and what is being implic-itly *denied*).' Accordingly, the gaps in these monologues (the issues the characters either raise and then leave hanging or, notably fail to raise) point to a politics of self-censorship and/or denial. Arguably, then, it is also that which remains unsaid as well as that which remains unseen in the series that can poignantly infect and affect stories, meaning and audience reactions to these seemingly honest character monologues.

The grammar of television, the fades to black, the angles of the camera, the facial close-ups of the actors and the refusal of characters to make the private public are teased out in these moments. Indeed, television as a medium here opens up the performance of the actors beyond the physical. Fiona's frequent refusal to nominate her pain (or shame) is expressed beautifully in the first episode of Season 1. Meeting upper-middle-class male Steve for the first time at a nightclub after having her bag stolen, the pair return to the cramped Gallagher household at 2 Windsor Gardens. Later, after sending her brothers and sister to bed, Fiona and Steve kiss hungrily in the half-light of the kitchen. As Fiona pulls off Steve's T-shirt he murmurs to her to go 'slower'. She looks down towards the floor and then into Steve's eyes in close-up. Their faces fill the screen, a small segment of light coming from behind the net curtain between them at the centre bottom of the screen. They kiss. Next, a medium shot from behind shows Fiona, her back to the camera, and Steve sitting on the kitchen floor propped against a dilapidated washing machine. They fuck hungrily and noisily.[4] Fiona is positioned sitting on top of Steve – her right hand shown in close-up holding onto the edge of a partially open kitchen drawer for balance. Fiona is red-faced, half-dressed and lost in her pleasure, her dress around her waist. As her groans become louder, a diegetic knock is heard penetrating the scene. She turns to face the camera: 'Shit, shit, shit', she says, still breathless. She stands up rapidly, clutching her hand over her exposed breasts, before bolting upstairs. Steve tries to pull up his trousers but falls over in the rush – injecting humour into the scene. When he finally manages to answer the door, a uniformed police officer looks him up and down before asking if Fiona is in. Fiona's response to his notifying her of the police's presence is flat: 'I know. I'll sort it.' Returning downstairs, Fiona is framed on the right-hand side of the screen watching two police officers carry a man, who appears to be unconscious, into the house. Looking at the unconscious figure and then Fiona, the police officer warns: 'I wouldn't put him anywhere near a carpet until his keks dry off a bit.' Fiona's face betrays both anger and pain as she looks down at the man whose wet trousers and unconscious state belie an alcoholic stupor. Steve also looks intently at the unconscious figure. Appearing shocked and confused through a shot-reverse-shot sequence, Steve asks: 'What the fuck's that?' 'That's mi Dad', Fiona replies flatly.

As the police place Frank in the recovery position and get ready to leave the house, Fiona speaks to one of the officers with a resigned familiarity: 'Thanks Tony, appreciate it.' 'Cheers, Fiona', Tony replies. The exchange of first names and intimate looks between Fiona and the officers indicates to the audience that this is a familiar occurrence. As

Tony and his partner leave, Fiona is seen in a medium shot, purposefully closing her eyes. In contrast, Steve stares at Frank: 'Hey, do you want a hand?' he asks, as Fiona approaches Frank. 'No, you're all right', she replies. In the next shot Fiona has returned to the kitchen. Steve walks in and subsequently pauses before asking: 'Do you leave him there all night?' Fiona's curt response indicates both the deep pain caused by Frank and the determined protection of her family from an outsider's judgements: 'He's never there when I get up.' While Steve is determinedly trying to engage Fiona's gaze and draw her back into their previous shared intimacy, Fiona remains defiant – looking only at the floor. The sharp posture of her shoulders, her curt tone of voice and her numerous repositionings (each time turning her back on Steve) culminate in her handing him a plastic bag. Wordlessly understanding the gesture, Steve removes the T-shirt he has obviously borrowed from Fiona and she gives him back his suit jacket. Steve's face demonstrates disappointment – at first his eyes searching to connect with Fiona's own before seemingly recognising that the connection between them has been surpassed by Frank's unspoken and unconscious demand that Fiona put him first. Fiona, now alone in the shot, looks down, and her previously defiant face crumples. She silently begins to cry. Her unspoken frustration, pain, or perhaps shame at Frank's alcoholism – the fact that she forces Steve to walk away from her – demonstrates her selflessness. Indeed, Fiona explicitly puts Frank's needs before her own and accordingly, through this scene, the medium of television acts to reveal a strong vision of emotional knowledge. As Joshua Meyrowitz (1994: 68) argues: 'Television has lifted many of the old veils of secrecy between children and adults ... The electronic society is characterized by more adultlike children and more childlike adults.' As such, the audience witnesses a parent/child role reversal – a reversal that is made visible throughout each series of *Shameless*.

Class, cultural choice and chaos

Through bringing to light the reversal of parental roles and responsibilities here and in countless additional episodes, Abbott is able to address the overlap between personal and familial ambitions and highlight the oscillation between individual and collective desires. In Episode 1:2 the positioning of the Gallagher family (minus Frank, who is positioned in his spiritual home, the Jockey pub) in the cramped lounge of the family home demonstrates and reconfirms a serious lack of individual space. Yet, this lack of space (understood via tight framing as well as through the positioning of Fiona, Lip, Ian, Liam, Veronica, Karen – Lip's new girlfriend – and Steve perching on all available surfaces while watching the television) points to a specific vision of intimacy. The characters within the scene do not acknowledge the lack of space but rather appear entirely at ease with the situation, with their 'reality' as it stands. Frank, the absent father, is in the pub doing what Fiona ironically calls a 'superb job ... sod-all', while she cooks for, organises and brings up her younger siblings with the little money she has available to her. Reminiscent of the television series *Bread* (BBC, 1986–91), however, the series also disclosed that the other siblings, like Fiona, contribute to the family 'pot' through various forms of legal and illegal work. The visible lack of money above and beyond what is needed to survive within the cramped house is further emphasised through the mise-en-scènic elements of the living space: the ragged furniture, old television set and mismatched teacups that the audience is encouraged to observe again through the eyes of Steve – a man new to the family.

With a comparatively 'posh' accent and an array of expensive cars in which he arrives at the Gallagher residence, Steve is ultimately positioned, for the purposes of the audience, as an 'outsider'. His gaze – his role as observer of the family – allows the audience to potentially recognise their own exterior fascination with the family on screen and identify with Steve's voyeuristic nature. Furthermore, the medium of television as both a locus of knowledge and a domestic character is shown to be ultimately powerful in this scene in that the family are silently watching a news report focusing on Tony Blair and Gordon Brown addressing the issue of British poverty which, according to the report, will affect one in three poor families adversely. This injection of what Corner (1999: 27) calls 'a direct account of the real' is amplified through a wide-angle shot of the family's intimacy – their social and physical proximity to one another explicitly made evident in the aforementioned cramped surroundings. Veronica (Maxine Peake; Fiona's friend and neighbour) and Karen (Rebecca Atkinson; Lip's girlfriend) can also be included in the nomination of social intimacy above via their geographic, socioeconomic and cultural similarities to the Gallaghers. As such, conventions of social realism – the potential for the family's disaffected response to their own plight – are at once brought to bear and then purposefully subverted by Abbott. Comparable to Frank's Christmas speech, the enforced intimate coda and explicit political concerns made visible here are again left hanging without resolution. As Tom Jennings (2008) argues: '*Shameless* invokes discourses relating to the nature and potential of working-class people, only to flout and undermine them.' Interestingly, reflecting on her interview with

Abbott, Aitkenhead (2008) also nominates Abbott's purposeful distance from known generic social realist conventions of galvanising external solutions to internal social problems. She writes: 'What is Abbott's real truth? His first attempt to dramatise his childhood produced 92 pages of a film script whose relentless bleakness horrified him: it was like [quoting Abbott directly] "a social worker's diary, or a Ken Loach case-book". So he ditched it and refashioned the amoral dysfunction into *Shameless*' comic episodes.'

Steve's observation of the family's silent understanding of further impending poverty and their refusal to engage with the 'doom' of the report culminates in Steve looking on in wonderment – his eyes wide and his smile arguably belying a respect which has previously been unknown to him despite his indicated privileged upbringing. Yet, as to be expected of Abbott, generic closure is not attained in this narrative sequence. Frank's sudden drunken return functions to flex the narra-tive, to create a further disturbance and generic oscillation for the audi-ence. Frank enters, dishevelled, angry, unsteady, before violently and inexplicably head-butting his son, Ian. Abbott's engagement with the televisual expression of the 'élan of underclass transgression', issues of poverty, self-respect, government policy and domestic violence operate in order to refuse a twee confinement of *Shameless* as a generic social realist text. Yes – the family are visibly poor and their lives are sometimes unpleasant, but, born from their determination to survive together, there is an intimacy which cannot be easily translated or even understood by outsiders. This unspoken subtext is perhaps the most poignant, most dramatic and most political message Abbott relays.

After witnessing the head-butt Steve stands and pushes Frank by his shoulders into the lounge wall, shouting: 'You're pissed, Frank. Don't do this to your kids.' Fiona's response is, however, altogether different: 'Dad, leave it. Steve, just go.' Debbie, Frank's young daughter, has seem-ingly exited the lounge during the fray and suddenly returns with a joint of frozen meat. The purpose of the domestic object is invariably under-stood to be to prevent further violence by being used to knock Frank out (echoed in the opening credits of each episode where Frank is shown to be knocked out by his children with a frozen loaf of bread). Steve, again witnessing the chaos Frank brings and angered by his violence towards Ian, laments that Frank is 'pathetic', branding him 'a total waste of organs'. Fiona's response is again one that demonstrates Steve's lack of understanding. She looks at him and demands: 'I mean it, Steve, leave now.' Domestic violence is thus shown to be contained within the family – a private family affair that does not destroy the Gallagher family but is invoked by Abbott to demonstrate their shared understanding and strategies for dealing with Frank's addiction on an everyday basis.

Interestingly, both Steve and Frank leave the family home – Frank presumably returning to the pub. The fact that he doesn't return to the house that night is only noted the next day when Fiona realises that Frank isn't back and, significantly, that it is Friday – Giro day. Knowing her father is possibly in danger as he has missed the arrival of and hasn't cashed his Giro cheque, Fiona alerts the police reporting her father missing. Frank, however, is shown waking up on a park bench drenched in sunlight. As the scene humorously unfolds (utilising disorientating, luminary and lumbering point-of-view shots representing Frank's bewildered perspective), the audience learns that Frank is inexplicably in France. Later, it is discovered that Steve, as an act of revenge, found Frank in the pub, bought him further drinks and, when he was comatose, put him in his car and shipped him from Dover to Calais. Fiona, furious after discovering Steve's unrequested redress, journeys to his affluent house to confront him. Explaining his actions, Steve unconsciously angers Fiona further by revealing his own familial background in an attempt to explain to Fiona his own escape from familial expectations and confinement. Revealing that his 'mum, dad, brother and sister' are doctors and that he himself 'quit medical school after two years' in order to escape the 'medical equivalent of a battery farm and find a personality that wasn't a carbon copy of his father's', Fiona points out the irony of Steve's previous accusation that Frank is a 'waste of organs': 'You nick cars for a living. Given the choices that you've had, it's a bit rich that you don't like other people living with theirs, innit, Steve!' she shouts.

Fiona's judgement regarding Steve's criminality is not the main issue here. Rather, Fiona points to the fact that Steve has been privileged enough, both financially and via his education, to have a choice. What of course remains unsaid here concerns both Fiona's own and her family's lack of choices as a result of poverty, addiction and social circumstance. Boiling over with frustration and in an effort to have Steve hear her, perhaps even feel an element of her pain, Fiona punches Steve in the face, bloodying his nose. This enactment of violence in response to Steve's self-ignorance operates affectively, encouraging a para-social, intimate engagement with the narrative and its characters. At once the audience is invited to understand Steve's actions and values and sympathise with his revenge in response to Frank's domestic violence. Just minutes later, however, after we are enlightened as to Steve's distinct and privileged choices, Fiona's punch (another instance of domestic violence) and her direct gaze at Steve – again sitting on top of him in his affluent kitchen and engaging passionately with him, albeit violently – forces the audience's sympathies and understanding regarding Steve's values to be undercut. Visually aligned with Fiona's gaze, the audience is encouraged to look at the situation from her social and personal perspective rather than Steve's. As such, the audience is in turn encouraged to feel complicit in a desire to hurt him. As Corner notes, this type of encoded engagement with narratives by televisual audiences operates to both 'affect' the viewer and impart narrative knowledge (in this case, relating to Steve's social background). Corner (1999: 49) argues:

> The affective dimension of narrative is a matter of the extent to which, and the ways in which, it seeks to create personal involvement, excitement, pleasure, fear, and desire in the viewer. The involvement with narrative is often a para-social one, in which engagement with portrayed characters leads to an imaginative investment in their actions and situations. But narratives often have an informational function too ... Knowledge, information of different kinds, and perhaps particular viewpoints are being advocated and projected through the instantiations of 'story'. Values are being variously advanced and undercut.

Again, then, while invariably domestic, *Shameless* refuses middle-class voyeuristic confinement, instead engaging with internal social concerns relating to the judgement or the 'shame' that outsiders place upon sink estate communities. As such, Steve's receiving a punch to the face can be understood as a form of poetic justice: a painful and violent reminder that as an outsider looking 'in', his judgements are middle-class, privileged and born from an ability to 'choose life, choose a job, choose a career, choose a family, choose a fucking big television, choose washing machines, cars and compact-disc players'.[5] Indeed, the irony of Steve's multiple choices, his purchase of a new washing machine for the Gallagher family after only his first meeting with Fiona, his multiple high-end cars and his own big television are to be read comparatively. In enacting his revenge on Frank, Steve unwittingly demonstrates the middle-class coda that he has previously expressed a determination to leave behind. In ignoring Fiona's assertions that he should allow the problem to be dealt with internally, Steve positions his own middle-class sense of judgement above Fiona's, thus making visible his belief that he, rather than she, is better equipped to deal externally with an internal problem. Fiona's emotional and violent confrontation of Steve thus serves to expose the ubiquitous anxieties associated with cross-class relations and differential political perspectives. Fiona refuses to allow Steve to 'have it all'; he cannot, she demonstrates, be a part of her community and yet, on occasion, consider himself above it. His bleeding nose can thus be understood as a literal symbol of the figurative pain he has caused the family; a poetic discernible signifier of the familial rupture he chose to enact by believing his judgement and perspective to be superior.

Poetry in motion, monologues and magnification

The notion of poetic justice dominates *Shameless* not only in such poignant and explosive moments of violent slippage but also through the lyrical, ironic and ultimately un/reliable narrative monologues of Frank. While undoubtedly positioned in part as a hapless addict and 'crap' father, Frank equally demonstrates his desire to be heard whilst simultaneously undermining his self-regard via hypocritical and yet ironically subversive speeches. The opening of each episode from Series 5 onwards is formulated explicitly as a poem; a lyrical, parodic and political comment by Frank on social status, policy, voyeurism, opportunity and desire. Furthermore, Frank explicitly imagines and acknowledges a middle-class viewer both watching and judging him, thus situating his poem as a response to the unspoken condemnation of him by others:

> Tickets this way to the Chatsworth Express!
> Come and watch pikeys making a mess,
> Of the lives they were given by Him upstairs!
> And kids, they're convinced, aren't actually theirs ...
> What sounds on earth could EVER replace,
> Kids needing money? Or wives in yer face ...
>
> 'Cause this, people reckon – and me included –
> Is why pubs and drugs were kindly invented.
> To calm us all down and stop us going mental.
> These are Chatsworth estate's BASIC essentials!
> We're worth every penny for grinding your axes ...
> You shit on our heads, but, you pay the taxes!
>
> Imagine Britain without Chatsworth buccaneers,
> Who'll cum on your face for the price of a beer ...
> Make poverty history! Cheaper drugs now!
> Make poverty history! Cheaper drugs now!
> Scatter! Paarty!

Arguably, Frank's poem demands that the unforgiving viewer 'gets their own house in order' before looking at his. Accepting his position as a figure who is likely to be looked down upon by viewers, a man who may potentially be denied the right to express his opinion (or at least have it heard), Frank's direct address to the viewer forces an engagement with the social via explicit mention of the systematic continuity of social divides in contemporary Britain. It is, perhaps, purposefully surprising that the form this demand takes is so beautifully lyrical; however, the dialectic accent of Frank paired with his derelict ability to contribute even to his own family kitty (instead, pissing his money away – literally – on drink and drugs) allows his political postulations to be partially dismissed as drunken drivel. Maybe this invisibility and inaudibility (he is consistently ignored by Chatsworth residents during his frequent self-indulgent speeches) in the diegetic world of *Shameless* at least, serves as Frank's poetic justice. Such speeches aid the audience's recognition of Frank's (mis)understanding of his community, or, more accurately, his subjective internal perspective of his community from within. As Creeber (2009: 432) argues: '*Shameless* immediately informs us that its narrative perspective is both unstable and unreliable, articulated through a narrator who is so much part of the community of which he speaks that he is clearly unable to be objective about it.' Invariably, Frank's monologues, as we have mentioned, also function to expose his ignorance, his own misplaced self-belief. Speaking of Frank to journalist James Rampton (2005), Abbott notes that 'Frank believes every word he says. He's never paid a penny of tax in his life but he feels he's got a right to comment on the government and the state of the nation – that total psychopathy of someone who really thinks he is a contributor to society.'

Alternately, it is possible to muse that Frank's voice is not heard because amidst his own community, his voice is not a particularly strange one. Arguably, then, the audible regionality of Frank's Mancunian dialect and slang operate to draw attention to the northern imposition and social attitude of *Shameless*. In short, Frank's accent makes audible the fact that such language is shared in *Shameless*, pointing to a shared and intimate experience of the everyday. The significance of ordinary language, ordinary life, operates to evoke pleasure and create a seamless dialogue of realism which does not draw attention to its own illusion. In Episode 1:1, the camera captures a close-up of the Gallagher family's corkboard in the kitchen being studied by Steve on his first visit to the house. As the camera focuses on the notes chaotically strewn across and pinned to the board, the audience is given access to the Gallaghers' shared life and domestic concerns: 'Buy milk'; 'Lip – Dentist Monday! Don't forget!!' Further down, following Steve's eye-line, the audience sees a scruffy envelope becoming the focus of the shot:

> 'Who's eating all the bread?' is written in blue biro.
> 'NOT ME' follows in red ink.
> 'Yes you are, Ian.'
> 'Fuck off, wanker!'

Such colloquial linguistic specificity demonstrates Abbott's regard to 'show', in various forms, interpersonal relationships. The arguments of Sarah Cardwell (2005a: 47) (writing of Andrew Davies's television series *Bavarian Nights*) seem applicable here: 'both the physical environment and the group dynamics that together constitute a social situation are revealed as influences upon the demeanour and states of mind of the characters'. While the aforementioned example could arguably be considered as insular in that it references the actual family members alone, several points of resistance to such insularity are exhibited by Abbott. Demonstratively, Abbott seeks to situate the Gallagher family as part of a larger 'Chatsworth' community. Other families made visible within the community are also shown to be equally flawed. For example, the Karibs are fronted by the wilful white Yvonne (Kelli Hollis) and her bisexual husband Kash (Chris Bisson), who has an affair with teenage Ian Gallagher in Series 1 before later faking his own death at Yvonne's insistence. The Fisher family includes Veronica who, along with her 'fake' husband Kev (Dean Lennox Kelly), are (in Series 4) jailed in Romania for attempting to buy a baby. The Fishers also extend to an introduction of Veronica's pathological kleptomaniac mother, Carol (Marjorie Yates), and her pyromaniac brother Marty (Jack Deam). Indeed, the linguistic and physical interaction between families and their reliance upon each other for everyday survival are positioned as an important mode of progression and change.

Within *Shameless* blood-family distinctions are eroded through slippage. For example, Frank, learning that Lip's girlfriend's mother, Sheila (Maggie O'Neill), is newly single, vulnerable, sexually ardent and in receipt of extensive benefits for her agoraphobia, purposefully sets out to seduce her in order to 'escape' the Gallagher household and move into a new home. Thus, both Lip and Karen and Frank and Sheila are soon situated as couples. Further slippage occurs, however, after Frank moves into Sheila and Karen's home. Unbeknown to Sheila and Lip, Frank and Karen engage in a sexual affair which, notably, the young Karen encourages as a response to being (as she sees it), 'pushed out' by her mother. Frank's inability to resist the sexual advances of his girlfriend's daughter once again reconfirms his unreliability as a father figure as well as concreting his inability to turn down anything which may accord him immediate pleasure. Poignantly, the affair is eventually discovered by Steve and then Lip. In response, Lip engages Frank in the language Frank knows and has previously dished out: a violent head-butt. Life, however, goes on. Frank's wife, Monica, briefly returns to the family home with her ex-lesbian lover in tow (a woman who later demonstrates a genuine love for the Gallagher children), thus extending the family yet again. Ian finds out that Frank is not his biological father and continues his love affair with a local married male shop-owner, Kash. Kev and Veronica act as surrogate parents to the Gallagher children when Fiona, heartbroken from her split from Steve and pregnant to another man, tearfully elopes with the blessing of her siblings. Lip impregnates his new girlfriend (the daughter of local drug dealers) Mandy Maguire (Samantha Siddall). In short, these extensions to the Gallagher family (and others) demonstrate the growth and shared experiences of the Chatsworth community, situating the residents of the Chatsworth as complex, resourceful and internally focused. Frank's repeated voiceover at the beginning of each episode and the accompanying images of the Chatsworth residents partying en masse around a burning car offer visual and oral confirmation of the Chatsworth as a shared community:

> A few things, see, are vital to a half-decent community – space, yeah, you need wide-open spaces where everyone goes mental and neighbourliness, fantastic neighbours, Kev and Veronica; lend you anything, well, not anything, but all of 'em, to a man, know that first and foremost one of the most vital necessities of in this life is, they know how to party. [*The police arrive in response cars, sirens blaring to the cheers of the residents.*] Scatter!

This repeated vision of togetherness, of a community functioning in opposition to controlling state apparatus, of a man subjectively believing in communal love, can, however, be understood as Frank's somewhat mythical vision of northern togetherness. Again, however, the gap between the mythic and the real can arguably be seen as a mode of meaningful and conscious political perspective. As Nelson (2007b: 51) states, such gaps 'invite viewers to pick up on the ironies pointed up by a gap between mythologies and actualities [making for] more politically active as well as more compelling television'.

Conclusion

While there are, then, no simplistic solutions to many of the political, social and class-based problems that the series presents, the success of *Shameless* can be attributed to Abbott and the writers' trust in contemporary televisual audiences to recognise the significance of the voids between various societal perspectives regarding what is and is not shameful. In essence, Abbott and his team make visible the problematic nature of supposedly objective perspectives. As such, the series augments a perpetual 'pulling back' from objective and simplistic solutions to complex problems. While the diegetic responses of the characters to various sources of trouble are frequently posited as chaotic and rapid (for example, Frank's head-butting Ian), the televisual grammar of *Shameless* encourages viewer restraint. As Cardwell (2005a: 185) notes, such cognition can also function to 'emphasise the active role ... we must undertake: a literal refocusing, a determined search for meaning'. The uniqueness of *Shameless* can, then, be attributed to its original 'way of seeing', a privileging of personal over political agency. Rather than focusing on the Chatsworth as a space of social exclusion and depravity, the estate is represented as a space of internal belonging. Such belonging is demonstrated aesthetically via consciously subjective televisual paraphs; signatures in the form of a hybridisation between realist and anti-realist techniques. Hand-held camera shots are combined in rapid edits with anti-naturalist techniques such as whip pans, over-exposed colours, surreal dream sequences, freeze-frames and flashbacks. As Stephen Baker (2009: 453) notes: 'without proper attention to television's diverse genres, visual styles and content we have only a partial understanding of how television makes the contemporary social world meaningful'.

Returning to the issue of performance, the frequency of close-up shots in the series allows for a drawing-out of the nuances of performance. In terms of Fiona and Frank in -particular, the close attention paid to their facial expressions is revealing, exposing the comedy of the tragic and the tragedy of the comic; in essence, the multiple layering so characteristic of quality, complex performance. While such an ability to articulate via facial expressions that which remains unsaid demonstrates a subtlety, in terms of Threlfall, his equally often over-exaggerated gestures (for example, raising of the eyebrows, pursing of the lips, deliberate closing of the eyes and shaking of the head) denotes an attunement to the mode of the melodramatic and the theatrical. In generic terms, the commonality of the close-up can also be understood as a convention of the soap opera, yet as discussed above, *Shameless* exhibits an unrelenting multiplicity of generic reference points from the comedic to the socially realistic. Abbott's ability and determination to combine differing genres is a trait that is recognisable throughout his work and demonstrates his vitality and desire to create new registers, to innovate rather than working within the confines of those already established.

Notes

1 This and all other unattributed quotations from Abbott are cited from specially commissioned interviews with the author in 2011 and 2012. Full extracts from the interviews are available in Appendix 1.

2 Paul Abbott, cited by Stuart Jeffries, 'Why I Write: The Monday Interview', *Guardian* [online], 7 February 2005, available at: www.guardian.co.uk/media/2005/feb/07/broadcasting.arts (accessed 09/09/2009).

3 Available at: www.youtube.com/watch?v=Jx3Zdl_V3z0 (accessed 03/01/2002).

4 For a more specific discussion of representations of sex in the series, see Beth Johnson, 'Situating Sex Beyond the City', in *Television, Sex and Society: Analyzing Contemporary Representations*, ed. Johnson, James Aston and Basil Glynn (London and New York: Continuum Press, 2012).

5 Narration from Mark Renton (Ewan McGregor) in *Trainspotting* (dir. Danny Boyle, 1996, UK).

AbbottVision, global reach and epilogue

At the time of writing (2012), the success of *Shameless* in the UK continues with an eleventh series of 14 hour-long episodes, commissioned to be shown in early 2013. Though the UK success of the series is, as noted in the previous chapter, connected, at least in part, to the ways in which Abbott's creation addresses British issues and concerns (indeed, the sociopolitics that the most recent opening titles depict include reflections on the Labour government's reclassification of 'scum' in a ruling period from 1997 to 2010, the power-related cock-sucking of the present coalition government, the 'yak, yak, yak' of the 'big society' and the need for social revolution), *Shameless* also has global reach. Recently remade in the USA, the first episode of 12, constituting Season 1 of *Shameless US*, was seen by audiences on Saturday 9 January 2011. Written by John Wells (renowned executive producer of *ER*, *Third Watch* and *The West Wing*), and with Abbott as an executive producer, US Episode 1:1 aired on the premium television service Showtime and achieved 982,000 viewers.[1] Its audience figures over Season 1 and Season 2 grew, and as a result of the show's continuing popularity, a third series has been commissioned and is due to air in 2013.

Set in the southside Chicago projects rather than the outskirts of Manchester, and focusing on a family that is more working-class than underclass, the Gallaghers are represented as the same, but different. Frank (played by William H. Macy), while still a drunk, is distinctly softer than his British counterpart, warmer in his relations with his children, though no less selfish in his behaviour. Though clear disparities are evident in terms of space – for example, the US Gallagher home in Canaryville is much bigger than 2 Windsor Gardens – *Shameless US* clearly signals its connection to or reframing of Manchester via subtle aspects of mise-en-scène. For example, in Episode 1:1, the youngest Gallagher member, little Liam (played by Brennan Kane Johnson and Blake Alexander Johnson), wears an Oasis T-shirt. After he has spilled most of his breakfast down it, the T-shirt is turned around rather than changed by his sister Fiona (played by Emmy Rossum), signalling perhaps a metaphorical repositioning of the working-class, 'Madchester' ethos of the indie band. Fiona, though clearly positioned as shameless by some of the more affluent Chicago residents (for example, when working in a burger van at a local sporting event, two middle-class jocks admire her body before one retorts to the other that he needs to remember that 'project girls don't abort'), is more polished and less 'real' in appearance than the UK's Anne-Marie Duff. Though still absolutely convincing in her performance of a teenage sister effectively playing a mother figure, Rossum (like Macy in comparison to Threlfall) is a little more polite, more apologetic and less gritty than Duff. In the remake, key colloquial terms are also of course Americanised. Rather than receiving a blow job from Karen Jackson (Laura Slade Wiggins), Lip (Jeremy Allen White) tells his brother, Ian (Cameron Monaghan), that he 'got a hummer'. The Jockey pub, the UK Frank's spiritual home, is renamed 'The Alibi Room' – making obvious reference to the criminality of its inhabitants. Despite these seemingly straightforward differences to Abbott's original UK creation, the US remake, while lacking in part the 'Brit-grit' amorality of its UK big brother, is not shy of making important sociopolitical points.

In Episode 1:1 for example, Asian shopkeeper Kash (Pej Vahdat) is reminded by his Muslim convert white wife, Linda (Marguerite Moreau), to 'Talk to your mother. I don't want the cops dragging me out of bed at 4AM again because she's in the alley yelling that the CIA is stealing her trash.' Interestingly, in response to this comment, Ian, also present at the time, notes: 'But that happened, didn't it?' at which point Linda concedes: 'Once. 4 years ago. Yes. But now she's locked in the basement making a helmet out of tinfoil.' In Episode 1:2, Frank is transported by Fiona's new boyfriend, Steve (Justin Chatwin), to Toronto rather than France (as in the UK version of the story) as a punishment for head-butting his son, Ian (though in the US episode Frank apologises, whereas in the UK series he does not). From his prison cell, reflecting on his hard luck, Frank makes insulting, part-humorous, warped and tragic social observations, arguing:

> Why would I want to come to Canada? So your national healthcare could make me wait 60 years for a new kidney? Whole country's a bunch of parka-wearing, draft-dodging, chicken-shit cowards who didn't have the balls to stay home and fight the Vietcong to preserve our American way of life.

Like the UK show, then, *Shameless US* demonstrates its ability to address the most complex sociopolitical problems and issues without dumbing down or offering simplistic solutions where none exist. Moreover, in the spirit of the original UK show, the US remake is both tragic and comic, able to turn rapidly from the devastating to the hilarious. In particular, the issues of poverty and othering are pushed front and centre in the American remake. As writer and producer Wells pointed out in a *New York Times* interview (2010), discussing the working-class Chicago setting of the show: 'We have a comedic tradition of making fun of the people in those worlds. The reality is that these people aren't "the Other" – they're people who live four blocks down from you and two blocks over.' Indeed, this can be identified as what Robin Nelson (2007a: 35) refers to as a 'concern with the marginal'.

Shameless US also retains the cinematic quality of Abbott's original UK series in its visual and sonic treatment. In particular the opening title montage of 1:1 is energetic, sharp and clear in its familial focus. Opening with white lettering on a black background announcing 'Showtime presents', a fade to black is followed by an audible drumbeat and a long shot of the Chicago skyline at night, illuminated by the glare of artificial car, street and high-rise office lights. As the camera pans to the right and then shakily downwards, a group of men, women and children in dark winter coats are revealed, drinking, smoking and chatting amidst the piles of frozen snow on the ground. Showing them huddled around a large street fire, the scene echoes frequent televisual representations of poverty in which the homeless are often envisaged attempting to keep warm via the heat of a fire in the dead of winter. Before the potential darkness of the situation is allowed to sink in for the audience, a voiceover interrupts the sequence. While slow in pace, the male voice speaks with energy and clear jovial intonation, transforming the tone of the credits:

> Nobody is saying our neighbourhood's the Garden of Eden, hell, some people think God avoids this place altogether, but it's been a good home to us, to me and my kids, who I'm proud of, 'cause every single one of them reminds me a little bit of me. Fiona – my rock – huge help, has all the best qualities of her mother, except she's not a raging psycho bitch. Lip – smart as a whip, straight 'A's in the honor role, the boy's definitely going somewhere. Ian – industrious, contentious, ambitious, an incredible work ethic (I don't have a clue where he got that from). Wants to be a paratrooper. Knows how to disembowel an enemy with a roll of dimes and an old gym sock. Carl. Erm, I don't really know that much about Carl. Oh, loves animals. Always dragging home some poor stray he found, taking them up to his room. Ahh, Debbie. Sent by God. Total angel. Raises money for UNICEF all year round, some of which she actually turns in. Liam. Gonna be a star. I'm no biologist, but he looks a little bit like my first sponsor. He and the ex were close. Kev and Veronica – fantastic neighbours. There's nothing they won't do for each

other, or to each other. I never realised how little sex I was having till V and Kev moved next door. And me, Frank Gallagher. Father. Teacher. Mentor. Captain of our little ship. We may not have much but all of us, to a man, know the most important thing in this life. We know how to fuckin' party. Wa haaa!

While this opening speech by Frank is purposefully similar in its content and scope to the UK version in that it clearly outlines the Gallagher family focus, it is the juxtaposition between the aural and the intercut visual images that aids the 'proper' reading of Frank's (at times warped) understanding of his world. In addition, the contrast between the different montage images themselves also helps to establish the interrelations between family members, allowing for what André Bazin (1967: 47) calls 'the creation of a sense or meaning not proper to the images themselves but derived exclusively by their juxtaposition'.

Via sharp editing, we are informed that Fiona is not only like her mother but *is* a mother figure to the rest of the siblings, as an image of her supervising Debbie and Carl completing their homework is followed by her simultaneously placing tissues on both of their noses and telling them gently to 'blow'. As Frank discusses Lip, he is seen on-screen, drinking from a can, with a steely and determined gaze. While Frank notes that he is 'definitely going somewhere', an intercut sequence reveals Lip running away from two US police officers while an emergency siren penetrates the aural soundscape. Though Frank notes Ian's industrious nature and implies that he is determined and skilled in his military ambitions, an intercut sequence again provides the viewer with an alternative perspective. Ian may enjoy wearing a military uniform (or seeing other males wearing uniform), but clearly, his weaponry skills leave a lot to be desired. Rather than Carl demonstrating a loving and caring nature towards animals as implied by Frank, a mini-sequence reveals Carl in his bedroom, holding a stray cat in one hand and a lit blowtorch in the other. As for Liam, Frank's comment regarding him resembling his first sponsor is shown to be an understatement, as the toddler is shown as clearly mixed race rather than white like his siblings. Kev and Veronica, Frank's fantastic neighbours, are seen engaging in BDSM (Veronica dominating Kevin rather than vice versa), and Frank himself looks nothing like the 'captain of the family ship' that he asserts himself to be. Instead, he is clearly aged, drunk and scruffy, with straw-like, tobacco-stained hair, and is positioned standing apart from rather than with his children. Following Frank's assertion that the family and friends all know 'how to party', the screen, at first alight with the Day-Glo ripples of orange heat from the fire, takes on a blue tinge as several police patrol cars and a fire engine disrupt the street party amidst a wail of sirens. Some of those gathered display two-fingered gestures in response to the disruption, providing, as the force attempt to break up the party, a volatile mix of sound and movement. Frank, rather than responding violently, however, wanders slowly away before the screen cuts to black with white lettering announcing the title card 'Shame*less*', with the letter 'l' visibly skewed.

The skewing of the word 'less' is significant on both a literal and thematic level. Indeed, as Angelina Karpovich (2010: 30) notes, the opening sequence of a television series works to 'address the wider over-arching thematic and narrative concerns' as well as the 'visual style of what is to follow'. The notion of the Gallagher family having 'less' is written into the visuals from the opening shot of the Chicago skyline. Clearly situated as a city with its make-up on, central Chicago twinkles as the lights suggest an urban lustre, beyond which we are invited to imagine high-flying city rollers, champagne bars and inhabitants with desires for upward mobility. In contrast, the Gallagher family is situated on the fringes of the city. Artificial lighting is not present here; rather the raw glow of the street fire illuminates the poor streets and abandoned parkland. Fancy clothing is replaced with fingers blue with cold poking out from beneath fingerless gloves, clutching cans covered in brown paper. Yet, while the notion of 'less' is framed as integral to our understanding of the socioeconomics of the community in Canaryville, the view of the residents is, following the ethos of the original UK series, not drab or colourless. Rather, to borrow a phrase from Robert Kolker (2000), it is 'coloured by the characters' perspectives'. Indeed, the space in which the characters choose to congregate is transformed from being icy-cold, silent, menacing and dark, to being bright, noisy, community-based and jovial. Akin to Frank's reclamation of England as a space no longer belonging to the government in the opening credits of UK Series 8 – 'It's not theirs any more. This is our England now!' – the residents of Canaryville reclaim and transform the darkness of the Chicago projects. Despite the interruption of the community party by police in the opening credits, Canaryville is, like Chatsworth, a place in which the residents refuse to be shamed by those external to it – be it the city slickers or the police. In terms of being without shame, then, the US Gallaghers are only perceived as 'less' in the eyes of those with more or in the minds of those who believe that their privilege is natural, deserved, a birthright rather than an act of random fate.

What Glen Creeber (2009: 431) refers to as the 'internal perspective' of the UK show (a perspective in which the characters from the community look outwards at their life, rather than the middle classes looking inwards towards families such as the Gallaghers and branding them shameless) can also be seen in the different credits that open Episodes 2 to 12. Repeated 11 times after the première credit sequence discussed above, the 'new' opening credit sequence is thus worth noting here. Situated inside the Gallagher home rather than outside it, the sequence opens as before with 'Showtime presents'. Following the momentary silence, a rock-pop drumbeat asserts an aural invasion, signalling the beginning of a music track aptly titled 'The Luck You Got' by the ironically named *The High Strung*. As the beat of the track continues to dominate the soundscape, a static, low-level shot of the Gallagher bathroom is introduced. Filmed inches above floor level, the whiteness of the suite and room is further highlighted by white toilet rolls stacked on the floor to the right of the frame and a child's white teddy bear to the left of the frame. The colour interruption comes in the form of Frank. Dressed in blue denim jeans and a shirt, he lies unconscious on the floor, dominating the audience's eye level, his head resting near the foot of the toilet and his feet by the bath. The stillness of the image is then disturbed by a pair of female, tanned bare legs entering the bathroom. Though the height of the camera does not change (thus we can see only the body and not the head of the figure), the slim legs clearly belong to Fiona, who is dressed in a black T-shirt. The brightness of the room, alongside Fiona's attire, signals that it is morning, the start of another day in the Gallagher household. After gently kicking her father to see if she can rouse him (Frank remains unconscious), Fiona bends down and, seemingly unperturbed, drags Frank by the feet out of the bathroom. In quick time, Fiona then lifts up the pan lid, pulls down her underwear and, we infer, urinates before rising and leaving the bathroom. In quick succession (and again in continuous quick time) other family members enter the bathroom. However, again the space of the bathroom is not rendered private (not once is the door closed or our vision obscured), rather, it is used as a space to drink, smoke, masturbate, clean wounds, play and have sex. What this opening sequence highlights is the everydayness of the family experience, the normalcy of not having the space or time or perhaps desire for privacy and the transformation of sterile places and spaces into fun and, at times, erotic ones.

The innovative visual and sonic treatment of the opening sequence discussed above is certainly a hallmark of what has been recently labelled as TVIII or 'quality' television. In addition, the alternative, fun, yet socially conscious subject matter of the show is also arguably aimed at a quality audience, an audience described by Catherine Johnson (2005: 58) as 'urban, 18–49, liberal, professional and culturally educated'. As a piece of quality or 'high-end' television, the global elevation of *Shameless*'s status can then, I contend, be understood as part of an ongoing trend in which quality television series (the likes of shows broadcast on Showtime and HBO) are being increasingly understood and appreciated as the new locale of storytelling in the twenty-first century. As Tim Goodman (1997) of *The Hollywood Reporter* argues: 'Television, not feature films, is the true home of storytelling, real filmmaking and the edgiest, best new movies.' The link between the American remake of the series on Showtime, and the much discussed quality of contemporary American cable television in recent scholarly research by academics such as Cara Louise Buckley, Marc Leverette and Brian L. Ott (2008), is interesting in that it points not only to the conceptual ambition of the series and its auteur, Abbott, but also the global reach of this originally British 'high-end' television fiction. The prestige of the show is also, however, achieved, in part, via its cinematic stylistic treatment – it is shot on film, showcases canny editing, precise grammar, taut writing, attentive composition and an expensive and expansive range of background actors, and demonstrates fastidious attention to mise-en-scènic detail. Additionally, though, and at times simultaneously, *Shameless US* also purposefully highlights its status as a work of televisual fiction, the episodes beginning each week with a 'catch-up' (sometimes with Frank directly addressing the audience with 'this is what you missed last week', prior to a montage) and ending with a 'next-week teaser'. The teaser is also showcased paratextually on the Showtime website, referring to the next episode and, at the end of a season, the following season. In addition, the Showtime website also contains key clips from the show (such as the finale of Season 2), quizzes, an episode guide, message boards where fans can interact, behind-the-scenes interviews and merchandise such as the *Shameless US* hoodie and a 'Frank the Plank' T-shirt and bottle opener. As argued by Catherine Johnson (2007: 19), in such a case 'each product is designed to convey and cohere the core values that [the] series epitomises' as well as to ask audiences to engage with the series as a fictional construct. One of the *Shameless US* T-shirt designs available shows a large image of a baby's bottle wrapped in a brown paper bag (intimating its alcoholic contents) and is advertised thus:

> This *Shameless* Baby Bottle T-Shirt is absolutely wildly unapologetically shameless. From the show about the family that writes their own rules. This comedic graphic reflects the basis of the show in which the head of the household is too drunk to take care of the kids. One of *Shameless*'s best traits is its ability to balance extremely dark plot lines with lighter ones. The *Shameless* Baby Bottle T-Shirt is proof positive of that.[2]

Shameless, then, can be understood as not only a show but a brand. Indeed, as noted by Mark Rogers *et al.* (2002: 48): 'TVIII, at least at this juncture, must be considered the age of brand.' Often explicit in its direct address of sex, sexuality, graphic violence and the common utility of the profane, Showtime's *Shameless US* is unique, distinctive and to a large extent escapes the typical censorship of 'regular' network television. Much of the merchandise pushes and plays on the liberal shamelessness of the show, frequently including on products the strapline 'Wildly, Absolutely, Unapologetically Shameless'. It is, then, this supposed 'excess', this difference from the norm that forms an integral aspect of the *Shameless* brand.

AbbottVision

Of course, all of Abbott's creations are branded to the extent that they communicate his unique vision, but, in 2008, Abbott literally branded his style of work and his authorial voice through the creation of his own company, AbbottVision. Describing it as a 'truly unique production company with an attached Writers' Studio', the official press pack for AbbottVision noted that one of the core goals of the company was to inaugurate a 'hugely creative environment for established and new writers to work and accelerate the turnaround from format conception to script, through to full production'.[3] Based both in the UK and the USA, and via the media of television and film, AbbottVision's first production was the mini-series *Exile*, in three one-hour episodes, created and executively produced by Abbott and written by Danny Brocklehurst, an early student of Abbott's mentoring and successful now in his own right. Shown on BBC One in May 2011, *Exile* dealt with complex social issues such as political corruption, illness and family secrets. Starring Abbott's muse, John Simm, playing a recently fired hedonistic journalist Tom, Olivia Colman as his sister, Nancy, and Jim Broadbent as their Alzheimer's-plagued father, the series tells a story of sociopolitical abuse, discovered through the unveiling of family violence and secrets. Speaking to Amy Raphael of the *Guardian* in 2011, Abbott noted that *Exile* was inspired by two main things – the memory of visiting his grandmother in a nursing home when she was suffering from Alzheimer's and a more recent event in which he watched a couple trading insults in a row:

> The row was the epitome of social deafness. It gave me the idea of writing about a character wanting to unpick a monumental event that happened many years earlier. But it's a unilateral argument – the other character hasn't got the capacity to argue because he's got Alzheimer's. I thought it would be interesting for a 40–year-old British male to return home and instead of it being the typical story in which the problem is fixed, he finds it's not fixable.

Abbott's nominated inspirations only hint at the violent, difficult and dark undertones of the series, set in the winter of 2009, which reveals that Tom fled to London following a severe beating from his journalist father after he was found snooping in his office years before. Unexplained and life-changing in its ferocity, Tom's beating (the abrupt end of the previously idyllic father–son relationship) and Sam's reunion with his father in the present day is not framed as a story of rediscovering familial love. Rather, Sam and Tom's story is represented as part of a psychological thriller in which Tom eventually uncovers the horror of his father's findings from years before (information that he was close to discovering in Sam's office prior to and thus pre-empting the savage beating). To Tom's horror, it is revealed that Sam is not his biological father, but rather, that Tom was born as the result of a rape at a local mental institution before being given as a 'gift' to Sam's wife, Edith (herself unable to have children and unaware of the torrid origins of her new son), by local doctor, Metzler (Timothy West). Later, after discovering and hiding for years Metzler's fraudulent practice of selling babies, Sam's beating of his (adopted) son is understood as an external act of emotional turmoil in which his lifelong anxiety and anger at the events of the past are revealed. Furthermore, Tom's investigations uncover additional abuses of power from the past – most notably that Metzler, now a politician, was, in his father's day, part of an active ring of abusers in which a violent male orderly at the mental hospital, Ricky Tulse (Ned Dennehy) was allowed and encouraged by Metzler to rape and impregnate vulnerable young female patients. Metzler went on to sell the babies, blaming the many pregnancies on male patients.

From the outset of *Exile*, the issues of memory and responsibility are highlighted and the father–son dynamic is represented as painful. The ending of the mini-series does not bring closure for Sam or Tom (though Abbott's creations rarely offer such closing comfort). In *Exile*, injustices are uncovered but are not solved or resolved through the salvation of the individual; indeed, as in the words of Abbott quoted above, such huge problems are not 'fixable'. *Exile* met with critical success, *Radio Times'* Alison Graham (2011) stating that it was 'A tremendous piece of drama; subtle, intelligent, powerful and adult. Writer Danny Brocklehurst and creator Paul Abbott have achieved something wonderful by blending a touching human story with a riveting thriller. This is as good as TV drama can be ... On every level *Exile* delivers.' Other reviewers associated the creation, originally envisaged by Abbott as an American indie film, with future US success. Akin to the filmic remake of *State of Play* (dir. Kevin Macdonald, 2009), the *Guardian's* Stuart Jeffries (2011) wrote in his headline review of *Exile*: 'The ingeniously plotted *Exile* is over –

steel yourself for a Hollywood remake.' Indeed, the writer, Brocklehurst himself, spoke in the same article, 'Paul Abbott's Exile: The Prodigal Returns', of Abbott's global reach or auteur branding: 'Paul's almost become a brand, with the movie of *State of Play* and *Shameless* going to America.'

Abbott's brand or vision has also been evidenced in his recent creation of the six-part drama series *Hit & Miss*. Backed by FremantleMedia Enterprises, produced by AbbottVision and Red Company Productions, written by Sean Conway (a prime example of another young writer mentored by Abbott through the AbbottVision writing studio) and broadcast in May and June 2012, *Hit & Miss* was Sky Atlantic's first UK drama commission. Starring Chloë Sevigny (nominee for Academy Award and Golden Globe Best Supporting Actress in the critically acclaimed film *Boys Don't Cry*, directed by Kimberly Peirce, 1999), the concept of the drama was certainly original and complex – a transgender hitwoman, Mia (Sevigny) receives a letter from her ex-partner, Wendy, telling her that she is dying and that Mia is the father of their 11–year-old son, Ryan (Jorden Bennie), and will soon be his legal guardian.

Travelling to a smallholding on the Yorkshire moors, Mia finds that Wendy has died, leaving Ryan and his three siblings – 16–year-old Riley (Karla Crome), Levi, aged 15 (Reece Noi), and the youngest, Leoni (Roma Christensen) – to await her arrival. Described as a story that conflates Mia's mix of killer and maternal instincts, *Hit & Miss* is, in essence, a

Figure 7.1 *Hit & Miss*, Sky Atlantic 2012: Mia (Chloë Sevigny) and son Ryan (Jorden Bennie)

story that bears Abbott's hallmarks – a story about complex families, unsuitable mothers and fathers, children acting as parents, internal struggles, abuses, everyday life, love and laughter. Speaking to Rebecca Leffler (2012) at the *Hollywood Reporter* about the familial focus of the drama, Abbott related the complexity of the family set-up envisaged in *Hit & Miss* to his own difficult childhood: 'I'm intrigued by close families, but I like not coming from anywhere. I like not belonging to a family. It makes me able to write family better.'

While the transgender and hitwoman elements of the drama allowed for sharp descriptions of the show (such as Abbott's designation of Mia as a 'glock with a cock'[4]), the drama is domestic in its focus, revealing the brutality, happiness and heartache of family relationships. Undoubtedly original in its concept, the drama (akin to *Shameless US*'s channel branding on Showtime) was seemingly a perfect fit for Sky Atlantic, whose director, Naomi Gibney, described the mission statement of Sky Atlantic as one concerned with investing in original drama and providing for and bringing to audiences 'original pieces, surprise, risk and world class television that is truly cinematic'.[5] Indeed, *Hit & Miss* is cinematic in that it is not only dialogue, but white space and high-definition images that tell the story. The pacing is also traditionally slow for television and the bleak Yorkshire moors landscape is represented as a poetic character within the drama. At its première, writer Sean Conway noted Terrence Malick (writer and director of the multiple Academy Award-winning film *The Tree of Life*, 2011) and Bruno Dumont as influences on the show's unique look. In particular, the Dumont reference seems fitting in terms of both the aesthetic focus on the environment and some of the more brutal sex scenes in *Hit & Miss*. Writing of Dumont's work (in particular his 2003 film *Twentynine Palms*), theorist Tim Palmer (2011: 74) notes the continual 'cuts away to extreme long shots of deserted landscape and the modern minutiae that litter them: wind turbines, distant roads, crumbling buildings … directing us to contemplate opaque or (increasingly) vaguely menacing objects of contemporary urban scenery'. Such a cinematographic pattern is certainly evident in *Hit & Miss*, with an almost obsessive focus on long, winding, deserted roads, barren moors and the crumbling walls and rotting doors of the smallholding itself. In terms of the aforementioned sexual brutality, while Dumont's work is certainly more extreme than Abbott and Conway's (for example, Dumont frequently includes real rather than fictitious sex and employs fragmentary storytelling in order to convey raw emotion, isolation and despair), *Hit & Miss* is certainly affective at times, in particular, through its representation of rape as a punctum of savagery. Akin to what Palmer (2011: 69) nominates as the 'stylized but unromantic sex acts, encounters often devoid of any emotional contexts except berserk aggression and rage' in Dumont's work, Episode 1:3 of *Hit & Miss* sees a constant and shocking conflation of sex and violence from its opening, culminating in a horrific scene in which John (Vincent Regan), the owner of the smallholding where the children and Mia live, rapes pregnant teen Riley in his cowshed in enraged revenge for being humiliated by Mia.

The actual rape scene itself begins with a clear indication of John's (sexual) violence towards women. Realising that she is likely pregnant by the owner of the smallholding on which she and her siblings live (a man with whom she has been having sex in lieu of paying rent to following the death of her mother), Riley walks to his farmhouse and knocks on the door. Opening the door only a few inches, John's pregnant wife, Penny (Erin Shanagher), is revealed, her left eye clearly blackened. As John comes to the door he violently grabs Riley's left arm, hissing: 'What are you doing here? Fuck off!' Riley, clearly scared and desperate, is framed in a medium shallow-focus shot, responding to his aggression with the innocent question: 'Why didn't you come to meet me?' Riley's face then comes into focus, seemingly indicating her realisation of John's ultimate selfishness. As John tells her 'It's over', Riley asks why, before saying, 'But we need to talk. It's important.' As Riley places her hands on John's shoulders, clearly attempting to find some comfort in their damaged relationship, John uses both hands to shove her literally off her feet onto the wet, muddy gravel. As she repeats his name and clings to his leg, the camera changes focus, momentarily framing the violent sequence from the window inside his house (presumably, from John's wife's perspective), before showing John brutally kick Riley, breaking the chain of a gold heart necklace that she wears (a gift from her mother), which she claws back before breaking down into loud sobs. Looking down at her, John suddenly grabs her arm, pulls her roughly onto her feet and takes her into his deserted cowshed (a shed in which he had, earlier that day, needlessly executed a cow with a shotgun). In a low-angle shot, we see the dark roof of the cowshed, its grey metal glinting coldly and with torn green netting hanging from the ceiling. A cut then takes us to a medium shot of Riley, facing a wall, with her hand against it, dominated by the shadow of John behind her. Speaking to John, Riley begs: 'Not now, John. I need to tell you something.' John, in response, shushes her before whispering: 'You know you want it.' As he begins to kiss the back of Riley's neck she closes her eyes before staring forward, seemingly resigned to the act that is about to occur. Next, a close-up shows John pulling up Riley's skirt from behind and ripping her knickers before fumbling with his own belt and spitting loudly onto his hand (before, we imagine, lubricating his penis with it – showing a clear awareness that Riley is *not* ready or wanting). The next shot is a medium one, showing Riley's tear-stained face being violently jolted by what we infer to be John's violent sexual thrusts. As he moans loudly, Riley quietly removes her right hand from the wall (the hand which is clinging on to her broken heart necklace) and places it tenderly on John's head.

Riley's gentle movement is problematic, as it serves on one level to show that she clearly has feelings for John, and thus blurs the line between the previous framing of this scene as a rape and a new understanding in which Riley might be seen to be in some way consenting (similar in many ways to the final scene of Catherine Breillat's brutal filmic text, *À Ma Soeur!*, 2001). For me, however, the necklace adds additional depth to the scene, intimating that what Riley is craving is love. As a 16–year-old girl who has recently lost her mother, Riley's actions can be understood to represent her brutal and painful experience of bodily intimacy – watching the decimation of her mother's body by cancer. In essence, Riley may desire the continuation of the relationship with John, however damaged, because the pain and heartbreak of love are all that she has known. Indeed, when John later find out that she is pregnant and refuses to abort the baby, as per his demands, he attempts to 'beat the baby out of her', forcing Riley to shoot him. The result of the murder again leads to increased desperation for Riley, who begins to self-harm – yet another motif of the type of sequence that Palmer (2011: 62) refers to as the 'farce and horror of brutal intimacy', a mixture of the banal and the extreme.

There are, however, also moments of clear comedy, parody and laughter in *Hit & Miss*. When Mia first goes out for a date with local Yorkshire lad, Ben (Jonas Armstrong), he takes her to a bierkeller bar in Manchester city centre, on his way out stealing a large biscuit heart with the words 'Ich liebe dich' written on it in icing and an attached ribbon so it can be worn around the neck. While in many ways this could be seen as a romantic gesture (the actual translation being 'I love you'), the necklace seems to take on a comic value in that in can be read as a declaration of intent in a more crude sense – 'I love dick.' While Mia's intermediate transexuality (she has female breasts but still has male genitalia) is never treated disrespectfully, Ben's stealing the necklace comically presages his later anxieties on finding out Mia's transgender status – an anxiety that causes him to say explicitly, 'You've got a cock? ... I'm not gay!'

Conclusion

To conclude, it is important to draw together the differing strands of argument that have been discussed in this study of Paul Abbott's work such as auteurism, genre reflexivity, political/social realism and iden‐ tity as performance. Analysing Abbott's work, the recurrence of specific themes and tropes (revealing the extraordinary from the ordinary, the empowerment of normally disempowered gender/class characters, parent/child role reversals, a sharp interest in sociopolitics, the connec‐ tion between environment and identity) demonstrates a homogeneous sensibility, a specific way in which Abbott views and shapes his tele‐ visual world. While his characters are dynamic and demonstrative of these concerns, their individuality and strength are garnered through the differing connections between their environments and identities. Frank Gallagher, for example, is shaped, in large part, by his existence on the fringes of society – his residence on the Chatsworth estate – an environment that represents the underbelly of modern Britain. With Frank (and as with all of Abbott's characters), the connection between environment and identity operates reflexively. That is to say, the envi‐ ronment within which characters live and work provides what Cardwell (2005a: 189) notes to be 'a commentary on characters' situations'. As such, characters cannot be separated from the sociopolitics of the spaces in which they spend their time. Time is also important in that the story‐ lines of Abbott's programmes tend to express the zeitgeist of the time in which they are created and produced. *Linda Green*, for example, can be understood as a commentary upon so-called ladette culture so prominent in twenty-first-century Britain, while *State of Play* clearly showcases concerns regarding the sleaze and spin of New Labour in the same period.

Identity as performance is also a key theme in Abbott's work. When Linda Green decides she's had enough of men and intends to 'try out' women, she has to relearn how to perform her identity as a gay woman – how to act, when and where to approach women, how to dress, and so on. Similarly, in *Reckless*, Dr Owen Springer is forced to perform a role of professionalism and perkiness for the camera in order to pass a personality assessment and attain a job that he so desperately wants. His refusal to perform the desired role almost costs him the post that he is well-qualified, if not overqualified for. In creating such charac‐ ters, Abbott demonstrates his acknowledgement of the fundamental expectations of performance in the everyday and links such demands to places, people and sociopolitics in the public and private spheres. To return to Frank Gallagher momentarily, it is also interesting to note Frank's resistance to and rejection of the performance of political correctness in *Shameless*. While at times (specifically, when visited by officials who have the power to stop his benefits) Frank performs a role as a responsible parent, in his frequent direct address monologues to the audience, he purposefully rejects the 'PC', as shown in Chapter 6 when he talks disparagingly about the elderly: 'They need stopping or topping!' In doing so, Abbott showcases his ability and desire to create a variety of voices, attitudes and performances. In addition, the device of direct address can be linked to the notion of generic reflexivity in that it is a method through which Abbott fractures continuity and stability, reminding the spectator of a drama's textuality and artificiality. In *Shameless*, Frank's hilarious and offensive direct-address monologues frequently expose Abbott's ability to (to borrow a phrase from Cardwell 2005a: 192): 'use comedy to offer ideological critique'.

Though all of the themes, tropes and techniques discussed above contribute to Abbott's authorial signature, it is important to point out here, as indeed Abbott himself does, that his close relationships with other industry professionals such as television executives and producers Nicola Shindler, George Faber and Sita Williams have been important to the development of his career. Constantly confronting difficult subject matter, Abbott has needed support to ensure that his work is commissioned and broadcast. During his career, Abbott's creations and visions have consistently pushed the envelope in terms of transforming demarcated boundaries regarding what is and what is not representable on television. Undoubtedly however, Abbott's clear passion for writing about the sociopolitics of families has remained at the heart of all his work, from his television beginnings on *Coronation Street* to the present day. On the back of huge national and international success, Abbott's name now holds significant weight in industry circles, allowing his original voice to be heard.

While I have attempted to cover most of Abbott's key works in this monograph, the expanse of Abbott's oeuvre has made this an impossible task; thus, several series and creations have not been addressed, such as the four-part soap opera *Springhill* (BSkyB, 1997), the six-part British crime drama *Touching Evil* (ITV, 1997–99), the two-part police drama *Butterfly Collectors* (Granada, 1999), the two-part drama *The Secret World of Michael Fry* (Channel 4, 2000), the three-part serial *Best of Both Worlds* (BBC, 2001) and the two-part crime thriller *Alibi* (ITV, 2003). In terms of Abbott's global success, as well as the export of his original British drama, Abbott has also had several of his works (besides *Shameless*) remade in the USA. Both *Touching Evil* and *Cracker*[6] have been remade as television dramas there (in 1997–98 on ABC and in 2004 on the USA Network). In addition, the UK TV drama series *State of Play* was remade as a hugely successful Hollywood film, directed by Kevin Macdonald and released in 2009, starring Russell Crowe, Ben Affleck, Rachel McAdams and Helen Mirren.

Television is where Abbott has earned his name. Abbott is an auteur who determinedly treats audiences with respect and aims to create, write and produce high-quality, high-resolution, high-intelligence works in a voice that is his own. Cited as continuously feeling like a 'resistance worker',[7] Abbott refuses to stand still or regurgitate the same story or creation time after time. He has demonstrated the ability to write, with agonising beauty, for all classes, creeds, sexualities and ages. His writing is political, spiky and unafraid, underpinned by a determination to be available for everybody. In his own words:

> A lot of people think it is only high middle class that can understand rich sophisticated drama and you can go and put anything in front of a regular television viewer. Rubbish. Their instincts will have worked it out.[8]

Abbott's authored drama speaks the truth of his world and his work is prolific, unstoppable, captivating and frequently devastating in equal measure. He is a writer, creator and artist whose work deserves to be acknowledged, discussed and analysed. He is violently original, confronting and hilarious in equal measure, and his power lies in exposing the extraordinary from the ordinary. Flecked with the real of sociopolitical and personal concerns, his drama, imagination and will to better the television industry have changed the landscape of British television. Not satisfied with his own success, however, Abbott is insistent on passing on the mantle, sharing good practice and mentoring new and promising writers. If only all artists had such ambition.

Notes

1 Première audience figures cited by Mike Reynolds online: www.multichannel.com/article/462230-_Shameless_Opens_As_Showtime_s_Top_Drama_Series_Debut_In_Seven_Years.php.

2 T-shirt advertisement on the Showtime website: http://store.sho.com/shameless-baby-bottle-t-shirt/detail.php?p=367903&v=showtime_t-shirts_shameless.

3 Cited from Deborah Goodman, 'ABBOTTVISION', publicity document, supplied by Deborah Goodman: www.dgpr.co.uk/about.

4 Abbott's 'Glock with a cock' strapline was referenced in Benji Wilson's interview with Chloë Sevigny entitled 'Queen of Kookiness', in the *Sunday Times* 'Culture' magazine, 13 May 2012, p. 5.

5 Quotation from Naomi Gibney, director of Sky Atlantic, introducing *Hit & Miss* at its world première at the Mayfair Hotel, London, 15 May 2012.

6 See, for example, Albert Moran, 'Americanization, Hollywoodization, or English-

Language Market Variation?' Comparing British and American Versions of *Cracker'* in C. Lavigne and H. Marcovitch (eds), *American Remakes of British Television: Transformations and Mistranslations* (New York and Plymouth: Lexington Books, 2011).

7 In the Foreword to *Suburban 100: Paul Weller Selected Lyrics* (revised edn, London: Arrow Books, 2010) Abbott notes: 'What I love most about loving his [Weller's] stuff is that he makes me feel like another resistance worker. Simple as that' (p. vii).

8 Abbott, cited in an interview with the author, 2011.

Appendix 1
Interviewing Paul Abbott

During the process of researching and writing this book, Paul Abbott very kindly agreed to partake in three specially commissioned interviews over 2011–12. Summaries of the interviews are noted below.

How do you think of your audience and what they want/need?

A lot of writers go, 'the audience won't spot that', and you go, well you spotted it, and I spotted it – who the fuck do you think the audience is? If you don't think the audience is at least as bright as you are, you can't win. You might win them over for a short length of time but when they spot it's a regurgitated pattern they might tune in but that will always come back to haunt you. Because, when you try to do something subversive with your next product, they'll go – 'we don't get that'. You've taught then to expect a lower level of grammar.

You show people getting things wrong – we all do – in common prosaic dialogue. It says to the audience that you are not taking the easy route and feeding them the first thing that came into your head. The minute the audience know they are being cared for, they will travel much further with you. That is one of the most fundamental identities of the way I write. I find things that aren't visible normally and the minute you put them in everybody knows what you are talking about. I get really bored with writers who use a five-inch brush and only write the story in headlines. I don't know whether it ever became a strapline on *Clocking Off*, but it's 'how well do you know the person next to you?' There's so much more drama in the microscopic stuff and so much more to be had as well as the story that you've got. All this stuff is gold dust. What it does is tell the audience that you're caring for them – yes, you've gone from there to there and audience expectations are for scaffolding for normal drama but, you've fed them three other things. That gets their trust so then you can be more patient and more sophisticated and more elegant about the way that you speak to them thereafter. You've got them onside – they're going be looked after, we're not going to trip them up, it won't be the guy with the beard that you saw in the first scene like it was in *Bergerac*. It was always the guy doing a new deal, in a certain type of suit driving a certain type of car – it was like *Scooby Doo* – and they called it sophisticated drama and it was an absolute pile of painting by numbers shite, except it was very popular and very watchable, but why can't they do that *and* the other? Certain things work, but if they're repeated it makes me go into the background of a scene and find something else, and that can be, unwittingly and unexpectedly, the biggest part of the scene. So, it opens up another part of the story that you're invisibly telling.

You're meant to take people to a place they didn't know they wanted to go in drama – and that's a fundamental part of your job as a writer. I wish I'd heard more than five writers say that in this country, because often they just want to take the audience to where they think they'd like to go because they loved it last year on that series! And that's where all the market research is woefully destructive!

You write better when you think of the audience. Nobody here, but most of the bad writers that I've worked with talk about the audience like, 'They'll never know' and I'm like, 'You're the audience, aren't you?' They're like, 'No.' What! Are they subhuman, sitting in deckchairs watching this shit? Of course they will know. They've watched more television that you've ever watched in your life. They are experts. I can think back to audiences that I've sat with in my past and go 'hmmm, druid, but, they're watching', so you've got to work for everybody. Some people go, 'I've got this thing and it's really good for blokes', and you go, 'But that's only a third of your audience. The rest are women and teenagers.' That kind of language just stinks like counterfeit.

I think I learned how to become a shepherd of my own stories at a higher value than other writers would write for the audience because I got sick of watching television that looked like it was television. It's not meant to feel like television. It's meant to feel like the world and you make it filmic – you spend a conspicuous amount of money on a tiny thing that you don't really need and the audience knows they are being looked after because that scene was bigger than it ever needed to be. Then, then, you can have two people sit in a room talking for half an hour because they think you're capable of spending money like that – you've chosen to do this and you're looking up. The minute your audience know that they are being cared for in a story, you win them over. They can often not describe why they love this above that but I know why I've put the little sausages in there.

Shameless costs about £10,000 a page. When you get from the top to the bottom of a page and you're reading stuff where nobody has moved and nothing's changed, they've just opened their mouths and noises came out but there's no drama in it and no food for the audience, even if they're talking about a plot shift you can still give the audience a three-course meal with that scene just having two people talking at a table. That's all drama is – people talking and how they talk, and how you let them talk, and the patience and sophistication that you provide them with (you give yourself patience to find sophistication for the way they talk). It's magnetic. It doesn't sound like stuff that came out a thousand times before. That's your job as a writer. Not to be so different that you lose the real, that's where you use your skill.

How did your writing emerge and how close is it to your own life?

Writing is about the extraordinary from ordinary – which we all are. We know things about ourselves that other people don't and we're all fascinating. When I worked on *Coronation Street* they gave me a hard time because I was so young. They treated me like a tea boy. The more they treated me like that the more I thought, 'I'll write a fucking script. I'll show them!' I pumped all my anger into the script. There was one episode of *Coronation Street* when I first got commissioned as a screen writer, not a story writer (I worked as a story writer for four and a half years and then left to set up *Children's Ward*), and of course they hated the fact that I was doing another show, so they treated me like shit and the writers either side of my episode stole all the main protein from my episode. I sat there and watched them, thinking, 'You think you've robbed me! You think that', and I wrote the best episode out of nothing and I got more pleasure out of rubbing salt in their wounds and that's the petulance of me. I find a massive second fuel tank when I think I've been wronged.

I wrote *Reckless* because I wanted to write a story about or, at least a version of, younger man–older woman. It was because my second wife was thirteen years older than me. We were together nearly ten years and in my opinion, it only fell apart because she thought that I was bound to go for somebody younger. We were as in love as we could have been forever and it just got racked with suspicion. I've never had an affair in my life. Suspicion is so powerful. The more it permeates, the less energy you've got to fight back and the more it looks like the other person is right. She used to say things like, 'Who were you talking to at work today?' I'd be like, 'It was a story conference. Barry was there and Steven.' She'd be like, 'Oh. No women?' And I'd say, 'Of course – half of our story-writing team are women.' She'd be like, 'But you didn't mention women first.' And I'd be like, 'Because you told me not to.' That's when we split. The power of suspicion tells you that people don't know how to ask questions. If you suspect, you live with torment until you ask the question. You either then believe the answer or you don't. You can't keep thinking that it's right because you keep thinking it. Sometimes you might be near the truth but it might be a mitigated truth. You have to ground stuff in real life. I wanted a romance. A younger man with an older woman – and then to put some bite into it.

Linda Green was based on one of my female friends who could drink any bloke under the table and she ransacked three of them in one night and they weren't even thinking about it and didn't know what had happened until she's banged them in the toilets. So, I wrote a little postcard to myself in a scrapbook saying, 'fat bird with a pint – and what's wrong with that?' I found the file three years after I'd created *Linda Green*.

There was a critic in *The Daily Telegraph,* James Walton, and the only reason I wrote *State of Play* was because he called me a 'warrior of white sliced bread' meaning I could only write working-class. I was like, 'Right, you fucker. I'm going to write something posh and you'll have to retract that.' After the first episode, he wrote that the episode was really good but that I'd got five hours to fuck it up – basically that was his summary, and I was like, 'Ha, ha, ha – I'm just going to wipe the floor with you now.' I wrote *Shameless* and *State of Play* in the same year to show I can do both things – don't pin me down. I'm never rude but I'm rude back and a lot of my work is stimulated by stuff people have said can't be done. So I get on the keyboard and put out stuff in a way that they couldn't admire as something else. It's part of me that is a little bit ugly, but I hope I never lose it because that's what drives me. I've just written a foreword to Paul Weller's new book, and what I said about his songwriting is that it makes me feel like another resistance worker – a resistance worker – and that absolutely summarises what I've felt like since I was fifteen.

In terms of *Shameless* the semi-autobiographical elements are well known. *Shameless* should have been quite repellent. I remember when the first series was going out and in all honesty I thought we'd only get away with the first seven episodes, but thought, 'I can watch it, or not watch it, but it will be in my pocket for the rest of my life and I will have done it, got away with it.' People presume that Frank is my dad and it's not that straightforward. I can tell you exactly who Frank is and he's based on three separate people. Like, my dad – he's a nice bloke, everybody likes him and yet he's vicious, a lot more vicious than Frank is. He has never gone out of his way to do anything wrong to me, he's done it from a chair and he does it in abstract. Frank was based on three people and I smell each one of them every time I write a line for Frank. My dad would be totally negligent on looking out for his children, but you put him in front of a nurse in a hospital, even though you haven't seen him for two years, he appears to sign a consent form. And he talks to nurses like he's a wage-earning carer of this young lad – and you can hear him in the office next to your bed.

When I got sectioned I heard him in the office next to my bed and I was in the acute-level isolated thing. I was fifteen in Burnley General and he came in and I heard them talking two per cent arbitration for nurses and he's going, 'Bloody ridiculous – you want more than that!' He's never worked a day in his life but he talks like a taxpaying grandfather of a brood of kids – he hadn't seen us for two fucking years!! In fact, after he had countersigned a consent form for my sectioning or countersigned for ECT or something, he never came to see me! He left the hospital and he'd forgotten to go and see the kid. He was professing to be so caring and it was actually a little scaffolding that he learned to play. If ever school wanted to get in touch he'd turn up in a suit to make him look dignified and professional. And you think, you abandoned all your kids and left your sixteen-year old daughter to bring them up and he's like, 'Well, fair dos, you had that house.' And I'm like, 'We had to pay for that house! And pay for our own upkeep – you absolute fucking rapist!' How to make that funny is one thing, but his biggest complaint when he saw *Shameless* was – 'When did I have long hair?'

Shameless is a big part of my landscape because it is investigating what you can't normally say. I wrote a version of *Shameless* in *Children's Ward* in 1992. I'd rehearsed telling a story about a bunch of kids with no parents fending for themselves. Then, in *Butterfly Collectors* I did the same thing. In *Butterfly Collectors* I alluded to kids with no parents in a classic BBC structure and you go, 'Well, social services need to get involved' and you go, 'But they can't! They can't.' In our family, nothing that happened would be reported back to the police or to anybody because if we got spotted we would be ripped apart.

You need to invite a bit of real life into a character and you can take the audience miles and miles and miles further if they know you haven't taken the easy road to tell a story.

How do you deal with negotiations with producers and executives?

Sharing is so important. Once you're into your story and your authorship, you may get blinkered to other available options. When you're sitting there with a producer like Nicola Shindler or George Faber or Tessa Ross, they just open your head up. George Faber always knows what I'm on about even when I don't sometimes. He will encapsulate what I've just said to him and I go 'Aha. I did make sense, or it makes sense.'

In *Shameless* storylines can still court controversy. Sex is often figured as celebratory. In the first episode when Lip finds that Ian is fucking Kash (the Muslim with the white fundamentalist wife), Lip says to Ian, 'That makes you a rent boy at best because he bought you stuff.' Ian smacks him and says, 'Ask me what I've bought him?' So, I make it a love story – with Beckham shin pads so it takes the piss out of United fans. I think most writers would end it on 'You're fucking him?' and mayhem. But Ian goes back and says, 'Let me tell you how much of an adult I've been, buying him presents and showing him stuff that he might like or doesn't know about and giving him music that I think he'd love.' You make it a love story and then nobody can contradict it.

In most television dramas you've got to battle with executives all the time. For example, we did an episode where Debbie is having an affair with the policeman and one of our execs went, 'Ohm. Do you think our audience can cope with that?' There was a big meeting and all the producers were sat around the table and one of them went, 'How can they kiss if they're not in love?' and I was like, 'It's called *Shameless*! You need to go out and get laid.' The executive reported me to Channel 4.

How do you think about the structure, pace and shape of your dramas?

A lot of people want to tell a story in a line. I don't. If I see a straight line I knock it off beam. Learning how to turn corners without spotting the bend, taking a left or right without knowing which way you're going to go is fantastic and it makes the writing process so much more refreshing for you.

When I was working on *State of Play* I didn't write a single storyline – I just wrote a paragraph per episode. I didn't know the characters at this point but I thought they (the audience) will think I'm going to go big there, so I'll go tiny, *tiny* – but, make it really nourishing and then I'll blow their tits off by going *big* when they think I'm just about to relax. It's perverseness and subversion and petulance. If I can see where I'm going, I don't like it. I like taking myself by surprise. I remember on *State of Play* I went downstairs [after writing] and said to Saskia, 'Oh my

God, Kelvin Stagg and Sonia Baker died on the same day and they had a conversation for nearly a minute that morning – what's that about?' And Saskia (my ex-wife) went, 'You're paid to write the script – what are you surprised about?' and I went, 'Because I didn't know that was going to happen.' I love it. I love it – wondering what this story is when it kind of drives itself. You've got to be capable of an enormous level of surrender to the story. You could say my next scene is this and my next scene is that but, if you dare to leave it freestyle, you've got to be a bit mad, a bit tilted to do it freestyle, but, that's kind of the way I write. I know in my head what the beginning, middle and end is – there will be three sentences but the one I'll drop is the end because I might not know where it's going to take us and you sacrifice that end bit to see what comes up in the beginning and the middle. It might be a completely different ending and all that you do is guarantee that you have a backstop and, if all else fails, you've got a really good structure. George Faber once said to me, 'You think three sentences is a structure?' And I said, 'It is for me.' I don't want to know any more because I want people to roll in – roll in in the most naturalistic fashion even though it's all constructed. Realism is a counterfeit trait when you write drama except it's not, because you keep pulling. The smallest things that people do are the most important to feed an audience.

Things don't have to be solved. I think that was the biggest secret weapon in *State of Play*. People go, 'There was so much in it!' But there isn't. In terms of plots, between Episode 2 and 3 there really isn't much distance. The script editor, Susie, is one of the highest-qualified script editors and one of the highest paid. She lives in Colorado but works for the BBC and she's like, 'Is there too much in it?' and I'm like, 'Do you know how much we actually reveal?' The best weapon I used was to get people intelligently asking questions which had no reply. In television, you ask the question and a reply comes back and people would kill for a life like that where they get an efficient reply to any question all the time. Well, make them ask questions that aren't easy, questions that are absolutely valid at that point in their investigation or in their demeanour as a character, but you don't have to answer them – and that doesn't make them a McGuffin or a red herring.

What do think has worked well and what went badly?

On *Clocking Off*, working with Nicola Shindler, there's an episode with Chris Eccleston and Sarah Lancashire [Series 1, Episode 2, 'Yvonne's Story']. I've said it so often, but I'm really proud of it. First off, I hated

Chris's character, and I sat down with Nicola. I was good at spotting my own mistakes and repairing them but I said, 'He just feels like a paedophile. He just wants a woman with kids to move in! I wouldn't trust him as far as I could throw him. He works at the airport, he's got a BMW, he's got a house to himself, the same five-bedroom size as hers – so why would he want to, why?' On that particular episode of *Clocking Off* there were five gaps that were bafflingly repellent and I went into a meeting with Nicola Shindler one day and she just turned to page 42 and said, 'I think that's the new page 1.' We'd started the story at the wrong entry point to make him justifiable and to make him as decent as I wanted him to feel. I was really frustrated because I was good at fixing mistakes, I had learned that over decades – to spot stuff – and Nicola just said page 42 – and we were shooting in about five days – and I rewrote the 42 pages in less than four days. We shot when we said we were going to and fixed it. I don't know anybody who would have dared to say, 'We're 5 days away from the shoot and your first 42 pages are void', but she did it. She was pregnant and then ran out of the room and nearly burst into tears because she said so. She was brilliant at spotting that we'd done nothing wrong with the characters but we'd started the story at the wrong axis, from the wrong axis to make him as viable as the rest of them. He was a free-floater, a bit of a catch, so he knew that he had airport wages and women permanently on tap because it's that kind of landscape. Suddenly, everything went right – everything about the story went right. It was such a genius suggestion from Nicola and even those 42 pages would have taken me a month to six weeks to write over five drafts, I didn't care. The minute I started at page 42 every tool was available to me because it made him look dignified, heroic (because he rescued them from a fire), and then you basically play the same scene over and over and over again with him coming back to his house in his BMW (that he now shares with her) and he comments on the floor and the food sticking to the table legs and we played 4 or 5 scenes of him just coming home and having to wash up. He's been a bit of a bachelor, black silk sheets-type and they dismantled him – whether he liked it or not – and he totally fell in love with her. And then I could understand why he would – because she told him everything as it was and gave him a real bullet between the eyes in that restaurant scene.

I loved the execution of that and Sarah Lancashire was just fucking stonking in that episode. She didn't care what she looked like – she wouldn't let make-up on to re-dress her hair, she looked feral because she is speaking for her family and he was just playing the game as a floating bachelor, a floating voter, and that's what she thought. What we had seen was him making an effort and coming back slightly early

– home – and that means a lot and there that is a love story because we know he could be anywhere – he could have gone to a bar but he comes home slightly early and fancies watching the match, and they're watching *Spiderman* or something so he's got to go upstairs to watch it, but he came home early to a family that are imported – cuckoos in his nest. That says he's in love for a start. He's galvanised by them and galvanised by her. The more truth he got delivered by her, the more he fell in love with her. That's the nicest way to do it because you make people feel what's going on before you tell them (well, you should never tell them but eventually you have to form a sentence).

One of the most well-written characters in *State of Play* was the newsroom secretary, Liz. Because there wasn't that much for her to do, we used to make her dialogue the most significant and the most memorable because we might not go back to her significantly for two episodes. And we didn't. Loads of people I know picked up on that – about how well she was written and she was deliberately well written so you'd never forget her, so that even when she's not in a scene, you remember her frequency and can imagine her life going on – because she was so outspoken. I've forgotten how it goes but in one scene she comes up and says, 'What are you talking about?' and Cameron says, 'Mind your nose.' And what does that tell you! Mind your nose – make it a witty limerick. And her presence is felt when she's not there. That's a way to develop a character. I didn't need Liz for that many scenes but then you've got to write her to be memorable and so that they think that she's in all of the scenes – so her frequency is carried in all of the scenes. And Cal teases her but she doesn't threaten to report him – she laughs it off. The fact that she doesn't says that they have arrived at that point. They have a history and you imply history whereas a lot of people just make characters. In most things I watch the characters sound like the writer sounds because the writer hasn't written them well enough to sound like themself.

You paint a picture from that. You could easily have her going, 'Here Mr Cameron, here are the papers', because it costs the same. But you've got a speaking actress, so give her a fucking part! She could have been equally vivid with the opposite personality, but at least give her something.

John Simm in *State of Play* is both witty and clever – our guide for the whole story – and woefully derelict because people are flawed. The only drink he's got in the house are miniatures because he's shagging a stewardess from easyJet and we see him go, 'I'm not seeing that girl any more', but he's got all these miniatures. All of these tiny miniatures are contradictions to his power, but it invited you to look into his past and to position it. You make him feel a bit reckless and a bit socially retarded but then you put him with the highest-ranking female in the story. But he make mistakes, still has the miniatures, and that speaks to an audience more than anybody knows. I think that is a big technique, miniaturisation.

I loved messing about with that kind of stuff – like Bill Nighy, where I wrote him like a twelve-year-old. He's fifty-odd – two years away from retirement, and of course he's the brightest bloke we meet in the story because he runs the newspaper and it's a broadsheet newspaper – he can't be thick, for a start, but you're allowed to play him as a petulant little juvenile. Because he's two years away from retirement he doesn't give a fuck what he says and of course he's allowed to joke – really childish jokes – and they all laugh at the fact that they laugh at him in front of him but that's a little construct that he uses to concede that he's their boss. He rarely changes his voice when he's cross – he's still the twelve-year-old; you don't break that rule. But, when he says, 'You can choose not to do it but I'll just sue you for your back lates', and you go, that's not a very grown-up way of delivering stuff, it's important to recognise that it is if he means it. And they know he means it and some people do talk like that. Television doesn't honour the way we all talk.

Shameless has worked well but there are downsides too. Here and in the States people go – we want another *Shameless*, and I go, 'You can't have one – there is only one. Get your own!' Take the frequency for the doors it opens and you find your own next thing. Some writers don't want to do that. They want to Xerox a previous version and it can never work. It's like all the period cop dramas they all copy because 'that one was really successful'. *George Gently* and *Foyle's War*. They're the same. It's OK if you've invested in a character that is completely different but if all you want to do is copy what you did last year it makes you a bit of a sap! It's the opposite of your job as a writer – you've got to keep looking for stuff that's protein, stuff that comes out of your higher respect for the audience.

How is the UK experience in TV different to that in the USA?

There are differences between UK and US television writers. In the US, we're looking at a business landscape that's twenty times bigger than ours. They've got more writers, more executives, more channels, more money and so it is bigger and so they have had to have a wider take on the gauge of what writers are. Writers have done more because there is more to be done and there are high-level writers. In Britain we have a pitifully low amount of writers, proper writers. There are loads of fucking typists earning money under false pretences but proper writers hone their skill so well. The difference is that we are so starved of writers that the minute we get somebody with voice, we isolate them to make them author – a named author – and dramatist. The high demand for things to feed their appetite means that there is a certain expectation that people will continue to work in teams. If you had six of me sat round a table you could really shift some mountains.

Sitting in the story room for the American *Shameless* there are three women round the table. All three women are the seniors (quite unusual in a writer's room). It's not unusual in production and we should be proud of the fact that in this country we've got a top end of highly skilled females running departments but, in writing there are so few females. We here at AbbottVision are a tiny company and target about three women per year – completely prejudiced towards women. Watching how they develop and how they are talked to (not by me), but when they step into the outside world, you watch them collapse or be made to collapse. It's fucking terrible.

I don't know what it is but in America, there is a huge amount of dross and we never get to see it because it's off-the-radar dross and even that is so much higher than we get. Most drama, well, eighty per cent of it, is stuff you'd pay not to have written. The stuff in Britain that we often discuss in terms of American drama is top-end because we only get to see top end because the world syndicates US top shows. So, we get to see something and they've got top writers, top people with a track record of ten shows. You just watch that roll out and the fluidity of the high quality in American drama is amazing. Like, when watching *West Wing* I'm like, 'Oh, wow. I wish we could even begin to be prepared for writing that kind of show.' We haven't got that many writers in this country who know how to do that. The ones that could in this country are all 'named' writers. They've got an identity as a top-ender and they won't talk to each other. We've got a different approach to the culture of writing and it's the same as writing homework with your arm around your page so that your friend can't see. If he knows what you know, you both grow and we haven't got that spirit. We're peevish in the way that we keep things to ourselves.

The American – I can't tell you – I'm still breathtaken by the standard of communication around the table. Alex Borstein plays Lois in *Family Guy* and she's one of our chief writers and producers (on *US Shameless*) and Nancy Pimental and Cindy Caponera both worked on *The Simpsons*, on *West Wing*, on *ER*. They've got a massive cache of real high-quality programmes so they bring all their skills to a brand-new title and we in the UK don't have that high range of writers to persuade to sit round a table. In fact, the BBC wanted to do a project of higher writers to do ten different things and not one of the writers wanted to sit in a room with the other one. What! What's the fucking problem? It's not competitive, by definition it's the opposite of competitive. If your voice is secure nobody can take it from you – it's a unique skill. Only when people are – well it's a symptom of their laziness and homogeneity when they won't talk frankly to other writers. It's a cause of our lack of ability to produce – well, the difference between British and American drama is a business model but, in the US, they aim for thirteen episodes or they aim for twenty-two and of course, that's got commercial imperative behind it, but, I wish we'd develop a stronger appetite – the balls to commit to something across twenty-six episodes in the UK. The audience may not like something when it first comes out, but stuff, people, they grow on us. It's like a boss – and you go, 'oh – she's a fucking nightmare, I hate going to work', and then eventually you go, 'she's not half bad, actually'. You sit down with British writers and nearly automatically, constitutionally, they're competitive – even six brand-new starters. We need to share.

Fifty per cent of the parts in British drama are people that can come in and say lines that any other character could say. I hate it. I hate that laziness and that homogeneity. The unforgivable bit is that homogeneity does get commissioned and they do turn in stuff that ought not to and they don't actually fix anything once they get it through. It's absolute bone-idle fucking uselessness from writers and commissioners. If you've got a scene where a commissioner says, 'What's the core scene next?', and you go, 'Libby and Jack split – marriage of five years falls apart, they've got kids, its messy', it's about how you write that. If you can write it in a fucking paragraph what's the point of having a three-and-a-half-minute scene that costs £25,000 to shoot?

Where should TV drama writing go from here?

If you sit still in this job, you go backwards, you can *only* go backwards. Writing is one of the hardest jobs to pull off, I reckon, because you're at a standing start. There is nothing on paper before you start typing. Keeping your head active at the same time that your logical brain is looking after the nature of its complexion is a really tough job and I don't know why anybody would want to do that unless they can move on to something bigger, more adventurous, more subversive, because you can use the magnetism of your name to get more difficult stuff through. There is so much stuff that I want to know and want to learn about.

It's important. Now, I tend to wrap things up too tightly, to coil them because I don't like things that sound normal because real people don't sound normal. They talk in fits and starts. It's so important to listen. You don't have to see someone's face to know what they look like. You can't be brave if you weren't scared, and that's a brilliant Buddhist mantra, and if you're scared of what's going to come out of you next, you'll look for much higher grammar in your storytelling.

I do get fed up some days of looking at writers and wondering why they wanted to take that commission at all because they've had no joy in showing off. That's what writers are meant to do – you're meant to show the way your voice carries when subdivided into the amount of characters you've got so people know it's the same voice. You've got to learn how, want to engineer. It's painting a background with the minimum amount of words. I love words, though, and dialogue, because it lets you spring things that aren't even being said but they're being felt, it lets that stuff rise like balloons, even when they're talking about something perfectly banal and you realise that something is wrong and you're already on the smell for it. That's how you treat an audience. That's how you reward an audience for their intelligence. A lot of people think it is only high middle class that can understand rich sophisticated drama and you can go and put anything in front of a regular television viewer. Rubbish. Their instincts will have worked it out.

Appendix 2
Television programmes and films by Paul Abbott

Hit & Miss
(AbbottVision/Sky Atlantic, 2012)
Creator, Executive Producer
6 x 60'

Exile
(AbbottVision/Red Productions/BBC, 2011)
Creator, Executive Producer
3 x 60'

US Shameless
(John Wells/Warner Brothers, 2011)
Creator, Writer, Executive Producer; three seasons
US adaptation of the UK Series for Showtime

Mrs In-Betweeny
(Tightrope Pictures, 2008)
Creator, Executive Producer
1 x 55'

The Girl in the Café
(BBC/HBO Films/Tightrope Pictures, 2005)
Executive Producer
1 x 94'

Shameless
(Company Pictures/Channel 4, 2004–)
Creator, Writer, Executive Producer; all 10 series

Alibi
(AKA & Monogram Productions/ITV, 2003)
Writer
120' two-parter

State of Play
(Endor Productions/BBC, 2003)
Creator, Writer
6 x 60'

Tomorrow La Scala!
(BBC/Film Council/Home Movies Ltd, 2002)
Writing consultant
1 x 108'

Linda Green
(Red Productions/BBC, 2001–2)
Creator, Writer; two series

Best of Both Worlds
(Zenith/BBC, 2001)
Creator, Writer
3 x 50'

Clocking Off
(Red Productions/BBC, 2000–3)
Creator, Writer; four series

The Secret World of Michael Fry
(Endor Productions/C4, 2000)
Creator, Writer
2 x 80'

Butterfly Collectors
(Granada, 1999)
Creator, Writer
2 x 90'

Love in the 21st Century
(Red Productions/Channel 4, 1999)
Writer
1 x 25'

Reckless: The Movie
(Granada/ITV, 1999)
Writer; based on Paul's earlier series
1 x 120'

Police 2020
(Granada/ITV, 1997)
Writer (screenplay)
1 x 120'

Reckless
(Granada/ITV, 1997)
Creator, Writer
6 x 60'

Springhill
(Granada/BSkyB/Channel 4, 1997)
Writer
4 x 30'

Touching Evil
(United/ITV, 1997)
Creator, Writer; three series

Medics
(Granada/ITV, 1995)
Writer
1 x 60'

Cracker
(Granada/ITV, 1994–95)
Producer, Writer; two series

Children's Ward
(Granada/ITV, 1989–2000)
Creator, Writer; twelve series

Dramarama
(ITV/Granada, 1988)
Writer – 'Blackbird Singing in the Dead of Night'
1 x 30'

Coronation Street
(Granada/ITV, 1983–89)
Story editor, Writer
53 x 30'

References

Abbott, Paul, cited by James Rampton. 2005. 'Paul Abbott: My Shameless Life', *Independent* [online], 20 December. Available at: www.independent. co.uk/news/people/profiles/paul-abbott-my-shameless-life-520219. html (accessed 09/09/2009).

Abbott, Paul, cited by Stuart Jeffries. 2005. 'Why I Write: The Monday Interview', *Guardian* [online], February. Available at: www.guardian. co.uk/media/2005/feb/07/broadcasting.arts (accessed 09/09/2009).

Abbott, Paul, cited by Amy Raphael. 2011. 'Paul Abbott's *Exile*: The Prodigal Returns', *Guardian*, 18 April. Available at: www.guardian.co.uk/tv-and-radio/2011/apr/18/paul-abbott-danny-brocklehurst-exile (accessed 02/06/2011).

Abbott, Paul. 2010. 'Foreword', in *Suburban 100: Paul Weller Selected Lyrics*. Revised edition, London: Arrow Books.

Aitkenhead, Decca. 2008. 'Estate of Play', *Guardian* [online], 12 July. Available at: www.guardian.co.uk/media/2008/jul/12/television (accessed 09/09/2009).

Akass, K., & McCabe, J. (ed.) 2007. *Quality TV: Contemporary American Television and Beyond*. London and New York: I. B. Tauris.

Akass, K., & McCabe, J. 2008. 'It's NotTV, it's HBO's Original Programming: Producing Quality TV' in Marc Leverette, Brian L. Ott and Cara Louise Buckley (eds), *It's Not TV: Watching HBO in the Post-Television Era*. London and New York: Routledge, pp. 83–94.

Altman, Rick. 1986. 'Television Sound', in T. Modleski (ed.), *Studies in Entertainment*. Bloomingdale and Indianapolis: Indiana University Press, pp. 39–54.

Ang, I., & Hermes, J. 1991. 'Gender and/in Media Consumption' in J. Curran & M. Gurevitch (eds), *Mass Media and Society*. London: Edward Arnold, pp. 307–28.

Annis, Francesca, cited by J. Selway. 1997. 'A Man in his Thirties is a Grown-up, not a Toy Boy', *Woman's Journal*, March. Available at: http://webspace. webring.com/people/df/francescasite/interview/WJournal0397.html (accessed 09/09/2009).

Annis, Francesca, cited by R. Barber. 1998. 'Francesca Annis on Love,

Therapy and Being a Sex Symbol', *The Times*, 30 September. Available at: http://fiennes.tripod.com/annis.html (accessed 09/09/2009).

Ashby, Justine. 2005. 'Postfeminism in the British Frame', *Cinema Journal*, 44:2, 127–32.

Auld, Tim. 2009. 'Francesca Annis interview', *Telegraph*, 14 April. Available at: http://www.telegraph.co.uk/culture/theatre/drama/5136654/Francesca-Annis-interview.html (accessed 09/09/2009).

Baker, Stephen. 2009. '*Shameless* and the Question of England: Genre, Class and Nation', *Journal of British Cinema and Television*, 6:3, 452–67.

Bazin, André. 1967. 'The Evolution of the Language of Cinema', in *What Is Cinema?* Berkeley: University of California Press.

Bignell, Jonathan. 2004. *An Introduction to Television Studies*. London and New York: Routledge.

Brown, Maggie. 1997. 'Review: *Reckless*', *Guardian*, 28 February. Available at: www.nothing-fancy.com/michaelkitchen/reviews/reckless.htm#rev4 (accessed 09/09/2009).

Buckley, C. L., Leverette, M. and Ott. B. L. (eds) 2008. *It's Not TV: Watching HBO in the Post-Television Era*. New York and Oxford: Routledge.

Cardwell, Sarah. 2005a. *Andrew Davies: The Television Series*. Manchester and New York: Manchester University Press.

Cardwell, Sarah. 2005b. 'Television Aesthetics and Close Analysis: Style, Mood and Engagement in *Perfect Strangers*', in J. Gibbs and D. Pye (eds), *Style and Meaning: Studies in the Detailed Analysis of Film*. Manchester and New York: Manchester University Press, pp. 72–80.

Cardwell, Sarah. 2006. 'Television Aesthetics', *Critical Studies in Television: Scholarly Studies in Small Screen Fictions*, 1:1, 72–80.

Cardwell, Sarah. 2007. 'Is Quality Television Any Good? Generic Distinctions, Evaluations and the Troubling Matter of Critical Judgement', in K. Akass & J. McCabe (eds), *Quality TV: Contemporary American Television and Beyond*. London and New York: I. B. Tauris, pp. 19–31.

Caughie, John (ed.) 1981. *Theories of Authorship: A Reader*. London and New York: Routledge.

Caughie, John. 2000. *Television Drama: Realism, Modernism and British Culture*. Oxford: Oxford University Press.

Clover, Ian. Blog response to Julia Reaside. 2010. 'Stop It, *Shameless*, We've Had Enough', *Guardian* [online], 26 January. Available at: www.guardian.co.uk/tv-and-radio/tvandradioblog/2010/jan/26/stop-it-shameless (accessed 26/01/2010).

Connolly, Paul. 2001. '*Linda Green* Review', *The Times* [online]. Cited in the *Guardian* [online], 31 October. Available at: www.guardian.co.uk/media/2001/oct/31/broadcasting (accessed 01/08/2011).

Cooke, Lez. 2003. *British Television Drama: A History*. London. British Film Institute.

Cooke, Lez. 2005. 'The New Social Realism of *Clocking Off*', in J. Bignell & S. Lacey (eds), *Popular Television Drama: Critical Perspectives*. Manchester and New York: Manchester University Press, pp. 183–97.

Corner, John. 1999. *Critical Ideas in Television Studies.* (Oxford Television Studies), Oxford: Clarendon Press.

Creeber, Glen. 2004. *Serial Television: Big Drama on the Small Screen.* London: British Film Institute.

Creeber, Glen. 2009. 'The Truth is Out There! Not!: *Shameless* and the Moral Structures of Contemporary Social Realism', *New Review of Film and Television Studies*, 4, 421–39.

Davies, Máire Messenger. 2005. '"Just That Kids' Thing": The Politics of "Crazyspace", Children's Television and the Case of *The Demon Headmaster*', in J. Bignell & S. Lacey (eds), *Popular Television Drama: Critical Perspectives.* Manchester and New York: Manchester University Press, pp. 125–41.

Davies, Russell. T., cited by V. Frost. 2011. 'My TV Hero: Russell T Davies on Paul Abbott', *Guardian*, 20 June. Available at: www.guardian.co.uk/ tv-and-radio/2011/jun/20/my-tv-hero-paul-abbott (accessed 21/06/2011).

Di Mattia, Joanna. 2006. 'What's the Harm in Believing? Mr Big, Mr Perfect, and the Romantic Quest for *Sex and the City*'s Mr Right', in Kim Akass & Janet McCabe (eds), *Reading Sex and the City.* London and New York: I. B. Tauris, pp. 17–32.

Duguid, Mark. 2009. *Cracker.* BFI TV Classics, Basingstoke: Palgrave Macmillan.

Dyer, Richard. 1997. *White.* London and New York: Routledge.

Games, Alex. 2004. 'Paul Abbott: Absolutely Shameless', *Independent* [online], 19 December. Available at: www.independent.co.uk/news/ people/profiles/paul-abbott-absolutely-shameless-694274.html (accessed 09/09/2009).

Garratt, Sheryl. 2001. 'The Likely Lass: Liza Tarbuck', *Observer*, Sunday 14 October. Available at www.guardian.co.uk/theobserver/2001/oct/14/life1. lifemagazine4 (accessed 09/09/2009).

Gibbs, John & Pye, Douglas. 2005. 'Revisiting Preminger: *Bonjour Tristesse*', in J. Gibbs and D. Pye (eds), *Style and Meaning: Studies in the Detailed Analysis of Film.* Manchester and New York: Manchester University Press, pp. 108–26.

Giddens, Anthony. 1991. *Modernity and Self-Identity: Self and Society in the Late Modern Age.* London and New York: Routledge.

Graham, Alison. 2011. '*Exile*', *Radio Times.* Available at: www.radiotimes. com/episode/zx6j/exile-series-1—episode-3 (accessed 11/12/2011).

Green, Robson, cited by F. Hardy. 2010. 'Robson Green's Highly Explosive Secret', *Daily Mail*, 22 January. Available at: www.dailymail.co.uk/femail/ article-1245032/Robson-Greens-highly-explosive-secret.html (accessed 03/05/2011).

Hallam, Julia. 2005. *Lynda La Plante.* The Television Series. Manchester and New York: Manchester University Press.

Hayward, Susan. 2000. *Key Concepts in Cinema Studies.* 2nd edition, London: Routledge.

Hill, John. 1997. *Sex, Class and Realism: British Cinema 1956–1963.* London: British Film Institute.

Jancovich, Mark & Lyons, James. 2003. *Quality Popular Television: Cult TV, the Industry and Fans*. London: British Film Institute.

Jeffries, Stuart. 2011. 'The Ingeniously Plotted Exile is Over – Steel Yourself for a Hollywood Remake', *Guardian*, 4 May. Available at: www.guardian. co.uk/tv-and-radio/2011/may/04/exile-the-secret-millionaire-review (accessed 10/05/2011).

Jennings, Tom. 2008. 'A Low-Down Dirty Lack of Shame', *Libcom.org*, 16 January. Available at: http://libcom.org/library/shameless-paul-abbott-series-1–2–channel-4–20034–television-review-%E2%80%93-tom-jennings (accessed 09/09/2009).

Johnson, Beth. 2012. '*Shameless*: Situating Sex Beyond the City', in Beth Johnson, James Aston and Basil Glynn (eds), *Television, Sex and Society: Analyzing Contemporary Representations*. London and New York: Continuum Press, pp. 3–16.

Johnson, Catherine. 2005. 'Quality/Cult Television: *The X-Files* and Television History', in Michael Hammond & Lucy Mazdon (eds), *The Contemporary Television Series*. Edinburgh. Edinburgh University Press, pp. 57–71.

Johnson, Catherine. 2007. 'TELE-BRANDING IN TVIII: The Network as Brand and the Programme as Brand', *New Review of Film and Television Studies*, 5:1, pp. 5–24.

Jordan, Marion. 1981. 'Realism and Convention', cited in R. Dyer, C. Geraghty, M. Jordan, T. Lovell, R. Paterson & J. Stewart (eds), *Coronation Street*. London: British Film Institute, pp. 27–39.

Karpovich, Angelina. 2010. 'Dissecting the Opening Sequence', in Douglas L. Howard (ed.), *Dexter: Investigating Cutting Edge Television*. London and New York: I. B. Tauris, pp. 27–42.

Klevan, Andrew. 2000. *Disclosure of the Everyday: Undramatic Achievement in Narrative Film*. Trowbridge: Flicks Books.

Kolker, Robert. 2000. *A Cinema of Loneliness: Penn, Stone, Kubrick, Scorsese, Spielberg, Altman*. 3rd edition, Oxford: Oxford University Press.

Lavery, David. 2002. '"A Religion in Narrative": Joss Whedon and Television Creativity', paper given at the *Blood, Text and Fears* conference, Norwich, England. Available at: www.slayageonline.com/PDF/lavery2.pdf (accessed 12/06/2012).

Lefebvre, Henri. 1991. *Critique of Everyday Life*. London: Verso.

Leffler, Rebecca. 2012. 'MIPTV 2012: "Shameless" Scribe Paul Abbott Aims High With Chloë Sevigny Transsexual Killer Drama', *Hollywood Reporter*, www.hollywoodreporter.com/news/shameless-miptv-paul-abbott-hit-miss-307395 (accessed 16/06/2012).

Lury, Karen. 1995/96. 'Television Performance: Being, Acting and "Corpsing"', *New Formations*, 27: 114–27.

MacKinnon, Kenneth. 2003. *Representing Men: Maleness and Masculinity in the Media*. London: Arnold.

Massey, Michael. 2010. *Studying TV Drama*. Leighton Buzzard: Auteur Press.

McFarlane, Brian. 1996. *Novel to Film: An Introduction to the Theory of Adaptation*. Oxford: Clarendon Press.

McKechnie, Kara. 2007. *Alan Bennett*. The Television Series. Manchester and New York: Manchester University Press.

Merritt, Bishetta, D. 1991. 'Bill Cosby: TV Auteur?', *Journal of Popular Culture*, 24:4, 89–102.

Meyrowitz, Joshua. 1994. 'Medium Theory', in D. Crowley and D. Mitchell (eds), *Communication Theory Today*. Cambridge: Polity Press, pp. 50–77.

Moran, Albert. 2011. 'Americanization, Hollywoodization, or English-Language Market Variation? Comparing British and American Versions of *Cracker*', in C. Lavigne & H. Marcovitch (eds), *American Remakes of British Television: Transformations and Mistranslations*. New York and Plymouth. Lexington Books, pp. 35–54.

Mulvey, Laura. 1975. 'Visual Pleasure and the Narrative Cinema', *Screen*, 16:3, 6–18.

Nelson, Robin. 2007a. 'HBO Premium: Channelling Distinction through TVIII', *New Review of Film and Television Studies*, 5:1, 25–40.

Nelson, Robin. 2007b. *State of Play: Contemporary "High-end" TV Drama*. Manchester and New York: Manchester University Press.

Nelson, Robin. 1997. *TV Drama in Transition*. Basingstoke: Palgrave Macmillan.

Palmer, Tim. 2011. *Brutal Intimacy: Analyzing Contemporary French Cinema*. Middletown, CT: Wesleyan University Press.

Pearce, Lynne. 2007. *Romance Writing*. Cambridge: Polity Press.

Pearson, Roberta. 2005. 'The Writer/Producer in American Television', in Michael Hammond & Lucy Mazdon (eds), *The Contemporary Television Series*. Edinburgh: Edinburgh University Press, pp. 11–26.

Peirse, Alison. 2010. 'In a Lonely Place? *Dexter* and Film Noir', in Douglas L Howard (ed.), *Dexter: Investigating Cutting-Edge Television*. New York: I. B. Tauris, pp. 189–204.

Phillips, Adam. 1994. *On Flirtation*. London and Boston: Faber & Faber.

Propp, Vladimir. 1968 [1928]. *Morphology of the Folktale*. Trans. L. Scott. Austin and London: University of Texas Press.

Rackham, Jane. 2003. '*State of Play*', *Radio Times*, 1 June, 57.

Radway, Janice. 1984. *Reading the Romance: Women, Patriarchy and Popular Literature*. Chapel Hill, New York and London: University of North Carolina Press.

Raeside, Julia. 2010. 'Stop it, Shameless, We've Had Enough', *Guardian* [online], 26 January. Available at: www.guardian.co.uk/tv-and-radio/tvandradioblog/2010/jan/26/stop-it-shameless (accessed 26/01/2010).

Rampton, James. 1998. 'An Actress in Her Prime', *Independent*, 10 October. Available at: www.independent.co.uk/arts-entertainment/an-actress-in-her-prime-1177415.html (accessed 12/09/2009).

Rogers, Mark C., Epstein, Michael and Reeves, Jimmie L. 2002. 'The Sopranos as HBO Brand Equity: The Art of Commerce in the Age of Digital Reproduction', in David Lavery (ed.), *This Thing of Ours: Investigating The Sopranos*. London: Wallflower Press, pp. 42–57.

Rolinson, Dave. 2011. 'The Other South Park: *Children's Ward* Series One

Review', Tachyon TV [online], 4 July. Available at|: http://tachyon-tv. co.uk/2011/07/the-other-south-park/.

Saïd, Edward. W. 1978. *Orientalism*. London: Routledge & Kegan Paul.

Segal, Lynne. 1994. *Straight Sex: Rethinking the Politics of Pleasure*. Berkeley: University of California Press.

Smith, Angela. 2011. 'Femininity Repackaged: Postfeminism and *Ladette to Lady*', in Melanie Waters (ed.), *Women on Screen: Feminism and Femininity in Visual Culture*. Basingstoke: Palgrave Macmillan, pp. 153–66.

Spicer, Andrew. 2002. *Film Noir*. Harlow: Longman.

Thompson, Robert, J. 1996. *Television's Second Golden Age: From* Hill Street Blues *to* ER. London and New York: Continuum.

Thornburn, David. 2007. 'Television Melodrama', in Horace Newcomb (ed.), *Television: The Critical View*. 7th edition, New York and Oxford: Oxford University Press, pp. 438–54.

Walters, James. 2006. 'Saving Face: Inflections of Character Role-Play in *Shameless*', *Journal of British Cinema and Television*, 3:1, 95–106.

Willetts, Philippa. 2010. 'Judging Other Women, Judging Ourselves', in *The F Word: Contemporary UK Feminism*. Available at: www.thefword.org.uk/ blog/2010/07/judging_other_w (accessed 05/03/2011).

Williams, Sita, cited by J. Rampton. 1998. 'An Actress in Her Prime', *Independent*, 10 October. Available at: www.independent.co.uk/arts-entertainment/ an-actress-in-her-prime-1177415.html (accessed 12/09/2009).

Yates, David. 2005. *State of Play: Complete BBC Series 1*. DVD Extra: Commentary on Episodes 1 and 6.

TV/filmography

Alibi. 2003. ITV. UK

À Ma Soeur! 2001. Dir. Catherine Breillat. France

Best of Both Worlds. 2001. BBC. UK

The Big Breakfast. 1992–2002. Channel 4. UK

Boys Don't Cry. 1999. Dir. Kimberly Peirce. US

Bread. 1986–91. BBC One. UK

Butterfly Collectors. 1999. ITV. UK

Children's Ward. 1989–2000. ITV. UK

Cleopatra. 1963. Dir. Joseph L. Mankiewicz. UK/US/Switzerland

Clocking Off. 2000–3. BBC One. UK

Coronation Street. 1960–present. ITV. UK

Cracker. 1993–96. ITV. UK

Dodger, Bonzo and the Rest. 1985–87. ITV.

Double Indemnity. 1994. Dir. Billy Wilder. USA.

Exile. 2011. BBC One. UK

Have I Got News for You. 1990–present. BBC One and BBC Two. UK

Hit & Miss. 2012. Sky Atlantic. UK

In a Lonely Place. 1950. Dir. Nicholas Ray. US

Linda Green. 2001–2. BBC One. UK

Macbeth. 1971. Dir. Roman Polanski. UK/US

Pride and Prejudice. 2005. Dir. Joe Wright. France/UK

Queer as Folk. 1999–2000. Channel 4. UK

Reckless. 1997. ITV. UK

Rhoda. 1974–78. CBS. US

Roseanne. 1988–97. ABC. USA

The Secret World of Michael Fry. 2000. Channel 4. UK

Sex and the City. 1998–2004. HBO. USA

Shameless. 2004–present. Channel 4. UK

Shameless US. 2011–present. Showtime. USA

She's Gotta Have It. 1998. Channel 4. UK

Six Feet Under. HBO. 2001–5. USA
Soldier, Soldier. 1991–97. ITV. UK
The Sopranos. 1999–2007. HBO. USA
Springhill. 1997. BSkyB. UK
State of Play. 2003. BBC One. UK
State of Play. 2009. Dir. Kevin Macdonald. USA
Superskinny Me: The Race to Size Double Zero. 2007. Channel 4. UK
Touching Evil, ITV. 1997–99. UK
Trainspotting. 1996. Dir. Danny Boyle. UK
The Tree of Life. 2011. Dir. Terrence Malick. USA
The Truth About Size Zero. 2007. ITV. UK
Twentynine Palms. 2003. Dir. Bruno Dumont. France/Germany/USA
Watching. 1987–93. ITV. UK
Women in Love. 1969. Dir. Ken Russell, UK

Index